The Interplay of Truth and Deception

New Agendas in Communication

Edited by

Matthew S. McGlone and
Mark L. Knapp

Routledge
Taylor & Francis Group

NEW YORK AND LONDON

First published 2010
by Routledge
270 Madison Ave, New York, NY 10016

Simultaneously published in the UK
by Routledge
2 Park Square, Milton Park, Abingdon, Oxon OX14 4RN

Routledge is an imprint of the Taylor & Francis Group, an informa business

© 2010 Taylor and Francis

Typeset in Sabon and Gill Sans by EvS Communication Networx, Inc.
Printed and bound in the United States of America on acid-free paper by Walsworth
Publishing Company, Marceline, MO

Library of Congress Cataloging in Publication Data
The interplay of truth and deception : new agendas in theory and research / edited by
Matthew S. McGlone and Mark L. Knapp. — 1st ed.
p. cm.
Includes bibliographical references and index.
1. Deception—United States. 2. Deceptive advertising—United States. 3. Truthfulness
and falsehood—United States. I. McGlone, Matthew S., 1966- II. Knapp, Mark L.
BF637.D42I58 2009
177'.3—dc22
2008055159

ISBN10: 0-415-99566-3 (hbk)
ISBN 10: 0-415-99567-1 (pbk)
ISBN 10: 0-203-88785-9 (ebk)

ISBN 13: 978-0-415-99566-5 (hbk)
ISBN 13: 978-0-415-99567-2 (pbk)
ISBN 13: 978-0-203-88785-1 (ebk)

The Interplay of Truth and Deception

During the past thirty years, there has been a steadily increasing number of scientific and popular publications dealing with lying and deception. Questions about the extent to which public officials are deceptive are standard fare in current magazines and newspapers. This volume aims to present a more precise conceptualization of this phenomenon, manifested in some well-known constructions like spin, hype, doublespeak, equivocation, and contextomy (quoting out of context).

The contents of the volume have been generated for the New Agendas symposium at The University of Texas College of Communication, and the authors are young, leading-edge researchers offering innovative perspectives and explorations of lying and deception in various contexts.

This volume will appeal to scholars, researchers, and advanced/graduate students in communication, media, and psychology. It is written to the level of advanced undergraduates, and it is appropriate for use in courses covering lying and deception.

Matthew S. McGlone (PhD Princeton University) is Associate Professor in the Department of Communication Studies at The University of Texas at Austin. He has published scholarly articles on euphemism, doublespeak, and contextomy. He has taught courses on persuasion, propaganda, and psychological warfare.

Mark L. Knapp (PhD Pennsylvania State University) is the Jesse H. Jones Centennial Professor Emeritus in Communication and Distinguished Teaching Professor Emeritus in the Department of Communication Studies at The University of Texas at Austin. Dr. Knapp has published several scholarly articles in the area of lying and deception, and has directed several dissertations on the topic. He has taught undergraduate and graduate courses in lying and deception, and is writing a book in the area as well.

New Agendas in Communication
A Series from Routledge and
the College of Communication
at The University of Texas at Austin

Roderick Hart and Stephen Reese, Series Editors

This series brings together groups of emerging scholars to tackle important interdisciplinary themes that demand new scholarly attention and reach broadly across the communication field's existing courses. Each volume stakes out a key area, presents original findings, and considers the long-range implications of its "new agenda."

The Interplay of Truth and Deception
edited by Matthew S. McGlone and Mark L. Knapp

Journalism and Citizenship
edited by Zizi Papacharissi

Understanding Science
edited by LeeAnn Kahlor and Patricia Stout

Political Emotions
edited by Janet Staiger

Media Literacy
edited by Kathleen Tyner

Contents

Figures and Tables

Figures

Tables

Contributors

Gary D. Bond is an Assistant Professor in the Department of Psychology at Winston-Salem State University. He has investigated decision making and language production in prisoner, parolee, and law enforcement officer groups. His research questions seek in part to discover the effect of context on cognition.

Zoë Chance is a graduate student in the Marketing Unit at the Harvard Business School. She holds a BA in English from Haverford College and an MBA from the Marshall School of Business at the University of Southern California.

Jeff T. Hancock is an Associate Professor in the Department of Communication and the Faculty of Computing and Information Science at Cornell University. His research is concerned with the intersection of deception and technology, and more generally with computer-mediated communication.

Brooks Jackson is Director of Annenberg Political Fact Check, a project of the Annenberg Public Policy Center at the University of Pennsylvania. A former journalist covering Washington for the Associated Press, *Wall Street Journal*, and CNN, he pioneered the "fact check" form of news stories debunking false and misleading statements in political speeches, debates, and advertisements. He is the author (with Kathleen Hall Jamieson) of *unSpun: Finding Facts in a World of Disinformation*.

Rachel K. Kim is a doctoral student in the Department of Communication at Michigan State University. Her research interests broadly involve interpersonal and intercultural communication with a specific interest in deception.

Mark L. Knapp is the Jesse H. Jones Centennial Professor Emeritus and Distinguished Teaching Professor Emeritus in the Department of Communication Studies at The University of Texas at Austin. He is a Distinguished Scholar and past president of the National Communication Association and the International Communication Association. Among other books, he is the co-editor of the *Handbook of Interpersonal Communication* and author of *Nonverbal Communication in Human Interaction* and *Lying and Deception in Human Interaction.*

Seow Ting Lee is an Assistant Professor in the Department of Communication and New Media at National University of Singapore. She is a media scholar specializing in the areas of journalism, public relations, health communication, leadership, and international communication. A former newspaper journalist, Lee received her MA and PhD from the University of Missouri-Columbia School of Journalism.

Paul Martin Lester is a Professor in the Department of Communications at California State University, Fullerton. He is the author or editor of several books including: *Visual Journalism: A Guide for New Media Professionals* (with Christopher R. Harris), *Images that Injure Pictorial Stereotypes in the Media* (with Susan D. Ross), *Visual Communication Images with Messages, Desktop Computing Workbook, Photojournalism An Ethical Approach, The Ethics of Photojournalism*, and is the editor of *Visual Communication Quarterly.*

Timothy R. Levine is a Professor in the Department of Communication at Michigan State University. Levine's research interests include deception, interpersonal communication, personal relationships, persuasion and social influence, intercultural communication, communication traits, and measurement validation. Levine has published more than 70 journal articles including approximately 30 articles in *Communication Monographs* and *Human Communication Research.* Levine is currently working on a new theory of deception to be called Truth Bias Theory. The theory will merge findings on the veracity effect, probability model, with work on deception motives and projective motives.

Clancy Martin, Associate Professor in the Department of Philosophy at University of Missouri – Kansas City, has published articles in *Harper's, The London Review of Books, The New Yorker, Ethics, Literature and Philosophy, NOON, McSweeney's,* and many other journals and magazines. He recently published a translation of Nietzsche's *Thus Spoke Zarathustra* and he is presently translating *Beyond Good and Evil.* He has edited, co-edited, and authored several books in philosophy, most recently *The Philosophy of Deception.*

Matthew S. McGlone is an Associate Professor in the Department of Communication Studies at The University of Texas at Austin. His research explores the linguistic strategies people use to overcome communication obstacles—i.e., the way people talk about things that are difficult to talk about (abstract concepts, taboo topics, social stereotypes, etc.). He is a former Distinguished Research Fellow of the Center for Research on Culture, Development, and Education at New York University.

Michael I. Norton is an Assistant Professor in the Marketing Unit at the Harvard Business School. He holds a BA in Psychology and English from Williams College and a PhD in Psychology from Princeton University. Prior to joining HBS, he was a Fellow at the Media Lab and Sloan School of Management of the Massachusetts Institute of Technology.

David Shulman is an Associate Professor and Head of the Department of Anthropology and Sociology at Lafayette College. He is author of *From Hire to Liar: The Role of Deception in the Workplace.*

Lassiter F. Speller is a Chancellor's Scholar affiliated with the Department of Psychology at Winston-Salem State University. Speller's interests are in the cognitive and emotional aspects of language produced in context. Most recently, his research has explored political deception in public venues and emotional expression in instant messaging and "texting."

R. Weylin Sternglanz is an Assistant Professor in the Division of Social and Behavioral Sciences at Nova Southeastern University. His primary research interests and publications are in the areas of nonverbal decoding accuracy, deception detection, and empathic accuracy. He teaches courses in social psychology, research methodology, interpersonal perception, and interpersonal communication.

Catalina L. Toma is a doctoral student in the Department of Communication at Cornell University. Her work examines the impact of new communication technologies on psychological processes, such as self-presentation and deception.

Series Editors' Foreword

We are happy to present this inaugural volume in the New Agendas in Communication series. Through this conference and publication initiative of the College of Communication at The University of Texas at Austin, we hope to advance our goal of defining communication education in the 21st century. For this series, selected College faculty members identify an interdisciplinary topic of broad appeal to the field of communication and then convene a group of the most promising emerging scholars to share and develop their ideas. Following this working conference in Austin, the faculty conveners edit a volume that brings the work together in a way intended to speak to a wide audience.

We hope each volume will provide a new and fresh perspective on the crucial questions of concern to the field.

Roderick P. Hart, Dean
Stephen D. Reese, Associate Dean for Academic Affairs
College of Communication
The University of Texas at Austin

Preface

Half-Truths and Other Fractions

Matthew S. McGlone and Mark L. Knapp

Children are taught to always tell the truth, journalists are obliged to report only the truth, and court witnesses take a solemn oath to divulge "the truth, the whole truth, and nothing but the truth." These imperatives may seem straightforward, but the notion of absolute truth they presuppose is elusive. What we believe to be true can be based on any of several shifting criteria (what we are told, what we feel, what we observe, what follows from reasoning, etc.), and the degree of certainty we attach to these beliefs can change with our circumstances. We also understand that the rules for communicating truths to others are more complex than absolute truthtelling imperatives stipulate. Thus a 10-year-old knows that she probably shouldn't tell Grandpa her true feelings about the savings bond he gave her for Christmas; a reporter highlights an actor's screen successes in his obituary, not his string of flops or DUIs; and a grand jury witness divulges all she knows about a defendant's attempts to bribe a public official, but is free to "plead the fifth" when asked about her own involvement in criminal activities.

Despite centuries of scholarly inquiry into the enigmatic nature of truth, a simplistic, dichotomous formulation of the construct persists in most communicative contexts: Statements are either true or not, and speakers who knowingly produce the former are being honest while those who knowingly produce the latter are lying. There are undoubtedly situations in which this conceptualization works, but there are many more in which we just act like it works even though we know otherwise. In particular, we know that all sorts of communications are passed off as truths that inspection reveals as possessing only some degree of truth. As philosopher Alfred North Whitehead observed, "there are no whole truths. All truths are half-truths. It is trying to treat them as whole truths that plays the devil" (Price, 1954). We don't always see horns and a tail on the teller of fractional truths; when we do, our decision to call attention to them depends on who we think is getting forked and how badly. Accordingly, Democrats are quick to cry foul when Republican attack ads wrench their candidates' words out of context to make them appear soft on defense, but stay silent about selective excerpting in Democratic attack ads that caricature their opponents as hard on the environment. On the other hand, no one is likely to feel put out by a lunch companion who excuses herself to "use the bathroom" but fails to disclose the particular use she has in mind.

The analytic difficulties encountered by scholars of truthtelling over the years have not discouraged others from holding deception up to similar scrutiny in recent times. Indeed, over the last 30 years there has been a steadily increasing number of scientific and popular publications dealing with lying and deception. Many of their authors hold that deception is on the rise in all aspects of human affairs. One recent book called the times we live in the "post-truth era" (Keyes, 2004). Callahan (2004) cites examples from sports, law, education, science, business, and journalism to document his belief that during the past 25 years a "cheating culture" has evolved in the United States. Exposés of people lying in public and private life have become standard fare in magazines and newspapers.

The preponderance of scientific studies of deception to date have focused on whether liars exhibit certain behaviors that distinguish them from truth tellers and the extent to which people can accurately detect liars and truth tellers (DePaulo et al., 2003). For purposes of control, these studies make a clear distinction between deceptive and truthful communication. In everyday life, however, there are a variety of message constructions that are more difficult to classify and seem to occupy a space between deceptive and truthful extremes—casuistry, doublespeak, equivocation, euphemism, flattery, innuendo, selective quotation, spin, etc. With all the recent attention being given to deceptive messages, communicators who intend to deceive may be driven more to these fractionally truthful constructions in order to avoid reproach while accomplishing their purposes. Consequently, we think the time is ripe for researchers to shift their attention from the endpoints of the truthtelling-deception continuum to the sizable gray area in between.

In October of 2007, we invited a group of likeminded scholars to the College of Communication at The University of Texas at Austin to participate in a 2-day conference we titled "The Interplay of Truth and Deception." Our goal was to launch a dialogue about fractionally truthful message constructions and attributions about lying, deception, and truthtelling that have been largely ignored in academic research but are nonetheless common in everyday experience. The conference was truly interdisciplinary, including representatives from behavioral economics, communication, journalism, marketing, philosophy, psychology, and sociology. Their contributions highlight the diversity of conceptual and methodological approaches to truthful/deceptive message hybrids, and we hope the present volume is a good representation of this diversity. All of the conference participants except one (Dan Ariely of MIT, who had published the work he presented elsewhere) contributed a chapter to this volume. Timothy R. Levine and Rachel K. Kim of Michigan State University did not attend the conference, but generously agreed to contribute a chapter on their research that fit well with our mission.

Professor Whitehead might have believed that all truths are half-truths, but an old Yiddish proverb maintains that "a half-truth can be a whole lie." A similar position is embraced by Brooks Jackson (chapter 1), our conference keynote speaker. As a journalist covering Washington for CNN in the 1980s and 90s, Jackson pioneered the "adwatch" news report genre exposing misleading claims in political campaign advertising. As the current director of the FactCheck.org project of the Annenberg Public Policy Center, he operates as a nonpartisan "voter advocate" calling public attention to lapses in the factual accuracy of statements by major U.S. political players in their ads, speeches, debates, interviews, and news releases. In his chapter, Jackson describes a variety of deceptive claims he has encountered in his debunking endeavors, from the "big fat lies" dietary supplement companies tell their customers to more subtle distortions in political ads containing claims that are literally true but still deeply misleading. When these distortions lead people to draw false conclusions, Jackson maintains, they are acts of deception, regardless of the artfully chosen "weasel words" that prevent them from being outright falsehoods.

Timothy R. Levine and Rachel K. Kim (chapter 2) agree that what is literally true can be deceptive, and also note that saying something false need not be, such as a sarcastic comment. They outline a new theory of deceptive communication that focuses principally on the deceiver's motives and the prevalence of deception in any given communicative context. Simply put, lies tend to serve a particular goal and also tend to occur less than truthful messages. These basic facts hold important implications for the study of deception detection, but have been largely overlooked by detection researchers preoccupied with issues of deception "leakage." The probability model they advance is intended to steer future detection research toward greater generalizability, particularly with regard to the variable base-rates of deception in different communication settings. Gary D. Bond and Lassiter F. Speller (chapter 3) are also critical of the conventional detection paradigm, noting that its reliance on clear-cut true or false messages is not representative of the "interspersed veracity" characteristic of much deceptive communication. These authors investigate the role of "displacements"—i.e., strategic alterations of descriptive details—in rendering otherwise truthful messages as vehicles of deception. They find not only that various forms of displacement (temporal, spatial, or affective) have different impacts on the manner in which people deliver fractionally truthful messages, but also that certain populations (e.g., college students) are more sensitive to these impacts than others (paroled felons). Their findings thus point to the importance of considering variability both in the composition of gray area messages and among the people composing them.

Matthew S. McGlone (chapter 4) explores a ubiquitous gray area message species he calls "contextomy," a form of citation traditionally (and redundantly, he notes) referred to as "quoting out of context." Contextomy can be used to create a false impression of a source's attitudes in the service of motives as harmless as selling movie tickets or as harmful as character assassination. Although remedying the problem would seem a simple matter of recontextualizing a misleading excerpt, his analysis of the uses and abuses of a single sentence from Dr. Martin Luther King's "I Have a Dream" speech demonstrates how enduring contextomy's contaminating influence can be. Professional journalists are duty-bound to fairly represent the public figures they quote from, but as Seow Ting Lee (chapter 5) points out, they sometimes resort to deception to gain access to the truth. The varieties of deceptive journalism she describes (insincere praise of a source, covert recording, impersonation, etc.) constitute a continuum, despite a professional code of ethics demanding that reporters tell the truth under all conditions. The results of her survey of professional journalists' attitudes regarding deceptive practices reveals this continuum to be subject to a complex interplay of organizational, situational, and moral pressure not easily captured by a set of truthtelling rules, norms, or values. Photojournalists and other visual media professionals are often portrayed as defenders of the "seeing is believing" rule of truth, but Paul Martin Lester (chapter 6) convincingly argues that deception is as common in and intrinsic to visual communication as it is in the verbal domain. With a tip of his chapeau to French cultural theorist Jean Baudrillard, Lester's survey of visual manipulation throughout history (from *trompe l'oeil* to spirit photography to film coverage of the Iraqi war) illuminates the murky boundary distinguishing deceptive visual effects that are received with delight by willing patrons and others met with scorn by professionals and the public. His analysis poses an intriguing question: If reality and its simulation are symbolically equivalent (á la Baudrillard), then isn't deception a mode of symbolism in its own right?

Clancy Martin (chapter 7) casts the relationship between sincerity and hypocrisy as one component of the broader interplay between truth and deception. Although hypocrisy may begin as a form of insincerity, the complexity of sincerity itself, coupled with selectivity of human memory, can subtly turn this ostensible virtue to the hypocritical purposes of deception and self-deception. Moreover, Martin argues that some forms of sincerity are perhaps best understood as self-directed hypocrisy from the outset. Hypocrisy and self-deception are often prompted by a discrepancy between one's behavior and cultural expectations; the exculpatory claims people formulate to camouflage these discrepancies are the subject of David Shulman's (chapter 8) contribution. The varieties of "social loopholes" (*I was distracted at the time, he had it coming*, etc.) he identifies do not reconcile the clash between conduct and cultural norms, but instead attempt to suspend normal rules of evaluative judgment. Although social loopholes can reduce strain on the social order, ubiquitous use conflates truth and deception in a way that can seriously harm interpersonal relationships. Zoë Chance and Michael I. Norton (chapter 9) also explore justifications for questionable behavior. Sometimes people justify questionable behavior preemptively, by using desirable behaviors in the past to license questionable ones in the present or future (e.g., *I was frugal all week, so it's ok to go on a shopping spree this weekend*); at other times they validate questionable behavior purely in the moment (e.g., *I buy* Playboy *to read the articles*); and at still other times they may simply perform the questionable behavior and then conveniently forget that it happened. The experimental evidence on behavioral justification (including a new study the authors report in their chapter) indicates that people are both facile and flexible at employing these strategies. Perhaps more telling, however, is the evidence suggesting that people are often blithely unaware that any rationalizing is going on!

Interpersonal interaction occurs increasingly online in blogs, social networking sites, and virtual environments such as *Second Life*. Jeff Hancock and Catalina Toma (chapter 10) investigate the forms of fractional truth that occur in a particular online context in which important personal relationships are now commonly forged—an Internet dating service. They provide a framework for operationalizing deceptive communication in this context and report an empirical study examining the deceptive practices of online daters. The study results indicate that these practices are, in the authors' words, "frequent, subtle, and strategic." The various forms of distortion they document—men overstating their height, women understating their weight, etc.—indicate a strong connection between the fractional truths people tell and selectivity in the public personas they wish to display. Repairing the damage to one's persona by an accusation of wrongdoing is the focus of R. Weylin Sternglanz's contribution (chapter 11). Specifically, he explores the possibility that people accused of a serious offense (e.g., cheating on an exam) might win back some credibility by admitting to a lesser offense (e.g., seeing someone else cheat on the exam without reporting it). The experiments Sternglanz reports indicate that, among strangers, confessing to a lesser offense elicits milder perceptions of guilt than simply denying a serious accusation. He also notes that the reparative efficacy of this strategy derives not from an alternative attribution the confession provides for the evaluator's concerns, but from the perception that someone who confesses to even a minor offense is "forthright" enough not to deny more serious guilt. Offenders take heed!

Over 30 years ago, award-winning novelist and journalist Arthur Herzog (1973) predicted that America would be "the first civilization to eliminate lies." Far from a bleary-eyed optimist, he was in fact an astute (if jaded) observer of human communication dismayed by the mounting frequency with which he encountered fractional truths of the sort described in this volume. In his words,

> Soon, in America, the lie will be superfluous, unnecessary, and will be buried. The lie is not vanishing because it is being killed off, like some hapless species of wildlife. It is not disappearing because it was legislated out of existence, like a noxious fume, or because it has atrophied from lack of use. Clearly, lies cannot be regarded as victims of higher morality. The lie is a casualty of progress ... The new device that is making the lie obsolete can be called the Fake Factor, or for those who require still more trenchant terminology, the B. S. Factor....this factor causes a subtle skewing of sense, a distortion of meaning, without ever becoming an actual lie. (p. 15)

Whether blatant lies will ever be obsolete in this country or anywhere else is debatable. However, it is indisputable that fractional truths are prevalent in contemporary discourse and are here to stay. The chapters in this volume map out just a few regions of the gray area between truth and deception, but we hope they might encourage other scholars to explore this largely uncharted territory.

References

Callahan, D. (2004). *The cheating culture: Why more Americans are doing wrong to get ahead*. Orlando, FL: Harcourt.

DePaulo, B. M., Lindsay, J. J., Malone, B. E., Muhlenbruck, L., Charlton, K., & Cooper, H. (2003). Cues to deception. *Psychological Bulletin, 129,* 74–118.

Herzog, A. (1973). *The B.S. factor: The theory and technique of faking it in America*. New York: Penguin.

Keyes, R. (2004). *The post-truth era: Dishonesty and deception in contemporary life*. New York: St. Martin's Press.

Price, L. (1954). *Dialogues of Alfred North Whitehead*. New York: Atlantic Monthly Press.

Chapter 1

Finding the Weasel Word in "Literally True"[1]

Brooks Jackson

My topic today is deception. The first thing I want to say about deception is that there is too damn much of it. And I say that knowing that if there were no deception, we wouldn't be having this conference, and a lot of us here would be looking for work elsewhere. I'll also be covering some other points about deception:

- First, the old saying "there's a sucker born every minute" doesn't begin to approach the truth. I say we're *all* born suckers, until and unless we train ourselves to listen carefully and think logically, something that's relatively new in human history.
- Second, and apropos of the theme of this conference, there are a bewildering number of *ways* to deceive—sometimes even including telling the literal truth, or some portion of it.

My colleague Kathleen Hall Jamieson and I recently published a book on the subject of deception. We titled it *unSpun* (2007), and we gave it the subtitle: "Finding facts in a world of disinformation." And we really do live in world of disinformation. Somebody out there may disagree—maybe a company with a lousy product and lousy sales, looking for a new advertising campaign. They might well think there's not *enough* deception. So let me offer some evidence.

Big Fat Lies

Pick just about any weight-loss product and you're likely to find a false or misleading claim. Bayer, for example, once claimed in TV ads that its "One-A-Day Weight Smart" vitamin pills could increase metabolism and bring about weight loss. When challenged to provide some evidence of that, they didn't. Instead, they agreed to jerk the ads off the air and pay a $3.2 million civil penalty to the Federal Trade Commission. By then, of course, they had sold a lot of these so-called "Weight Smart" pills (Dizdul, 2007). Today, Bayer calls the product "Weight Smart Advanced," as though it could bring about *more* weight loss. And it's again being advertised on TV. But read the fine print on their Web site and they grudgingly admit—I quote—"It is *not* a weight control product" (Bayer HealthCare LLC, 2007). After their run-in with the ad cops, they carefully pitch the product as one that can help the body withstand diet and exercise, not as something that will magically boost metabolism and burn off weight *without* effort or sacrifice. Yet the very name, "Weight Smart Advanced," implies otherwise. And who reads the fine print? Bogus weight-loss claims are so prevalent that the FTC in 2004 launched something it called "Operation Big Fat Lie," starting with a round-up of half a dozen companies (Mack, 2004). But "Operation Big Fat Lie" has had, I submit, little to no effect.

And for a heaping helping of weight-loss deception, Google up "Hoodia." An entire industry has sprung up selling powders, pills and patches, and even liquid drops and gel caps that somehow are supposed to be derived from a rare Kalahari Desert cactus called Hoodia Gordonii. CBS's *60 Minutes* made it famous when it showed Leslie Stahl nibbling a morsel of fresh cactus cut for her by a San tribesman (Stahl, 2004). In that form, it does seem to work as a natural appetite suppressant. The San Bushmen have used it for that purpose for generations. But you can't get fresh Hoodia cactus at your supermarket, and major drug companies have been trying for years to figure out how to make an effective, marketable pill from this plant—so far with no success (Phytopharm PLC, 2006). Pfizer publicly gave up on it (*Consumer Reports*, 2006). Can you imagine any drug company giving up on the profits that a truly effective and marketable appetite suppressant pill would bring in, if there was a remote chance of success? And yet, dozens of hucksters are marketing supposed Hoodia products using all manner of false and deceptive claims. In our book, we call it "Hoodia Hoodoo."

Beauty products are another obvious area where advertising is prone to contain empty or wholly false promises. In *unSpun*, we give an example that sounds ludicrous, and is: Emu oil. That's the supposedly active ingredient in a face cream that is supposed to get rid of wrinkles, and whose marketer claims it is "much better than Botox!" (Deception Wrinkle-Cheating Cream, 2004). In fact, it "makes wrinkles almost invisible to the naked eye" and—get this—"it is possible your wrinkles will no longer even exist." Oh yeah? The fact is there is zero scientific evidence that Emu oil has any—repeat, any—effect on face wrinkles. When we hounded the marketer for some proof of her claims, we got exactly one study of its cosmetic properties (Zemtsov, 1994). It was, of course, sponsored by Emu ranchers and reported the subjective opinions of a grand total of 11 test subjects. But more importantly it did not even attempt to assess effects on wrinkles. We searched the scientific literature for ourselves, and found zero studies of Emu oil as a wrinkle-reducer—and, of course, nothing comparing it to Botox. The claims for this product are pure hokum. The name of the product, appropriately enough, is *Deception* Wrinkle Cream.

In fairness to Emu-oil hucksters, deception is the foundation, if you will, of the entire cosmetics industry. Without deception, companies like Revlon, Estée Lauder, L'Oréal, and even Procter & Gamble wouldn't be where they are today. What are the odds that *your* hair will ever look like the long, shiny tresses of those models in the TV ads, even if you buy whatever hair goo they're advertising? The fact is—according to a former cosmetics-industry chemist—all cosmetics companies are basically using the same chemicals and producing products of approximately equal quality (Harden, 1982). Much of what you pay for when you buy cosmetics, he said, is "make-believe."

The same can be said of many other industries. Whole companies have been built on systematic bamboozling of the public. In *unSpun* we give the example of Listerine (Jackson & Jamieson, 2007), a product that was originally a not-very-good hospital antiseptic, until a legendary advertising campaign turned it into a hugely profitable household cure for bad breath. The trouble is, as medical authorities have been saying for decades now, Listerine does nothing to cure bad breath, and never has. No mouthwash is effective against bad breath—not according to the American Dental Association or any medical authority we can find (ADA, 2008). But I'll bet that any teacher who asks their class what a good product is to use for bad breath will receive "Listerine" as a common answer. Eight decades of false advertising have had their effect.

Advertising is just full of deception. A few more examples:

- Bayer—again—once advertised its Aleve painkiller as "prescription strength relief without a prescription," which it wasn't. The *maximum* recommended dose for Aleve is actually *half* the normally prescribed dose for its prescription counterpart (NAD Report#4323, 2005).
- NetZero claimed its dial-up Internet access worked at "broadband-like speeds." Actually, cable modems are several times faster (NAD Report #4413, 2005).
- An over-the-counter cold medication called Cold-Eeze (2005) advertises that it is "clinically proven to cut colds by nearly half," which just is not so. Cold-Eeze has been clinically *tested* any number of times, but the studies are inconclusive. They're about evenly divided between those showing it has some effect and those showing none at all.

The Right to Lie

The Federal Trade Commission tries hard to police this area. But it has only a tiny staff devoted to this (FTC Organizational Directory, 2007). It also must grant the deceivers due process of law, with the result that false ads can air for months before any action takes effect. My guess is that the public *thinks* it is better protected from false ads than is the actual case. How often have we seen the words "As Seen on TV" used as a selling point, as if anything that appears on television must be true? Still the public at least has *some* legal protection against false advertising for products.

But not when it comes to politics. There's no federal law preventing a candidate, or anybody, from making a false political claim (Jackson, 2004, June 3). A handful of states have tried this—I'm aware of three—and none of them have had much practical success. Either the courts strike down their laws as a core violation of the First Amendment, or they are too weak to provide a truly effective remedy, such as denying office to anyone found guilty of lying to get it. When it comes to political advertising, candidates have a legal right to deceive voters just about as much as they please. The only deterrent is the possibility of the falsehood being discovered and voters reacting with enough disgust to elect the opponent.

Not surprisingly, then, candidates do a lot of deceiving. In 2004, President Bush ran ads telling voters that John Kerry would take healthcare decisions out of the hands of doctors and have "bureaucrats in Washington" making them instead. That was just false. In fact, 97% of those who now have health insurance would have kept the same coverage under Kerry's plan, according to neutral experts who analyzed it (Jackson, 2004, October 4).

Kerry, in turn, ran an ad accusing Bush of harboring a "secret plan" to cut Social Security benefits by up to 45%, another big deception. The plan in question wouldn't have affected anyone already getting benefits, and would have allowed benefits for future retirees to *grow*, and grow fast enough to maintain current purchasing power. Benefits just wouldn't have grown as fast as under current law, which pegs them to wages rather than inflation (Jackson, 2004, October 18).

There's a lot of this—too much. Here are some more examples.

- In 2004, a radio ad by a pro-Kerry group claimed that members of the bin Laden family were allowed to fly out of the United States "when most other air traffic was grounded." Actually, commercial air traffic had resumed a week earlier. The same ad also claimed that the bin Laden family members were not "detained." Actually, 22 of them were questioned by the FBI before being allowed to leave, and their plane was searched as well. By the way, this ad stated—as fact—some falsehoods that were slyly implied but never stated outright in Michael Moore's film *Fahrenheit 9/11* (Jackson, 2004, October 27).

- In 2006, the National Republican Congressional Committee ran a number of false or misleading ads, of which the most memorable was one accusing a Democratic House candidate of billing taxpayers for a call made from his hotel room to an adult "fantasy hotline." The ad showed the candidate seeming to leer while a woman's silhouette gyrated suggestively behind him. Actually, the call was a wrong number—one digit off from a New York state office the caller had meant to dial. The call lasted less than 1 minute and the charge to taxpayers was $1.25 (Jackson, Novak, Bank, Ficaro, & Kolawole, 2006).

- Another example from 2006—this one from a Democratic group—accused a number of Republican senators of voting against modern body armor for U.S. troops in Iraq. It showed bullets ripping into the torso of a dummy wearing the old-style flak jackets, as though these Republicans wanted GIs to die. In fact, the amendment these Republicans voted against contained not one word about body armor and body armor wasn't mentioned once during the debate. And anyway, at the time the Pentagon already was buying up all the body armor the economy could produce (Jackson & Bank, 2006).

- And just in case you think candidates have gone straight in 2007, let me say they haven't. On the Republican side, Rudy Giuliani is fond of claiming that when he was mayor, adoptions rose 65 to 70%. In fact, adoptions were just 17% higher in his final year than they were the year before he took office. Giuliani arrives at his 70% figure by using cherry-picked statistics aggressively enough to leave an entire orchard bare (Novak & Miller, 2007).

- On the Democratic side, Bill Richardson has been claiming for months that he created 80,000 jobs in New Mexico since becoming governor. Actually, figures from the Bureau of Labor Statistics put the gain at 68,100. In fairness, the total is still growing and will no doubt eventually reach the 80,000 figure. But you could say the same thing about a stopped clock: It will be right, too, eventually (Jackson & Banks, 2007).

These political deceptions matter, more than the jaded Washington press corps probably realizes. Voters really are deceived, and deceived about important matters of public policy. As we documented in 2004, majorities of voters go to the polls believing some of the false notions fed to them by campaign advertising. The National Annenberg Election Survey asked a large national sample of adults—about 1,700—about some partisan claims we had found to be false (Romer, 2006).

Two thirds of them said they believed the statement—repeated again and again by Kerry—that new jobs created under George Bush paid $9,000 a year less than the jobs they replaced, a claim unsupported by evidence. And nearly as many—62%—said they believed Bush's often-repeated claim that Kerry's tax plan would raise taxes on 900,000 small business owners (Romer, 2006). Not true, unless you count George Bush and Dick Cheney both as "small business owners" by virtue of their small amounts of outside business income, the ludicrously misleading standard used by the Bush campaign to define "small business owner" (Jackson & Jamieson, 2007). You can find other examples of our polling findings in *unSpun*. To be more specific, when I say voters "believed" these falsehoods I mean that they said they found them to be either "very truthful" or "somewhat truthful," as opposed to the other choices which were "not too truthful" or "not truthful at all" (Romer, 2006). But you get the point. Deceptive advertising works. It really does deceive. Modern political campaigns, I submit to you, have become in effect multi-million-dollar disinformation efforts that succeed in misinforming the public. Now, as you might suppose, Republicans were somewhat more likely to accept a false claim as truthful if it came from a Republican, and vice versa. But we found plenty of Democrats who swallowed the Bush campaign's falsehoods, and plenty of Republicans who believed Kerry's spin (Romer, 2006). This isn't just partisan bias at work.

You would think the public would be more skeptical. Jokes about lying politicians have been a staple of humorists for a long time. We all know the standard answer to the question, "How can you tell when politicians are lying?" When their lips are moving—ha, ha, ha. But the reality is no joke. However skeptical the typical voter *thinks* he or she might be, the reality is that false claims become accepted as truthful when they are repeated over and over in these massive advertising campaigns. Falsehoods, when backed by big money, trump the truth.

I suspect this problem is getting worse. I can't give you any scientific measurements over time to prove that, but we all know that political campaigns are getting longer, advertising budgets are getting larger and the number of ads is increasing (Jackson et al., 2006). So unless there's been a change in the ratio of truth to fiction, the number of *deceptive* political ads is increasing too.

It has come to this: FactCheck.org has begun a special effort for 2008 to monitor the ads of candidates running for judgeships in the 23 states that elect their appellate judges. You would think that if anybody had a deep respect for facts it would be a state supreme court judge, and yet we've found examples of ads by judicial candidates that are little better than those we see in congressional campaigns. In 2006, one such ad falsely implied that a candidate for the Kentucky Supreme Court paroled a rapist who 12 hours later raped a 14-year-old and forced her mother to watch (Novak, 2006). As the unfortunate Michael Dukakis can attest, that sort of thing was once reserved for presidential campaigns. Another 2006 ad portrayed a Georgia candidate for judge as soft on crime, even though independent reviews found that she usually sided with the prosecutor and was tough on defendants in death penalty cases (Novak, 2006). Sad to say, the day of the mudslinging judge is upon us.

Barnum Would Have Been Wrong

Why do people believe this stuff? P.T. Barnum would have been on to something if he'd really said "There's a sucker born every minute," but he would have been very wrong. It's more like 4.2 suckers per *second*. That's the number of humans expected to be born in the world this year, according to the U.S. Census Bureau (2007). That's 252 suckers born every minute.

Actually, it wasn't Barnum who said "There's a sucker born every minute," according Barnum's biographer. He credits a confidence man named Paper Collar Joe Bessimer (Andrews, Biggs, & Seidel, 1996). I've also seen the quote attributed to a competitor of Barnum and even to Mark Twain, who gets credit for a lot of clever things he never really said. What's important, for our purposes, is that many people *believe* Barnum said it even though he didn't. That itself is evidence in support of my thesis that *all* humans are born suckers.

I don't need to remind this audience what the past half-century of cognitive science has shown us about the natural human tendency to believe what we want to believe in spite of contrary evidence. Our tendency is to cling to whatever bits of information come our way—however gossamer or spurious they may be—if they support our biases. We hold desperately onto whatever can shield us from the unpleasant necessity to change our minds and utter those awful, terrible, painful three words: "I was wrong." You also know what the research has told us about our tendency to believe something simply because we've heard it repeated many times, whether it's true or not and regardless of whether any evidence supports it. You know the mental shortcuts we all use—you scholars like to call them "heuristics"—which so often lead us to incorrect conclusions. As humans, we're just not wired to be rational.

This was brought home dramatically in some 2004 experiments by Drew Westen, a psychologist at Emory University (Cox Clark, 2006). He lined up a number of strong partisans, some for Kerry and some for Bush, and gave them some hypothetical statements to think about. First, he read to them a statement from their favored candidate that seemed to be a flip-flop, a gaffe that would surely lose many votes. Later, he told them that new evidence had surfaced that might make the offending statement less of a political problem. Here's the unique bit—the test subjects were undergoing brain scans while these statements were being read, so that the researchers could watch the physical reactions inside their brains. And as Westen put it, "We did not see any increased activation of the parts of the brain normally engaged during reasoning.... What we saw instead was a network of emotion circuits lighting up" (Cox Clark, 2006).

In short, these partisans didn't employ much of their grey matter trying to reason through whether the statements were true or not. When they heard something that threatened their candidate, their fight-or-flight centers kicked in. And when they heard information that favored their candidate, the parts of the brain that lit up were roughly those that light up when a drug addict gets a fix. We republished Westen's brain-scan images under the heading, "This is your brain on politics."

The Caveman Brain

There are probably good, evolutionary reasons for the way our brains work. Those mental shortcuts we take work most of the time, and save us from a lot of needless mental effort. Early hominids may have gotten themselves eaten if they stopped to ponder too long whether hearing a lion's roar meant a lion was nearby. Those whose brains automatically associated a roar with a lion after a few repetitions may have had an advantage: Maybe they just took off running without bothering to think too deeply about it, and thus lived to have children who also were wired to react without thinking. Maybe. I don't know. I wasn't there. What we do know is that what we call logic is a relatively recent invention. Humans have been walking the earth for perhaps 200,000 years, but our modern notions of logic only showed up about 2,500 years ago, if you accept Aristotle and the ancient Greeks as the inventors of logic. And the scientific method—systematically testing our theories of what's real and true against the hard evidence and forcing ourselves to reject what can be disproven—is an even more recent invention than that. Small wonder that humans often react emotionally, unthinkingly, illogically—ignoring evidence—and get suckered as a result.

It's even worse when clever marketers and political consultants have read the cognitive research and use it to push the buttons in our caveman brains. In the book we quote a marketing consultant who had read and understood a classic study by Harvard psychologist Ellen Langer (Langer, Blank, & Chanowitz, 1978). She found unsuspecting test subjects were more likely to let one of her researchers barge in front of them at the copying machine if they gave a phony reason: "because I'm in a rush." That's no reason at all if you think about it. Of course they were "in a rush," otherwise they wouldn't be queue-cutting. Yet, just saying "because I'm in a rush" made people much more likely to allow somebody to cut in than if they had just said "May I?" Langer and colleagues concluded that humans operate much of the time in a state she called "mindlessness," not really thinking. Hearing the word "because" triggered the same reaction as though a real reason had followed.

I suppose most people don't know that their brains are wired this way, but people who want to deceive us do know this. The marketing consultant I mentioned had this advice for those who want to sell their products: "Because," he said, "is a magic word that literally forces people to buckle at the knees and succumb to your offer.... Give your prospects the reason why, no matter how stupid it may seem to YOU" (Neocleous, 2007).

The Weasel Word in "Literally True"

With humans so ripe for deception, and marketers so knowledgeable about how to fool us, and with elections to be won or dollars to be made when deceivers succeed, it should be no surprise that there are many, many ways to accomplish deception. But here I'm going to talk about one broad category that seems to fit the theme of this conference. I call it the "literally true" falsehood.

The notion of a literally true falsehood may seem like a contradiction, but it isn't. I've employed a bit of deception here myself. I use the word "literally" as a weasel word, a qualifier that sucks the meaning out of a phrase the way a weasel sucks out the contents of an egg. "True falsehood" would be a contradiction, but "literally true" isn't the same thing as "true." Allow me to demonstrate, with a few 30-second ads. They all make statements that are true, or at least partly true. But the statements are strung together in a way that is designed to leave a false impression. In other words, they convey a false message.

Example #1: MoveOnPAC's (2004) "Assault Ban" Advertisement[2]

ANNOUNCER: "This is an assault weapon. It can fire up to 300 rounds a minute. It's the weapon most feared by our police. In the hands of terrorists it could kill hundreds. That's why they're illegal. John Kerry, a sportsman and a hunter, would keep them illegal. But on Sept. 13th, George Bush will let the assault weapon ban expire. George Bush says he's making America safer. Who does he think he's kidding? MoveonPAC is responsible for the content of this advertisement."

As you can see, this ad invites viewers to think that George Bush was somehow going to legalize fully automatic weapons than can fire "up to 300 rounds a minute" and kill hundreds. Actually, *all* fully automatic weapons have been illegal to own without a federal license since 1934, and they remain illegal to own today (Jackson, 2004, September 14). What the ad failed to mention is that all the so-called "assault weapon ban" covered were *semi*-automatic versions of those fully automatic military-style weapons. There might have been good arguments in favor of keeping the ban in place—but this ad didn't make them. Instead, by sly insinuation—reinforced by frightening pictures and sound effects— it conveyed a totally false message: that Bush was going to let terrorists get hold of machine guns. By the way, Bush's stated position was that he would have signed an extension of the ban had Congress produced one, which it didn't (Jackson, 2004, September 14).

Example #2: Kerry's (2004) "Truth on Taxes" Ad[3]

Here's another example of a political ad that makes a literally true statement, and yet misleads and the average viewer:

JOHN KERRY: "Here's the truth on taxes. After nearly four years under George Bush, the middle class is paying the bigger share of America's tax burden and the wealthiest are paying less. It's wrong, we need to cut taxes on the middle class, not raise them. We also need to get healthcare costs under control and lower the nation's deficit. I don't believe the wealthy need another tax cut. I believe ordinary Americans need someone who will fight for them."

It is a true statement that "the middle class is paying a bigger *share* of American's tax burden and the wealthiest are paying less." The key word is "share." The truth was, and is, the middle class is paying *lower* taxes (Jackson, 2004, October 23). But Kerry implied otherwise by immediately saying—his words—"It's wrong, we need to cut taxes on the middle class, not raise them." Bush *did* cut them. It's true that the rich got bigger cuts and—though Kerry would never mention this and the press seldom did either—*low*-wage earners also got bigger rate cuts. The tax burden went down for everybody who paid income taxes, just not quite so much for those in the middle. By the way, the *share* of the total tax burden—or the middle one fifth of all earners—according to projections by the Congressional Budget Office, went up from 10.5% of all federal taxes to—wait for it—10.7%. Not much of an increase, but enough to make Kerry's misleading statement literally true (Harris & Weiner, 2004).

Example #3: Bush's (2004) "Wolves" Ad⁴

I've just given you two of Democratic examples, now here are two ads from Republicans. Political bunk knows no party boundaries, in my experience.

ANNOUNCER: "In an increasingly dangerous world ... Even after the first terrorist attack on America ... John Kerry and the liberals in Congress voted to slash America's intelligence operations. By 6 billion dollars ... Cuts so deep they would have weakened America's defenses. And weakness attracts those who are waiting to do America harm." (On screen: *wolves eye the camera, as if preparing to attack.*)

BUSH: "I'm George W. Bush and I approve this message."

It's literally true that Kerry proposed to cut intelligence spending after "the first terrorist attack on America," which was in 1993. Our polling showed most voters believed Kerry proposed cuts after 9/11. The $6 billion figure is close—but it was spread over 4 years, and it amounted to about 4%. That's more of a trimming than a "slashing," and I'd reprimand any reporter who described a 4% reduction as a "slash." Would it have weakened America's defenses? The man George Bush appointed to head the Central Intelligence Agency didn't think so (Jackson, 2004, October 23). When Porter Goss was a congressman he proposed a similar cut around the same time, when everybody was trying to figure out how to get a handle on an out-of-control federal deficit. So this is another ad that uses true statements to send a false message.

Example #4: Republican National Committee's (2006) Internet Advertisement⁵

My final example of a literally true falsehood is from last year. It's a Republican National Committee video that was posted on their Web site and widely distributed by e-mail. Listen for Congressman John Murtha's words: "We're more dangerous to world peace than North Korea or Iran." It's true—Murtha really said that. Here he sounds like he's a retreat-happy "Blame America Firster," doesn't he? He was speaking at Florida International University. Now, listen to *all* of what Murtha said:

REP. JOHN MURTHA: "Fifty-six percent of the people in Spain think it's more dangerous, the United States is more dangerous in Iraq than Iran is. Every one of our allies think that the United States being in Iraq is more dangerous to world stability and world peace, every one of our allies, Great Britain, every single country, they think it's, we're more dangerous to world peace than North Korea or Iran. That says something."

As you can see, Murtha wasn't asserting that the United States is more dangerous to world peace than North Korea or Iran. He was citing international public opinion polls showing people in other nations *think* that, and he obviously disagrees (Jackson et al., 2006). When future dictionaries define the term "contextomy," they might consider using this RNC Internet ad as an example. We seldom see such an extreme case of editing a person's words to change their meaning.

There are so many ways to deceive, some of them blatant, others more subtle. Matt McGlone and Mark Knapp organized this very conference to examine some of the many varieties, including—quoting from their original proposal—"spin, hype, bullshit, doublespeak, equivocation," and the just-mentioned "contextomy" or quoting out of context. The idea is to examine what they originally called the "blood relatives of deception," less-than-factual claims that fall somewhere on a scale between an outright lie and the God's honest truth.

Now, to my perhaps too simple, journalistic mind, spin, hype, bullshit, and the rest are not "blood relatives" of deception, they *are* deception. If something deceives, it's deceptive. If it leads people to a false conclusion, it's misleading. We define spin in our book as just "a polite word for deception."

I can even cite a legal authority for this. When it comes to false advertising, the courts have upheld the Federal Trade Commission's position that a literally true statement can nevertheless constitute false advertising and be banned. That happened in the famous case of Doan's pills. Ads said—"Doan's is made for back pain relief with an ingredient [other] pain relievers don't have. Doan's makes back pain go away." Well, yes, Doan's did have a unique ingredient. And yes, Doan's was effective against back pain. But that wasn't because of the special ingredient. And Doan's was no more effective against back pain than other pain relievers, like Aspirin (Jansen, 1996).

And Bill Clinton didn't fare very well in the courts with his famous defense of the statement, "There is absolutely no sex of any kind" with Monica Lewinsky. Literally true—he wasn't having sex with her at the moment that statement was made in court. But Clinton ended up getting disbarred for such statements (DeMillo, 2006).

So where does this leave us? We humans are born inherently vulnerable to deception, and we can be deceived in many different ways. And worse, modern technology multiplies the *means* by which deceivers get over on us. If you don't believe that, allow me to introduce you to a former finance minister of Nigeria who is just aching to deposit 10 million dollars in your bank account. But it is also true that technology hands us the potential—and I stress *potential*—for avoiding deception. Thanks to the Internet, it is now possible to tap into more human knowledge more easily than ever before in human history. If only we will learn to use it properly.

At the Annenberg Center, we believe that schools should teach, as a regular part of their curriculum, the skills we all need to recognize deceptive messages, to understand the techniques that spinners and deceivers use against us, to navigate through the informational mine fields of the Internet to find reliable, authoritative facts, and finally to think analytically and logically about the evidence—something we don't do unless we're trained to. We've launched a new site—FactCheckED. org—to provide teachers with lesson plans and other tools for doing this. I hope you'll look it over.

And this conference is another step in the right direction. The more we learn about deception the better equipped we'll all be to sort through life's malarkey and see things as they really are. I'm really looking forward to these next two days. No fooling.

Notes

1. This chapter is an edited transcript of Mr. Jackson's keynote lecture at the "Interplay of Truth and Deception" conference at The University of Texas at Austin on October 5, 2007.
2. A recording of this advertisement is available in FactCheck.Org's' Internet Video Archive: http://www.factcheck.org/a_false_ad_about_assault_weapons.html
3. See http://www.factcheck.org/kerrys_tax_ad_literally_accurate_but misleading.html.
4. See http://www.factcheck.org/video/wolves.wmv
5. See http://www.factcheck.org/video/RNCwebad81606lo.wmv

References

American Dental Association. (2008). *Oral health topics: Bad breath (halitosis)*. Retrieved January 13, 2008, from http://www.ada.org/public/topics/bad_breath.asp

Andrews, R., Biggs, M., & Seidel, M. (1996). *The Columbia world of quotations*. New York: Columbia University Press.

Bayer HealthCare LLC. (2007). *One-A-Day WeightSmart Advanced frequently asked questions*. Retrieved January 7, 2008, from One-A-Day Web site: http://www.one-a-day.com/faqs_wsa.html

Cold-Eeze. (2005). *Cold-Eeze — the original one-of-a-kind zinc cold remedy*. Retrieved January 13, 2008, from http://www.coldeeze.com/

Cox Clark, B. (2006, January 24). *Emory study lights up the political brain.*

Retrieved January 13, 2008, from Emory University Web site: http://news. emory.edu/Releases/PoliticalBrain1138113163.html

Deception Wrinkle-Cheating Cream. (2004). *Deception wrinkle-cheating cream.* Retrieved January 7, 2008, from http://fdbuy.stores.yahoo.net/decept. html

DeMillo, A. (2006, January, 18). *Clinton eligible to get Arkansas law license back, but there's no indication he's trying.* New York: The Associated Press.

Dizdul, J. (2007, January 4). *Federal Trade Commission reaches New Year's resolutions with four major weight-control pill marketers.* Retrieved January 7, 2008, from Federal Trade Commission Web site: http://www.ftc.gov/ opa/2007/01/weightloss.shtm

Drugs and herbs. Hoodia: Worth trying for weight loss? (2006, February). *Consumer Reports on Health, 18*(2), 10.

Federal Trade Commission. (2007). *Organization directory.* Retrieved January 13, 2008, from http://www.ftc.gov/ftc/orgdirectory.pdf

Federal Trade Commission. (2007). *FTC Bureau of Consumer Protection – Division of Marketing Practices.* Retrieved January 13, 2008, from http:// www.ftc.gov/bcp/bcpmp.shtm

Harden, B. (1982, May 30). Vanity fare. *The Washington Post,* p. 8.

Harris, E. & Weiner, D. (2004). *Effective federal tax rates under current law, 2001 to 2014.* Retrieved January 13, 2008, from Congressional Budget Office Web site: http://www.cbo.gov/showdoc.cfm?index=5746&sequence=0

Jackson, B. (2004, June 3). *False ads: There oughta be a law! — or maybe not.* Retrieved January 13, 2008, from http://www.factcheck.org/specialreports/ false_ads_there_oughta_be_a_law.html

Jackson, B. (2004, September 14). *A false ad about assault weapons.* Retrieved January 13, 2008, from http://www.factcheck.org/a_false_ad_about_ assault_weapons.html

Jackson, B. (2004, October 4). *Bush mischaracterizes Kerry's health plan.* Retrieved January 13, 2008, from http://www.factcheck.org/bush_mischar- acterizes_kerrys_health_plan.html

Jackson, B. (2004, October 18). *Kerry falsely claims Bush plans to cut social security benefits.* Retrieved January 13, 2008, from http://www.factcheck. org/kerry_falsely_claims_bush_plans_to_cut.html

Jackson, B. (2004, October 23). *Would Kerry throw us to the wolves?* Retrieved January 13, 2008, from http://www.factcheck.org/elections-2004/would_ kerry_throw_us_to_the_wolves.html

Jackson, B. (2004, October 27). *Media fund twists the truth more than Michael Moore.* Retrieved January 13, 2008, from http://www.factcheck.org/arti- cle294.html

Jackson, B., & Bank, J. (2006, October 27). *False claims about body armor.* Retrieved January 13, 2008, from http://www.factcheck.org/article438. html

Jackson, B., & Jamieson, K. H. (2007). *unSpun: Finding facts in a world of disinformation.* New York: Random House.

Jackson, B., Novak, V., Bank, J., Ficaro, J., & Kolawole, E. (2006, October 27). *Republican mudslinging on an industrial scale.* Retrieved January 13, 2008, from http://www.factcheck.org/article460.html

Jansen, B. (1996, June 26). *FTC charges marketers of Doan's Pills with marketing deceptive back-pain relief claims.* Retrieved January 13, 2008, from http://www.ftc.gov/opa/1996/06/doans.shtm

Langer, E., Blank, A., & Chanowitz, B. (1978). The mindlessness of ostensibly thoughtful action: The role of 'placebic' information in interpersonal interaction. *Journal of Personality and Social Psychology, 36,* 635-642.

Mack, B. (2004). *FTC launches 'Big Fat Lie' initiative targeting bogus weight-loss claims.* Retrieved January 7, 2008, from Federal Trade Commission Web site: http://www.ftc.gov/opa/2004/11/bigfatliesweep.shtm

National Advertising Division. (NAD). (2005). *Bayer Healthcare (Aleve®),* Report #4323.

National Advertising Division. (NAD). (2005). *United Online, Inc. (NetZero "HiSpeed 3G"),* Report #4413.

National Institutes of Health. (2002). *Zinc and the common cold.* Retrieved January 13, 2008, from http://dietary-supplements.info.nih.gov/factsheets/cc/zinc.html

Neocleous, A. (2007). *More leads... more clients...and greater profits in your business guaranteed!* Retrieved January 15, 2008, from http://www.kaizen-marketingsystem.com/

Novak, V. (2006, November 20). *Judicial campaigns: Beginning to look a lot like Congress.* Retrieved January 13, 2008, from: http://www.factcheck.org/article470.html

Novak, V., & Miller, J. (2007, October 12). *Mitt & Rudy's cherry orchard.* Retrieved January 13, 2008, from http://www.factcheck.org/mitt_and_rudys_cherry_orchard.html

Office of Independent Counsel. (1998, September 9). *Independent Counsel's Report.* Retrieved January 13, 2008, from http://thomas.loc.gov/icreport/7grounds.htm#L83

Phytopharm PLC. (2006). *Hoodia Factfile.* Retrieved January 7, 2008, from http://www.phytopharm.co.uk/hoodiafactfile/#q10

Rep. John Murtha (D-PA) Speaking at Florida International University. (2006). Retrieved January 13, 2008, from http://video.google.com/videoplay?docid=5718988031914303903&q=murtha+florida+international

Romer, D. (2006). *Capturing campaign dynamics.* Philadelphia: University of Pennsylvania Press.

Stahl, L. (2004, November 21). *African plant may help fight fat.* Retrieved January 7, 2008, from CBS News 60 Minutes Web site: http://www.cbsnews.com/stories/2004/11/18/60minutes/main656458.shtml

U.S. Census Bureau. (2007). *World vital events.* Retrieved January 13, 2008, from http://www.census.gov/cgi-bin/ipc/pcwe

U.S. Department of Justice, Bureau of Alcohol, Tobacco, Firearms, & Explosives. (2004). *Semiautomatic assault weapon — questions and answers.* Retrieved January 13, 2008, from http://www.atf.gov/firearms/saw-faqs.htm

Zemtsov, A. (1994). *Moisturizing and cosmetic properties of emu oil: A double blind study.* Retrieved January 12, 2007, from Aussiepol Trading Web site: http://homepages.tig.com.au/~aussiepol/cosmetic.html

Chapter 2

Some Considerations for a New Theory of Deceptive Communication

Timothy R. Levine and Rachel K. Kim

Scholarly books, chapters, and articles on the topic of deceptive communication often begin with the assertion that deception is frequent, ubiquitous, and commonplace. For example, readers of the deception literature encounter claims such as "communicators frequently decide that honesty is not the best policy" and "deception and suspected deception arise in at least one quarter of all conversation" (Buller & Burgoon, 1996, p. 203). Careful consideration of the probable prevalence of deception, however, requires considering the question of relative frequency in comparison to some standard.

Perfect estimates of the prevalence of deception do not exist, and the overall frequency of deceptive communication in a society is probably not the sort of fact that is discoverable through the scientific method or otherwise. Just how does one create a representative sample of communication and then reliably ascertain truth and deception? Nevertheless, there is good reason to believe that (a) successful deception is substantially more prevalent than discovered deception, but (b) overall, while a daily occurrence, deceptive communication probably occurs with much less frequency than nondeceptive communication. Explaining the reasons behind these educated guesses requires defining deception and reviewing what is known about deception.

Consideration of definition and reliable research findings will lead to the main thesis of this chapter, namely that current theoretical approaches to deception are lacking and new theoretical directions are needed to understand deceptive communication and its detection. This chapter selectively reviews the research on deception and deception detection in an effort to suggest new and alternative perspectives on the topic. The chapter ends with a rough sketch of what a new theoretical perspective might look like.

Defining Deception

Deception involves knowingly or intentionally misleading another person.

Although this definition is simple, many important implications follow from defining deception in this way.

For a start, truth and deception are not polar opposites and deception and falsehoods are far from synonymous. For example, a so-called "honest mistake," that is, saying something that one incorrectly believes to be true, is not deception. Or, saying something known to be false is not deceptive if it is said in such a way that the hearer should know it is false. Sarcasm is an obvious example. None of these cases involves an intent to mislead. However, saying something that is literally true in a sarcastic way so that the listener infers something false can be deceptive. In short, what is literally true can be deceptive and saying something false need not be.

Following this line of thought, useful distinctions can be made between actual deception, deceptive attempts, messages perceived as deceptive, and messages that are functionally deceptive. Actual deception is meant to deceive, and achieves this end; the target person is misled by design. In deceptive attempts, someone tries to deceive, and there is deceptive intent, but the target is not actually misled. This situation may be thought of as failed deception. In perceived deception, the target person attributes deceptive intent and thinks that someone has or is lying regardless of the actual intent. Finally, messages that are functionally deceptive mislead others regardless of the actual or perceived intent. Functionally deceptive messages lead to the same outcome as deception without getting into the message source's head.

A related implication is that message features, message intent, and message function or impact need to be distinguished because these things do not map perfectly onto one another. So, someone can say something that is objectively false, omit information, change the subject, and so forth, in a manner that is either likely to, and intended to, deceive or not. The objective truth or falsity of messages may or may not actually function as deception, and such messages may or may not be perceived as deception. In short, speaker intent and message consequence in conjunction define deception, not the objective qualities of messages or information dimensions.

Deception Prevalence

Because deception, by definition, involves deceptive intent, many if not most messages that depart from the whole truth and nothing but the truth fall well short of deception. Most communication, for example, is by necessity truncated. If someone asks how you are, a simple "fine" will usually suffice, and a fully disclosive answer is typically inappropriate. After all, Grice's (1989) maxim of quantity also applies to refraining from providing too much information in addition to providing sufficient information. As a consequence, studies assessing the prevalence of "information control" (e.g., Turner, Edgley, & Olmstead, 1975) are not necessarily informative about the frequency of deception. Turner et al. find that omission, evasion, and inaccuracies are commonplace in conversation. While this is no doubt true, these forms of information control are not equivalent to deception because deceptive intent is unknown.

The impossibility of sampling deception has already been mentioned, but at least two studies provide some idea of how often people lie. DePaulo, Kashy, Kirkendol, Wyer, and Epstein (1996) had 70 college students and 70 nonstudents keep a lying diary for 1 week. During that time, the vast majority of respondents (95%) reported at least one lie, and on average, college students reported two lies per day while nonstudents reported a single lie per day. For the students, a lie was told in 30% of all interactions, and 20% of conversations for the nonstudents. These findings suggest that lying is an everyday occurrence, but also that it is relatively infrequent compared to nondeceptive communication. If one considers the sheer amount of communication we engage in during the course of a day, one to two deceptive messages is proportionally small.

More recently, Serota and Levine (2008) tried to access the prevalence of deception in American life with a different methodology. They asked a nationally representative sample of 1,000 individuals (stratified by age, sex, education, income, and region of the country) if they had lied in the last 24 hours. The mean number of lies per day was slightly less than two, a value similar to that reported above. The distribution, however, was highly skewed. Sixty percent of respondents reported zero lies in the past 24 hours, but a few of those who did lie reported as many as 54 lies. These findings suggest that many people may not lie each and every day, although we strongly suspect that almost everyone lies sometimes. More interestingly, if these findings are accurate, the findings suggest that most lies may be told by a relatively few very prolific liars. Together with the earlier findings, the conclusion seems to be that lying is prevalent in that we are likely to encounter lies on a daily basis, but infrequent in comparison to everyday honest communication. In other words, most people do lie at times, but most people are much more honest than not.

Deception Motives

Despite widespread social and moral prohibitions against deception, deception nevertheless occurs. The question that naturally arises is why do people deceive others?

The answer is that people lie for a reason. More precisely, we believe that people often deceive others when the truth poses some obstacle to goal obtainment. Absent some psychopathology, people do not deceive when the truth works just fine. In short, most people follow the maxim "Do not lie if you do not have to" most of the time.

This maxim is consistent with what noted philosopher and ethicist Sissela Bok (1999) has labeled the "principle of veracity." According to Bok, there exists a moral asymmetry between truth and deception. The telling of truth requires no justification, deceit does. Honesty and trust provide a necessary foundation for human relations and symbolic exchange. Violating these requires ethical justification whereas adherence does not.

Previous work has sought to classify deception motives in a variety of ways. For example, Turner et al. (1975) list five motivations including (a) to save face, (b) to manage relationships, (c) to exploit, (d) to avoid tension/conflict, and (e) to control situations. More commonly, motives are classified by the locus of benefit; that is, whether the deception primarily benefits self, other, or the relationship (e.g., Hample, 1980; Metts, 1989).

Examining existing typologies, it appears that none of the goals achieved through deception are at all unique to deception. That is, the various category systems delineating various motives for deception do not differ from more general social motivations guiding nondeceptive behavior. For example, consider face goals. The goal of a face-maintaining message is not to deceive per se, but to manage self and other's face needs, and these ends can be accomplished through both honest and deceptive means. Similarly, virtually all instrumental and relational goals can, depending on the situation, be achieved through both honest and deceptive actions. Thus, deception is best thought of as a possible tactic, strategy, or means for goal attainment rather than a desired end in itself.

The probability of using deceptive rather than honest means for goal attainment is likely conditional on situation features and constraints, and not on the nature or type of the goal pursued. According to Bok's (1999) principle of veracity, the moral culpability associated with deception creates an initial imbalance in the assessment of deceptive and truthful alternatives, and adopting deceptive means requires justification that is not necessary for truthful means. So, although deception is in almost everyone's social repertoire, it is generally employed as a tactical or strategic option of last resort or path of least resistance. People will not be deceptive when the truth is sufficient, efficient, and effective for goal attainment. It is only when the truth poses an obstacle to goal obtainment, regardless of what that goal might be, that people entertain the possibility of being deceptive. That is, people are deceptive only when truthful alternatives are more effortful or less efficacious.

We tested this thinking in a series of three studies (Levine, Kim, & Hamel, 2008). In Studies 1 and 2, participants considered what they would say in a set of common situations where motive to deceive was varied by making the truth problematic or not for goal obtainment. In Study 1, participants ($N = 66$) selected honest or deceptive messages in response to situations, while Study 2 ($N = 68$) replicated the first with open-ended responses coded for deceptive content. Consistent with pre-dictions, the selection or generation of deceptive messages was virtually nonexistent in situations where deception motive was absent (Study 1 = 1.6%, Study 2 = 0.0%) but substantial when such a motive was present (Study 1 = 62.5%, Study 2 = 64.3%).

The self-report findings of the first two studies were supplemented with behavioral observations in Study 3, where 126 participants were given an opportunity to cheat for monetary gain and subsequently inter-rogated about cheating. For noncheaters, sincere honesty was enough for attaining goals, but being truthful was problematic for cheaters. Once again as predicted, a substantial number of cheaters (60%) chose to lie about cheating while not a single noncheater did so. These three studies provide evidence consistent with Bok's (1999) principle of veracity. The findings indicate that people lie for a reason and generally avoid decep-tion when truth will suffice for goal attainment. On the other hand, those with a motive to deceive do not always choose to lie. The consis-tency of the findings across our three studies can be seen in Figure 2.1.

We also tested a projected motive model explaining deception detec-tion upon the idea that people not only often act in accordance with the veracity principle, but they likely believe that others adhere to it too (Levine, Kim, & Blair, 2008). That is, when people consider whether a

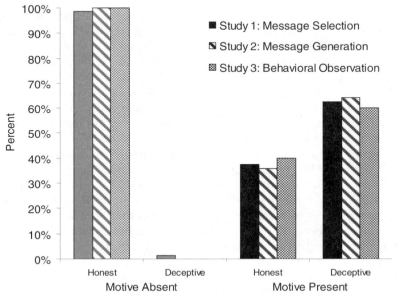

Figure 2.1 Honest and deceptive message production in Levine, Kim, and Hamel (2008).

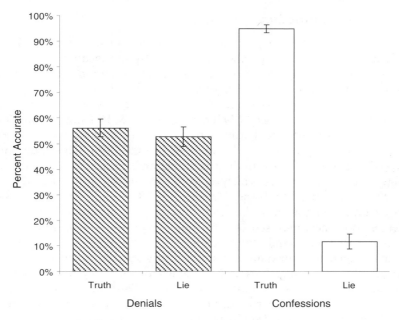

Figure 2.2 Detection accuracy for confessions and denials in Levine, Kim, and Blair (2008), Study 1.

message might be deceptive, they consider if the message source has reason to lie. If there is no perceived motive for deception, then honesty is likely presumed. Consistent with this reasoning, Levine Kim, and Blair (2008) found confessions were judged as honest more frequently than denials (η^2 = .64), and while detection accuracy was just above 50% for denials regardless of message veracity, it was 95% for true confessions, and only 12% for false confessions (see Figure 2.2). These findings also highlight the importance of the content-in-context in judgmental processes, which is generally lacking in extant deception research and theory.

Taken together, these findings have important implications for theory and research in deception. For one, motive plays a crucial role in deception, yet most studies of deception typically lack proper context reflecting the centrality of motive. For example, in many cue studies the only motive for deception is following instructions and held constant, and potential liars in detection studies often have no apparent motive at all. Another implication is that situational factors may have a stronger impact than individual differences in the probability of producing deceptive messages. Aside from perhaps a few prolific liars, people generally eschew deception unless situation features and constraints make being truthful problematic for attaining goals.

Deception Detection Accuracy

Perhaps one of the most reliable and well-documented findings in all of social science is that people are statistically significantly better than chance, but only slightly more so, at detecting deception. Meta-analysis of more than 200 separate lie detection experiments finds that people are, on average, about 54% accurate in assessing message veracity when they have a 50–50 chance of being right (Bond & DePaulo, 2006). The results of most individual studies fall within 10% of this across-study average (i.e., approximately between 45% and 65%). Thus, the only-slightly-better-than-50% finding is stable and consistent. Not surprisingly, it has become very widely accepted among deception researchers.

More recently, Bond and DePaulo (2008) looked at the variance in accuracy judgments rather than just average accuracy levels. They decomposed accuracy scores into four components: demeanor, truth-bias, transparency, and ability. *Demeanor* is the tendency of a person being judged to appear honest (or deceptive) independent of whether or not they are lying. Variance in demeanor means that some people are just more (or less) believable than others. *Truth-bias* is the tendency to believe others whether or not they are telling the truth. Variance in truth-bias means some people are more gullible than others; others are more skeptical. *Transparency* refers to how good or bad people are at lying. That is, people who are transparent tend to leak the fact that they are lying and are therefore relatively easier to distinguish when they are lying or telling the truth than those who are less transparent. Finally, *ability* is an individual difference in skill at telling if someone is lying or not. Thus, demeanor and transparency reflect variance in the message source, while truth-bias and ability reflect variance in the message judge. Further, demeanor and truth-bias reflect variance in *bias*; i.e., are tendencies to believe (or not) that are independent of actual veracity, whereas transparency and ability reflect variance in *skill* in presenting or discriminating between honest and deceptive messages.

Bond and DePaulo (2008) found that variance in demeanor is huge, both in an absolute sense and relative to the other sources of variation. Some people are just more believable than others, and this aura of believ-ability has a large impact on judges. There are also substantial individual differences in truth-bias, with these differences being much smaller than the variance in demeanor, but much larger than the two. Finally, the variance in transparency is much larger than the variance in abil-ity. Individual differences in ability contribute little (maybe only plus or minus 1% or 2% in overall accuracy). Thus, variance in believability and accuracy stems more from the message source than the person judging the message, and the variance in bias swamps variance in accuracy. This explains why accuracy values across studies are so stable. The lack of individual differences in judge ability leads to small standard errors and stable findings.

As just noted, looking across individual studies, there is relatively little between-study variance, with almost all studies reporting accuracy rates between 45% and 65%. The 4% improvement-over-chance finding is highly statistically significant and thus clearly reflects some systematic mechanism. An interesting question is why this 54% ±10% finding occurs so reliably. Why not higher accuracy? Why not lower? Why is accuracy so stable if it is not just due to mere chance?

The finding that people detect deception better than chance is not especially surprising. Most of us believe that people generally have at least some skill at reading others. What is perplexing, however, is why people systematically do better than chance, but never much better than chance. That is, a viable explanation for this reliable finding must not only account for why people systematically exceed chance, but also why people never, ever, seem to exceed chance by very much. A close look at current interpretations of these findings suggests that, while intuitive, currently accepted views really do not mesh very well with extant data.

In line with cultural inclinations associated with individualism, there is a tendency to interpret and explain detection accuracy in terms of the individual's skill, competence, and ability to ferret out lies. That is, accuracy findings are most frequently interpreted as informative about people's ability to detect deception, with a myopic emphasis on the message recipient's ability. The message recipients, after all, are the subjects in these experiences, and consequently their performance is the focus. However, all communication, including deception, requires at least two people, and there is no reason why the basis for the accuracy findings might not reside more in the message source or message itself than in the message recipient. In fact, this is just what the Bond and DePaulo (2008) findings suggest. In short, accuracy findings tell us more about the source and nature of messages being judged than the people doing the judging.

A Test-Taking Analogy

Many readers are likely familiar with giving and taking tests. Imagine that a class of 100 students is given four 100-question true-false exams over a semester. The typical interpretation of scores on tests like these is that scores of 50% reflect mere chance performance and no knowledge of class material, and that as scores approach 100%, nonrandom increases above chance levels reflect increasing mastery of course content. There is no reason to expect scores systematically below 50% because surely students would not intentionally seek a low grade by purposely missing a question they know. That is, test scores tell us about the student; how much they studied, how effectively they studied, how smart they are, their testing-taking ability, and so forth.

Now, imagine that students take a series of tests like the one described above, and the average score on each of the tests is around 55%, with all four tests producing approximately the same outcome and distribution score. The average student performs significantly better than chance, but in an absolute sense, fails miserably. Also, the standard deviations are small, so that over the four tests, all students tend to hover around the mean. Given that students tend not to do systemically worse than chance, there are few outliers on the low end to pull the mean down. What kind of explanation might best explain this pattern of test scores?

The first explanation that may occur to many readers is that the students studied a little but not very much. They learned something, but only a little. For example, the students may have learned and remembered only about 10% of the class content. So, if students knew the answers to 10 questions and guessed on the other 90 questions, then they would get the 10 they knew for sure right and get 50% of the 90 they guessed on and thus receive a 55% on the exam (10 + 45 = 55). So, a "little bit of knowledge" model can explain the outcome. But, it seems odd that *all* the students would only know a little.

An alternative explanation is that the scores tell us more about the test then the test takers. Imagine a true-false test with 90 questions that are impossibly difficult (thus necessitating guessing) and 10 questions that are so easy that everyone gets them right whether or not they took the class, studied, and so forth. This test tells us nothing at all about what was learned. Such a test, however, produces a reliable average of 55%. Further, now the lack of test-taker variance is not at all odd. It is expected. The nature of the test makes test-taker ability irrelevant. Further, to the extent that little test-taker ability variance is observed, the "test is the explanation" account is more plausible than the "little bit of knowledge" model. The test-based explanation is predicated on the idea of variance in test-item difficulty rather than in test-taker ability and is nicely consistent with the new Bond and DePaulo (2008) results.

We propose that most deception detection experiments involve an ecology very different from how people really detect lies. In most laboratory deception detection experiments, there is no motive for deception, and if there is, it is held constant. Also, the type of information people usually use to detect lies outside the lab (consistency with prior knowledge, confession, information from third parties, physical evidence, etc., see Park, Levine, McCornack, Morrison, & Ferrara, 2002) is withheld by research design. It is little wonder that people mostly guess, except when there is the occasional totally transparent liar. The 54% findings reflect the ecology of the experimental design; motive is constant, there is little external information, and there is an equal number of truths and lies.

Reasons for (In)accuracy

Much of the current thinking about deception detection has evolved from Ekman's (2001) idea of *leakage*. The idea is that there are emotional correlates of deception, that emotions are conveyed nonverbally, and that emotional expression is not entirely under conscious control. Compared to the honest message source, deceivers are apt to experience guilt, fear of detection, and so forth. Deceivers try to control behavioral displays so as not to give themselves away, but nonverbal cues to deception leak out anyway, often through nonverbal channels that are more difficult to control. Consequently, the message recipient who actively looks for the right leaked cues should be adept at distinguishing truths from lies.

The leakage idea was expanded upon by Zuckerman, DePaulo, and Rosenthal's (1981) four-factor theory of deception. The four-factor framework specifies four internal states that differentiate truths and lies: arousal, emotions, cognitive effort, and over control. Because relative to truth-tellers, liars are more likely to experience heightened internal states of arousal, emotions like fear and guilt, cognitive effort, and over control of nonverbal displays, and because each of these internal states is thought to be associated with specific nonverbal behaviors (e.g., increased cognitive effort leads to long response latencies), clues to deception are leaked nonverbally.

The most recent iteration of this thinking is reflected in Interpersonal Deception Theory (IDT; Buller & Burgoon, 1996). Liars strategically present themselves as honest, but nonstrategically leak deception cues. Message recipients pick up on these cues and become suspicious. Liars, however, pick up on leaked suspicion, and strategically adapt. In turn, so do receivers. Net accuracy depends on the liar's encoding skill (i.e., transparency) relative to the receiver's decoding skill (i.e., ability) and how the interaction progresses over time.

Thus, according to these dominant theoretical perspectives, the reason people are systematically better than chance in accuracy is that verbal and nonverbal cues indicative of deceit are inadvertently leaked, these leaked behaviors signaling deceit are then perceived, and consequently truth is correctly distinguished from lie. Accuracy is generally a function of a message judge's ability to recognize valid leakage.

From this perspective, the reason people are far from perfect is that (a) there is an imperfect link between any given behavioral display and veracity, and (b) people rely on cues that lack diagnostic utility in addition to valid cues. That is, there are no perfect cues to deception and people often look for the wrong indicators. For example, research finds that the most common belief about deception is that liars avoid eye contact whereas meta-analysis finds no link between gaze and honesty (Bond & The Global Deception Research Team, 2006; Depaulo et al., 2003).

IDT further adds that liars engage in strategic countermoves, constantly adapting their performance to appear more honest and mislead weary judges. The net result is above chance accuracy that is far from perfect.

There are good findings consistent with this view. Meta-analysis of deception cues finds that there are behaviors that probabilistically distinguish truths from lies, but no behavior or set of behaviors does so perfectly (DePaulo et al., 2003). Further, there is less than perfect correspondence between what people look for when detecting deception and the behaviors that have actual utility. Thus, above chance but less than ideal accuracy makes much sense from this perspective, and there are many supportive findings that can be cited as evidence in favor of this stance.

Not all findings in the literature, however, are in line with the ability-to-spot-leakage account. First, the Bond and DePaulo (2008) meta-analysis suggests relatively little variance in transparency and especially ability. At least on the surface, these new findings seem at odds with the skill- and leakage-based accounts. Important here is Bond and DePaulo's finding that variance in transparency in detection accuracy studies is massively larger (by a factor of 10!) than variance in ability. This suggests that accuracy is not so much a function of a person's ability to recognize leakage, but instead much more a function of individual differences in what is leaked independent of who is doing the judging. In terms of our previous test-taking analogy, the variance in accuracy is attributable to differences in test question difficulty rather than student knowledge. Back to deception, most people can lie seamlessly, but a few people's lies get detected by everyone. Accuracy findings tell us more about the liar than the detector. Clearly, this conclusion is at odds with current theory, especially IDT's cat and mouse account.

Second, efforts to enhance accuracy through nonverbal training have failed to document much in the way of improvement. For example, meta-analysis finds only marginal improvements from nonverbal training, and studies offering additional controls find even more meager results (Frank & Feeley, 2003; Levine, Feeley, McCornack, Harms, & Hughes, 2005). If low accuracy simply involved looking for the wrong cues, one would expect much better results from training studies.

Finally, a leakage and judge ability account would also predict that professional expertise would be a strong determinant of accuracy. If accuracy is a skill, people should get better with practice and experience. Police, military interrogators, customs officials, and so forth, should be better at detecting deception than the average college sophomore. Yet, meta-analysis suggests that this is not the case (Bond & DePaulo, 2006).

In short, while there is considerable evidence consistent with leakage-based accounts, there are also findings that are at odds with these accounts. Ideally, good theory should keep analogous findings to a minimum. Thus, there seems to be room for theoretical improvement.

Truth-Bias

Another reliable finding from the accuracy literature is the prevalence of truth-bias. Truth-bias is the tendency to judge messages as honest independent of actual message veracity (Levine, Park, & McCornack, 1999; Levine, Kim, Park, & Hughes, 2006). So far, truth-bias has been discussed as a source of individual variance in judgments, and Bond and DePaulo (2008) report substantial individual differences in truth-bias. Truth-bias, however, is not just (or even mostly) an individual difference. It also has a strong situational component, and it varies considerably based on situational priming (Kim & Levine, 2008; McCornack & Levine, 1990). But most importantly, truth-bias is reliably observable and has substantial impact across both individuals and situations. Bond and DePaulo (2006) found evidence for the existence of a general truth-bias across studies, and a truth-bias has been observed in every experiment we have conducted. That is, truth-bias varies in degree from person to person and situation to situation, but despite these differences, most people are truth-biased most of the time.

Consistent evidence for these claims can be seen in Table 2.1 where truth-bias rates in our research are presented in the first column. As the

Table 2.1 Truth-Bias and Veracity Effect Results

Study	Truth-Bias	Truth and Lie Accuracy	
McCornack & Levine (1990)	72%	81.8%	31.3%
Levine et al. (1999), Study 4	68%	68.5%	37.5%
Levine & McCornack (2001)	72%	75.0%	31.0%
Study 2	69%	76.7%	39.2%
Study 3	56%	56.8%	44.1%
E. Park, Levine et al. (2002)	66%	67.0%	37.0%
Levine et al. (2005), Study 1	63%	65.3%	38.6%
Study 2	62%	66.4%	43.0%
Study 4	62%	66.4%	43.2%
Levine et al. (2006)	66%	67.1%	34.3%
Levine et al. (2008), Study 1	72%	74.5%	32.1%
Study 2	68%	74.2%	37.7%
Study 3	70%	62.9%	22.5%
Kim & Levine (2008)	71%	73.8%	32.3%

reader can see, truth-bias scores range from a low of 56% to a high of 72%. In every case, the percent of messages judged as honest is greater then the 50% that is expected from nonbiased processing. We have even found a truth-bias when 100% of the messages judged were lies (Levine et al., 2006) and when judges were made highly suspicious (Kim & Levine, 2008; McCornack and Levine, 1990).

We believe there are at least three important reasons behind the strength and persistence of truth-bias. First, truth-bias stems in part from innate, hard-wired cognitive systems that govern how we process incoming information. Gilbert (Gilbert, 1991; Gilbert, Krull, & Malone, 1990) makes a convincing case that belief is a mental default, and while people can reject information as false, doing so requires additional cognitive resources and processes subsequent to comprehension. Doing otherwise would require a less efficient cognitive system, and thus there is likely an evolutionary basis for truth-bias. Second, communication requires truth-bias. If one questioned the veracity of everything others told them, communication could not operate. As Grice (1989) demonstrates, making sense out of what others say requires a presumption that they are communicating cooperatively. Finally, humans are social, and getting along with others requires some degree of trust, coordination, and consideration. Consistent with Goffman's (1955) observations, people give others considerable leeway so that social interaction is not disrupted.

Now it becomes necessary to make a brief digression. The widely accepted and incredibly reliable 54% accuracy plus or minus 10% finding has already been noted. The deception detection experiments leading to this conclusion, however, share some important elements that impact these findings. Accuracy is calculated by averaging across an equal number of truths and lies. The pervasive existence of truth-bias has important implications for the generality of the accuracy conclusions given these common research design features. These implications stem from a set of findings we call the "veracity effect" (Levine et al.,1999).

The *veracity effect* holds that, because people are truth-biased, people are more accurate in judging truths than lies, and therefore source veracity affects detection accuracy. Recall that meta-analysis suggests that (a) people are significantly, but only slightly better than chance, and (b) people tend to be truth-biased. If both are true, since people in deception experiments usually judge messages of which half are truths and half are lies, then people must be getting the truths right more frequently than the lies and truth accuracy must be greater than lie accuracy. Levine et al. (1999) found that the veracity accounted for between 30% and 60% of the variance in several detection accuracy rates in previous studies. Based on these findings, Levine et al. (1999) speculate that in many situations a priori message veracity may be the single biggest factor of deception detection accuracy. Examples of the veracity effect in our findings can be seen by comparing the second and third columns in Table 2.1. To date, the veracity effect has been evident in every deception detection experiment conducted by Levine and colleagues. More than a dozen replications to date means this is a nicely reliable finding!

Because of the veracity effect, a very different understanding of the literature is obtained when truth accuracy and lie accuracy are scored and reported separately. Just because average accuracy is better than chance does not mean that people can pick out lies more than 50% of the time. In short, different conclusions are reached when considering truth and lie accuracy separately, or when the ratio of truths and lies are unequal.

The findings consistent with the veracity effect led us to the issues of truth-lie base-rates and the Park-Levine probability model (Levine et al., 1999; Levine et al., 2006; Park & Levine, 2001). The idea is that if a priori message veracity predicts subsequent accuracy as suggested by the veracity effect findings, then the ratio of truths to lies is crucial. If the veracity effect is true, then the 54% accuracy findings from the meta-analyses reviewed at the beginning of the chapter are strictly limited to averaged rates under conditions of exactly half truths and half lies. Of course, outside the lab the probability of deception is seldom precisely 50–50. Therefore, a common design feature of 40 years of deception detection experiments has led to meta-analysis results with very limited generality.

The Park-Levine (2001) model was designed to model average detection accuracy rates at different truth-lie base-rates. That is, it seeks to answer the question, what if the base-rate is something other than exactly 50–50? According to the model, detection accuracy at any specific base-rate can be determined by the following formula:

$$\text{Average accuracy across truths and lies} =$$
$$P(H \mid T) \times P(T) + P(\sim H \mid \sim T) \times P(\sim T)$$

In words, the model predicts that observed total accuracy will be the product of truth accuracy times the proportion of messages that are true plus the product of lie accuracy times the proportion of messages that are lies where the proportion of true messages equals one minus the proportion of messages that are lies. This formula predicts linear effects and, so long as people are truth-biased, a positive slope. The more truth-biased people are, the steeper the slope. If judges are lie-biased, the slope would be negative. The y-intercept is a direct positive function of truth-lie transparency.

An initial test of the model yielded promising results. Levine et al. (2006) had one set of randomly selected subjects in a control group view a series of truths and lies with a 50–50 truth-lie base-rate. This condition

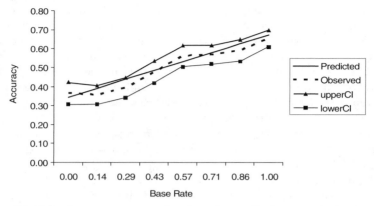

Figure 2.3 Detection accuracy as a function of truth-lie base-rate in Levine et al. (2006).

simulated previous experiments. The results were entered into the model as estimates of P (H | T) and P (~H | ~T). Then another set of subjects participated in an experiment in which the base-rate P(T) was experimentally manipulated. Participants made veracity judgments in 1 of 8 different base-rate conditions ranging from all honest to all deceptive messages. The accuracy in the eight base-rate conditions was predicted based on the formula, which condition participants were in, and the estimates obtained from the control group data. The base-rate induction substantially impacted accuracy explaining 24% of the total variance in accuracy (it explained 21% of the variance in the earlier Levine et al., 1999, Study 4). The effects were linear, with the linear contrast accounting for 95% of the base-rate effect (98% in Levine et al., 1999). The correlation between predicted values and those obtained was $r = .97$. The model predicted the slope and the intercept of the line best fitting the data to within two decimal places. Raw accuracy was predicted to within a couple percentage points. The results are portrayed in Figure 2.3. These results are exciting because they reflect a degree of prediction and precision not often seen in experimental communication research. An interesting next step will be to see if the model generalizes to interactive deception experiments.

How People Really Detect Deception

A final important consideration into deception detection comes from our "How People Really Detect Lies" study (Park et al., 2002). The idea is that deception detection experiments are restrictive in another even more fundamental way than just a common P = .50 base-rate. Whether the messages are taped or interactive, in most of these experiments all there is for judges to rely on is at-the-time verbal and nonverbal behavior of message sources. Outside the lab, however, people can fact check, talk to others, and so forth. Consequently, we expected that most lies outside the deception lab probably get detected well after the fact and by discovery methods other than utilizing verbal and nonverbal source behaviors at the time of deception. Park et al. (2002) simply asked participants to recall a lie that they had detected, to describe what happened, how they found out that the person was lying, and how much time had elapsed between the telling of the lie and its detection. Only 2% of the recalled lies were caught at the time of the telling based on source verbal and nonverbal behaviors. Most were detected after the fact, often much later, and discovery methods often included information from others, physical evidence, and subsequent confessions.

Conclusion: A Preliminary Sketch of Truth-Bias Theory

In this chapter, we offer a view of deception that departs considerably from current theory and conventional takes on the literature. Little emphasis is placed on nonverbal behaviors, leakage, and the mechanisms that produce leakage such as arousal, cognitive effort, guilt, and the like. We even will go so far as to suggest that the 54% detection accuracy finding is limited to only a very specific experimental paradigm that departs in important ways from the ecology of deception in nonresearch settings.

Our view begins with motives. Most people deceive for a reason, and would not deceive if a nondeceptive message would work just as well. The reasons people deceive are generally the same that guide nondeceptive behavior. Deception and truth are both means to goals. Deception is seldom an end in itself.

People presume others deceive for a reason. People project the motives of others, and if there is not an obvious motive for deception, people tend to believe. In contrast, many deception detection experiments do not provide a context for people to project motives, or if they do, motive is a constant so it cannot be used to distinguish between messages.

Deception, as opposed to information management, and relative to truth, is infrequent. We would ask the reader "How many times have you lied today?" We asked a nationwide sample this question, and 60% answered that they had not lied in the last 24 hours. Perhaps there is a reporting bias, but we believe that true deception is very infrequent relative to honest messages, but by no means infrequent in an absolute sense. If only 1% of messages were deceptive, given the sheer quantity of messages we receive, we would likely encounter lies daily. Nevertheless, most of what we encounter is probably honest and lacks deceptive intent.

Everyday deception is not especially arousing, emotionally charged, or cognitively effortful, and people worry little about detection unless the stakes are high. People learn to lie in childhood, and by the time they are teenagers most people can lie seamlessly most of the time. In fact, in the situations where people do lie, deception may often be an easier option than honesty (see McCornack, 1997). Further, at least for everyday deception, between- and within-individual variation in nonverbal behaviors swamps any deception-specific behaviors (see Levine et al., 2005). As a consequence, there are few diagnostically useful behaviors that reliably distinguish everyday deception from nondeceptive behavior. This may or may not be true of high-stakes situations, but those are unusual.

Consequently, additional information (e.g., confessions, prior knowledge inconsistent with a statement) is needed for deception to be detected accurately. And, this is the type of information people most often use outside the lab. As a further consequence, most deception is detected well after the fact by means other than at-the-time communicative performance of the source.

Message recipients do not actively consider the possibility of deception unless suspicion is aroused. A state of nonsuspicion is the default or status quo. Suspicion is most often a function of projecting a motive, information from an outside source, or message inconsistency with prior receiver knowledge. Absent this, there is little suspicion.

Even if suspicious, truth-bias nevertheless generally predominates. Truth-bias is likely to be especially strong in communication with close others, face-to-face (or other interactive) communication, in nonresearch settings, when there is no external information suggestive of deceit, and when an obvious motive for deception is absent.

As a consequence of deception being a low frequency event and message recipients seldom considering it as even a possibility, most people are correct in their assumption of honesty most of the time. This is adaptive and allows communication to function. However, deceptive messages slip through undetected. As a further consequence, at-the-time accuracy is a function of truth-bias and truth-lie base-rate; average accuracy approximates 50%, truth accuracy is higher, and lie accuracy is lower.

References

Bok, S. (1999). *Lying: Moral choice in public and private life.* New York: Vintage Books.

Bond, C. F., & The Global Deception Research Team. (2006). A world of lies. *Journal of Cross-Cultural Psychology, 37*, 60–74.

Bond, C. F., Jr., & DePaulo, B. M. (2006). Accuracy of deception judgments. *Review of Personality and Social Psychology, 10*, 214–234.

Bond, C. F., Jr., & DePaulo, B. M. (2008). Individual differences in judging deception: Accuracy and bias. *Psychological Bulletin, 134*, 477–492.

Buller, D. B., & Burgoon, J. K. (1996). Interpersonal deception theory. *Communication Theory, 6,* 203–242.

DePaulo, B. M., Kashy, D. A., Kirkendol, S. E., Wyer, M. M., & Epstein, J. A. (1996). Lying in everyday life. *Journal of Personality and Social Psychology, 70,* 979–995.

DePaulo, B. M., Lindsay, J. J., Malone, B. E., Muhlenbrick, L., Charlton, K., & Cooper, H. (2003). Cues to deception. *Psychological Bulletin, 129,* 74–118.

Ekman, P. (2001). *Telling lies.* New York: Norton.

Frank, M. G., & Feeley, T. H. (2003). To catch a liar: Challenges for research in lie detection training. *Journal of Applied Communication Research, 31,* 58–75

Gilbert, D. T. (1991). How mental systems believe. *American Psychologist, 46,* 107–119.

Gilbert, D. T., Krull, D. S., & Malone, P. S. (1990). Unbelieving the unbelievable: Some problems in the rejection of false information. *Journal of Personality and Social Psychology, 59,* 601–613.

Goffman, E. (1955). On face-work: An analysis of ritual elements in social interaction. *Psychiatry, 18,* 213–231.

Grice, P. (1989). *Studies in the way of words.* Cambridge, MA: Harvard University Press.

Hample, D. (1980). Purpose and effects of lying. *The Southern Speech Communication Journal, 46,* 33–47.

Kim, R. K., & Levine, T. R. (2008). *The effect of suspicion on deception detection accuracy: A reconceptualization and replication of McCornack and Levine (1990).* Manuscript submitted for publication.

Levine, T. R., Feeley, T., McCornack, S. A., Harms, C., & Hughes, M. (2005). Testing the effects of nonverbal training on deception detection accuracy with the inclusion of a bogus training control group. *Western Journal of Communication, 69,* 203–218.

Levine, T. R., Kim, R. K., & Blair, J. P. (2008). *(In)accuracy at detecting true and false confessions and denials: An initial test of a projected motive model of veracity judgments.* Manuscript submitted for publication.

Levine, T. R., Kim, R. K., & Hamel, L. M. (2008). *People lie for a reason: Three experiments documenting the principle of veracity.* Manuscript submitted for publication.

Levine, T. R., Kim, R. K., Park, H. S., & Hughes, M. (2006). Deception detection accuracy is a predictable linear function of message veracity base-rate: A formal test of Park and Levine's probability model. *Communication Monographs, 73,* 243–260.

Levine, T. R., Park, H. S., & McCornack, S. A. (1999). Accuracy in detecting truths and lies: Documenting the "veracity effect." *Communication Monographs, 66,* 125–144.

McCornack, S. A. (1997). The generation of deceptive messages: Laying the groundwork for a viable theory of interpersonal deception. In J. O. Greene (Ed.). *Message production* (pp. 91–126). Mahwah, NJ: Erlbaum.

McCornack, S. A., & Levine, T. R. (1990). When lovers become leery: The relationship between suspicion and accuracy in detecting deception. *Communication Monographs, 57,* 219–230.

Metts, S. (1989). An exploratory investigation of deception in close relationships. *Journal of Social and Personal Relationships, 6,* 159–179.

Park, E., Levine, T. R., Harms, C., & Ferrerra, M. (2002). Group and individual accuracy in deception detection. *Communication Research Reports, 19,* 99–106.

Park, H. S., & Levine, T. R. (2001). A probability model of accuracy in deception detection experiments. *Communication Monographs, 68,* 201–210.

Park, H. S., Levine, T. R., McCornack, S. A., Morrison, K., & Ferrara, M. (2002). How people really detect lies. *Communication Monographs, 69,* 144–157.

Serota, K., & Levine, T. R. (2008). *The prevalence of deception in American life.* Unpublished manuscript, Michigan State University.

Turner, R. E., Edgley, C., & Olmstead, G. (1975). Information control in conversations: Honesty is not always the best policy. *Kansas Journal of Sociology, 11,* 69–89.

Zuckerman, M., DePaulo, B. M., & Rosenthal, R. (1981). Verbal and nonverbal communication of deception. In L. Berkowitz (Ed.), *Advances in experimental and social psychology* (Vol. 14, pp. 1–59). New York: Academic.

Chapter 3

Gray Area Messages

Gary D. Bond and Lassiter F. Speller

> Falsehoods committed by people who are mistaken or self-deceived are not lies, but literal truths designed to mislead are lies. (DePaulo et al., 2003, p. 74)

Adolescents tend to think about the world in absolute terms: true/false, right/wrong, good/evil (Perry, 1999). We believe that the idealism peculiar to youth springs from dualistic thinking. Like the wily detective in the interrogation room, we can extract the truth after sifting through layers of fabrication. Like Don Quixote, we can venture out and try to right the wrongs of the world. Like Michael the archangel, we can wage a winning battle against evil. When we cross the ambiguous threshold into adulthood, however, we realize that dualistic thinking is, well, sort of naïve. We begin to perceive the world as a conundrum filled more with shades of gray than with neat rows of absolute black and white. When we talk specifically about deception and truth in this chapter, we will assert that those endpoints are not black and white opposites, but are rather crude, arbitrarily-drawn communicative boundaries. Even the definitions of deception and truth carry with them several exceptions, as noted next.

Many definitions of deception include the deliberate intention to mislead others (DePaulo et al., 2003; Ekman, 2001; Ekman & O'Sullivan, 2006), but intentional misleading is sometimes not deception. For example, one might joke or use irony or sarcasm without intentionally misleading another if one believes that the listener knows one's intent (Taylor, Lussier, & Maring, 2003). If the listener has the necessary cognitive capability, coupled with an accurate shared mental model of the conversation, then the messenger may safely assume that the joke or sarcasm will be "got" by the listener. Ekman (2001) and Ekman and O'Sullivan (2006) define "lie" as the deliberate intention to mislead "without prior notification of the target of the lie" (Ekman & O'Sullivan, 2006, p. 674). This definition excludes jokes, irony, and sarcasm, but incorporates "lie" in the definition of the same construct. Transmitting information to a listener to create a false conclusion (Buller & Burgoon, 1994) is also advanced as a definition of deception, but sometimes the transmittal of inaccurate information is not deliberate. The reader can see that though intentional misleading without notifying the target is deceptive, and creating a false conclusion in others is deceptive, these definitions invite caveats, casting the definitions in gray like the concept.

Conversely, what is truth? Philosophers have debated definitions of truth for centuries. Avicenna defined truth as what corresponds in the mind to that which is outside it, and Aquinas said that truth is conformity of the intellect to the "things" (Aertsen, 1988). Each of us holds versions of what we believe to be truthful depictions of events in our memory stores, and when contrasted with "reality," which is external and sometimes tangible (Ekman & O'Sullivan, 2006), internal and external truth are often at odds. If we are describing what we believe to be a true episodic event verbatim from memory, for example, we may experience the problem of reconstruction (Bartlett, 1932). If we present the recalled memory to another, we may faithfully and vividly reproduce some elements of the event; however, we will probably fill in some information by presenting the gist of the remainder of elements that makes our story seem mostly true. Thus, internal truth based in memory sometimes ranges far from external truth.

All Messages Are Gray Due to the Motivation of Self-Presentation

Given that truth and its opposite are abstractions surrounded by dense fog, we propose that the majority of language produced in conversation is composed of gray area messages—messages which have probabilistic veracity: mostly true, somewhat true, equally true and false, somewhat false, and mostly false—messages which lie between ambiguous absolutes. Scholars have argued that the line between truth and deception is often blurred in human interaction (e.g., Bavelas, Black, Chovil, & Mullett, 1990; DePaulo et al., 2003; McCornack, 1997): people do not usually state the whole truth and nothing but the truth, and they do not usually completely fabricate messages. Subtly shading message information (McCornack, 1988) is a uniquely human linguistic art honed over thousands of years. Why has communication evolved to the point that we shade almost all messages in conversation? DePaulo et al. (2003), following a perspective presented by Schlenker (1982, 2002) and Pontari and Schlenker (2000), argued that all truthful and deceptive messages are motivated by self-presentation, where people attempt to control impressions that others make of them (DePaulo et al., 2003, p. 77). Whether these impressions are being formed in informal, brief meetings between strangers in a grocery store, between students in a university library, or in a lengthy and formal interrogation between suspect and detective, most people will seek to manage their self-presentations to others. Arguably, the motivation to make ourselves appear to be greater than what we think ourselves to be is a stronger motivation than to faithfully follow the maxims of communication (Grice, 1989). DePaulo (1992) and DePaulo et al. (2003) reasoned that the self-presentational approach is central in understanding nonverbal communication and in predicting cues to deceptive behaviors, respectively. DePaulo et al. (2003), however, do not constrain the self-presentational perspective solely to nonverbal behaviors.

Self-presentation in verbal behavior has been studied in terms of presenter strategies and attributions that others make of the presenter, and in terms of the quantity and types of lies told when self-presentation is the goal of a conversation. Godfrey, Jones, and Lord (1986) looked at differences in the verbal behaviors of participants who wished to ingratiate and those who wished to self-promote, both of which are strategies used in self-presentation. The researchers found that people who are self-promoters show more proactive behaviors, whereas people who use the strategy of ingratiation use more reactive behaviors. Feldman, Forrest, and Happ (2002) evaluated the self-presentational goals of likeability and competence in assessments of verbal behaviors in a study, and found that people who held those self-presentational goals lie more in interactions with others than people who merely "act as they normally [do] when they meet someone new" (Feldman et al., 2002, p. 164). The researchers reported that people who were told to appear to be likable and competent told an average of two lies to their conversational partners over a 10 minute interaction, and those statements mainly involved lies about feelings.

Arguably, all verbal and nonverbal communication is motivated by self-presentation. We will note that self-presentation is not always managed in a positive direction. People do not always present gray area messages to favorably manage others' impressions of themselves. People also manage their impressions unfavorably in attempts to seek rewards. People seek sympathy from others by exaggerating negative events or situations to strengthen feelings of self-worth, or they seek some tangible or intangible gain in presenting themselves unfavorably to others. We believe that the motivation to present ourselves favorably (or unfavorably) to others is associated with the prevalence of gray area messages in human communication.

Maintaining Others' Face

People manage their "face" to others through self-presentation, but many of us seek to maintain others' self-presentations, or face, as well. Editing our comments about other's actions, achievements, plans for the future, and a variety of other behaviors, is commonplace. If we care about the person asking for our opinion about their future career plan to become a physician, and we are aware that their grades, work ethic, and area of previous study are incompatible with that goal, we will probably be gentle yet ambiguous when making remarks about their self-relevant goal (Bavelas et al., 1990). We would probably avoid presenting the hurtful truth, which is that their grade point average is mediocre, they often miss classes, and they are majoring in graphic design. We would probably prefer not to lie to them and say "go for it—you have the grades, work ethic, and background to become a physician." In situations where we truly care about the person asking for our guidance, we would probably equivocate truthfully (Bavelas et al., 1990), presenting somewhat true or mostly true gray area messages.

Tall Tales and Bullshit

In certain situations, people tell tall tales to each other to pass the time and sometimes to practice "one-upmanship." Self-presentation may not be the greatest motivation to shade messages in these situations, although self-presentation is still an underlying motivator. The reader can imagine that prisoners with time on their hands tell tall tales or stories to one another, mostly to avoid monotony, to bond, or to entertain each other. In studies conducted with prisoners, the first author held lengthy interviews with prisoners to talk about deception in that context. One inmate said that most of the lies he hears in prison are stories of no great consequence. "But the distrust is not so much verbal as what they're gonna tell you or what they're gonna say to you, but what they're gonna do to you" (Bond, Malloy, Arias, Nunn, & Thompson, 2004, p. 9). Other prisoners mentioned similar experiences of hearing stories about intimate relationships, criminal activity, or dealing with elements of the legal system.

Acquaintances in a bar or beer house will also be inclined to exaggerate or play the "I can top that accomplishment" conversational game. When the stated accomplishment exceeds some threshold of believability, we might just say that the speaker is presenting a certain blend of truth and deception which in common parlance is termed "bullshit." We include tall tale telling, exaggeration, and bullshit (for lack of a more acceptable term) as gray area message presentations which involve the self-presentational motivation as an underlying goal.

Interspersed Veracity

Long ago, Augustine (395/1887) described a liar who, at a loss for something "sweet," would interweave truthful information into a deceptive message, in order to continue the message through to conclusion (p. 466). Since the dawn of time, or at least since Augustine's formal description of this interweaving-of-veracity phenomenon, we have had gray area messages comprised of *interspersed veracity*. McCornack (1997) makes reference to hybrid truth + lie messages, noting that most deception manipulations in the laboratory are contrived and artificial, and that in real life, people actually present hybrid messages when deceiving. If people do this in real life, and they are brought into a research setting, one would expect that people would behave in much the same way. This would contribute to lower rates of detection in experiments designed to test how accurate people are at detecting truth and deception. In the lab, researchers often ask participants to tell an absolute truth or an absolute lie, sometimes without knowing whether the participants actually did so (see Sporer, 1997, for an example). If a person is asked to state the opposite of an opinion, such as their attitude toward the death penalty (O'Sullivan & Ekman, 2004), a "true" opinion may be influenced by what the person believes the experimenter wishes to hear, and the opposite of that opinion composed on-the-fly is really just a gray area message constructed opposite another gray area message. A truthful opinion (and a deceptive opinion) about the death penalty may merely follow a familiar script (DePaulo et al., 2003) recited from gist knowledge derived from a political science course or from political statements.

Displacements

In real life, people report that more than half of the time they base their lies on experiences from their own lives, but alter critical details in order to deceive (Malone, Adams, Anderson, Ansfield, & DePaulo, 1997). This finding led us to explore specific gray area messages which are presented in a form that we will call *displacements*. Displacements are literally true, mostly true, or somewhat true messages with strategically altered critical contextual details or information. *Context* can represent many things (e. g., Lee, Bond, Scarbrough, Gillan, & Cooke, 2007), but what often comes to mind when we think of contextual details or information are specific environmental elements, such as time, space, or emotion. Although there are many types of contextual details or information that a speaker might displace to present gray area messages, we decided to test temporal, spatial/setting, and affective displacements in an experiment which we will describe at the end of this chapter. Before we describe the experiment and our measures of displacements, we will discuss each displacement in turn.

Temporal Displacements

A temporal context can be thought of as a time span or temporal setting, such as one workday, one event of limited duration, a season, the decade of the 1970s, etc. In autobiographical memory studies, time is represented as a context or a framework within which we may cue and recall memories (Conway & Pleydell-Pearce, 2000). Episodes of our lives have an event-general timeframe ("When I was a teenager...") and/or an event-specific timeframe ("On my 16th birthday..."). We are aware of temporal details as an autobiographical context and as a framework for current and future details in our lives.

Literal truths designed to mislead are technically lies (DePaulo et al., 2003), and we believe that most literal truths are gray area messages presented in the form of temporal displacements. They are certainly not complete fabrications but they are interspersed veracity statements in which only one critical detail is displaced—the time that the event took place. These literally true messages are used to manage self-presentation and to create alibis.

Suppose we wish to present ourselves as younger than we truly are in an effort to manage others' impressions of us as a vibrant, energetic, youthful person, though in reality we fit squarely within the bounds of middle age. One way to manage a youthful impression is to displace time—we vividly describe a true event in our lives, such as our high school graduation, but we subtly displace the time that the event occurred—"I graduated from high school in 1990," rather than a true 1980 graduation date. We tell the literal truth yet strategically displace a critical temporal detail in order to appear to be younger than our true age, with the goal of managing other's impressions of ourselves.

Temporal displacements are also used to create effective alibis. A college student misses an important exam, and she comes to the professor in tears the day after the exam is scheduled, saying that a grandparent has passed away, and she was unable to take the exam. The student remembers the emotions and the setting within which the grandparent died, and vividly recalls the truthful heart-wrenching details to the professor. She alters only one critical contextual detail: time. The grandparent actually passed away over a year ago, but the time of the event is displaced to the date of the scheduled exam. Perhaps the student has not studied for the exam, and hopes that the professor will grant a make-up sometime in the future. In this case, the literal truth is pulled from the past and plugged in at a convenient time to create an alibi.

Spatial/Setting Displacements

A spatial context represents settings, objects, or arrangements in an environment. A city, a hotel room, weapons of mass destruction, the layout of a hedge maze on an English estate, or the placement of buildings in a downtown district all represent spatial/setting contexts. Liars present mostly true statements describing some vivid memory, but alter spatial/setting details to create false impressions in others, and to create alibis.

In a contemporary American example, O. J. Simpson and others were arrested for going into a hotel room in Las Vegas, Nevada, to retrieve what Simpson believed were stolen sports-related items and memorabilia that belonged to him. Mr. Simpson is a widely-known American public figure noted for his former football, sports reporting, commercial acting, and film acting careers. He also gained notoriety when he was tried but not convicted in the 1994 murder of his wife, Nicole Brown Simpson. In the Las Vegas case, Simpson denied to the police that accomplices had brought weapons into the room to threaten the alleged memorabilia thieves, but others involved in the event said the Simpson group wielded weapons in the hotel room. Simpson was convicted on several charges, including conspiracy to commit a crime, robbery, assault, and kidnapping with a deadly weapon, and sentenced to 33 years in prison. Although Simpson maintained that there were no weapons involved in the retrieval of items, some of Simpson's accomplices admitted that they had weapons when going into the hotel room, indicating that perhaps Simpson used a spatial/setting displacement to create an alibi. Simpson stated that he went into the hotel room to retrieve what he thought to be stolen items belonging to him, so he did present mostly-true information to the police, with the critical spatial/setting detail, weapons, possibly displaced for the sake of minimizing the consequences of the alleged criminal action.

Affective Displacements

Emotional context is an ever-changing environment within one person. Sexual attraction, the experience of death, winning a major match or game in sports, or the experience of skydiving all create an emotional context within a person. Affective displacement involves transposing affect from one situation or person and applying that affect to another situation or person in order to deceive, or it involves denying one's true emotion toward a situation, event, or person, or displaying a different emotion from what is truly felt. We present affective displacements to others mainly for self-presentation or to maintain other's face.

DePaulo and Rosenthal (1979) asked participants in a study to tell the truth about how they felt about an important person, and participants were asked to lie about their feelings toward an important person. The person spoken about was either a positive or negative figure in the speakers' lives. The important person paradigm has been used in several studies to create lies and truths for detectors, in order to assess how accurate people are at detecting deception (e.g., Bond, 2008; Sporer, 1997). However, these statements are not absolute lies and truths; they are gray area messages. Even if one feels mostly positive toward a person, such as one's mother, the positive feelings are probabilistic, in that there are negative events we experience even with the kindest people in our lives. Shading statements to create an all-positive, no-negative impression of a loved one is not a presentation of the absolute truth, but is a select collection of gray area statements designed to paint a glowing picture that is mostly or somewhat true, but involves omissions (McCornack, 1992) of negative information. In everyday life, we speak of events involving social others or we talk about other's traits, intentions, motivations, beliefs, and attributes. If we want to explain one of our own attributes, such as a tendency to be choosy when it comes to dating the right person, we may attribute this tendency to be cautious in love based on a perception of our parents' poor relationship. In this example, we paint a gloomy picture of our parents' relationship to our friends in order to explain away our conservative romantic tendencies. However, our parents probably did not experience all negative events in their relationship. Speaking negatively about others is one way to explain our dating behavior, but when we speak generally in negatives about others, we are omitting some positive information, creating gray area messages in the form of affective displacements.

An Empirical Test of Displacements

How different are gray area messages from "absolute" messages—truth and complete fabrication? We decided to test temporal, spatial/setting, and affective displacements in an experiment focused on the verbal dimensions of gray area messages, and the emotional arousal associated with making those statements, in order to explore linguistic and acoustic characteristics of displacements. Are gray area statements closer to absolute truth, or are they closer to completely-fabricated statements? In verbal accounts of truly-experienced events, truth-tellers present perceptually-based details of those events while liars, who are fabricating events from internally-generated thought processes or imagination, show more evidence of cognitive processes in their verbal accounts (Masip, Sporer, Garrido, & Herrero, 2005). In deception research, the analysis of verbal details is derived from basic memory research and theory presented by Johnson and Raye (1981), described in more detail below. Truth-tellers also do not show the heightened emotional arousal that people show when they completely fabricate messages (Zuckerman, DePaulo, & Rosenthal, 1981). Autonomic responses under increased arousal, such as pupil dilation, increased blinking, and higher voice pitch, may be due to a generalized undifferentiated arousal, or may be due to the specific emotion felt by a person when lying (Zuckerman et al., 1981). DePaulo et al. (2003), in a meta analysis of cues associated with deception, reported that higher voice pitch, in identity-relevant situations, was significantly higher for liars versus truth-tellers. People lie to make themselves appear to be greater than they think that they are (DePaulo, Kashy, Kirkendol, Wyer, & Epstein, 1996) in identity-relevant goal situations, and voice pitch is higher under those circumstances.

In sum, people who lie tend to provide fewer verbal details based on perception to others; they provide more evidence of cognitive processes in their verbal accounts; and their voice pitch is higher in deceptive identity-relevant situations. We wonder if displacements lack those critical verbal details and whether they are highly arousing, like deceptive statements, or whether they are more like telling the truth. We will describe the measures of verbal details next, and then we will describe the voice pitch measure used in our experiment.

Effect of Gray Area Messages on Reality Monitoring Coding Systems

In examining memories, various Reality Monitoring (RM) attributes, such as sensory, spatial, temporal, cognitive operations, and affective information, help to validate source authenticity (Johnson, 1988; Johnson, Foley, Suengas, & Raye, 1988; Johnson, Hashtroudi, & Lindsay, 1993). Although memories consist of many attributes, there are sensory characteristics, characteristics of the type of cognitive processing used (e. g., imagery), semantic content attributes (e. g., emotional connotation), and contextual attributes (time and place; Johnson & Raye, 1981). Memories originating in thought should be composed of more cognitive operations such as reflection and decision processes (Johnson et al., 1988).

RM has been applied to the coding of natural language and text in deceptive and truthful communications because there is evidence that truthful communication shows greater sensory, temporal, spatial, and affective information, while deceptive statements exhibit lower frequencies of those kinds of terms, following the Reality Monitoring literature which examines source memory. Thus, in studies that code deceptive and truthful statements, a speaker's message is examined for RM attributes, and the same RM categories used to identify a false memory in Reality Monitoring studies can be used to identify a deceptive statement. Further, RM categories used to identify a true memory can be used to identify a truthful statement. Over several studies that have coded RM characteristics of natural language, deceptive statements show lower sensory, spatial, affective, and temporal information (e. g., Sporer, 1997; Vrij, Edward, Roberts, & Bull, 2000), and show greater numbers of cognitive mechanism words (Bond & Lee, 2005; Newman, Pennebaker, Berry, & Richards, 2003). However, since much of our language involves the production of gray area messages, this suggests reasons why linguistic coding of deceptive statements is sometimes a difficult enterprise, resulting in findings that are minimally significant (e. g., Sporer, 1997) or in the wrong direction (e. g., Bond & Lee, 2005). In our experiment, Linguistic Inquiry and Word Count software (LIWC; Pennebaker, Francis, & Booth, 2001) was used to code some of the

Reality Monitoring categories of words in paroled felons' and university students' language produced under three conditions: an interrogation about a mock crime, a simulated job interview, and a description of a liked or disliked person. Those conditions are described in more detail in the experiment's Method section. RM categories used to code "absolute" truths, "absolute" lies, and temporal, spatial/setting, and affective displacements are senses, time, space, affect, and cognitive mechanism (cognitive operations) words, which are some of the built-in categories that LIWC uses to automatically code words. Words such as "appear," "call," and "speak," are coded as sensory words by LIWC. Temporal word examples are "during," "age," and "noon." Space word examples are "wide," "under," and "high." Some examples of affect words are "warmth," "love," and "bother." Cognitive mechanism words (cognitive operations), which should be higher in fabricated statements, are "cause," and "know," for examples.

Paroled felons and students are included in this study for several reasons. Bond and Lee (2005) found that although prisoners used greater sensory words in their truthful statements, they used more space words in their deceptive statements, unlike several studies in which students used greater sensory, temporal, spatial, and affective terms in their truthful statements and more cognitive operations words in their lie statements (e. g., Sporer, 1997; Vrij, Akehurst, Soukara, & Bull, 2004). Bond and Lee (2005) suggested that prisoners were highly aware of their context (e. g., being locked up; living in concrete and razor-wired rectangles; etc.), and so space, being in mind, was used frequently as a setting for fabricated events. Most deception research has been conducted with university students who are easily accessible to researchers. Scholars who do not elect to go out in the field to work with other populations believe that university students are generally representative of the population, but we believe that most people with a criminal background, and/or people who are repeat offenders, often do not even complete high school (Bond, Thompson, & Malloy, 2005) and few probably enroll in or complete university studies. If we wish to understand truthful and deceptive language as produced by people with a criminal background, as well as by people who represent a noncriminal population, it is necessary to sample and study people from each population.

Gray Area Messages and Voice Pitch

How does the inclusion of displacements challenge assertions that deception researchers have made over the years regarding arousal, cognitive complexity of deception, and attempted control of verbal and nonverbal behaviors while lying? Any type of deceptive action might increase emotional and physiological arousal; although without conducting voice pitch analyses (e.g., Streeter, Krauss, Geller, Olson, & Apple, 1977; Zuckerman, DeFrank, Hall, Larrance, & Rosenthal, 1979), or incorporating other measures of autonomic arousal, researchers would not know if participants in one or more of the displacement categories would exhibit greater undifferentiated arousal and/or more specific affect experienced while lying (Zuckerman, DePaulo, & Rosenthal, 1981). In terms of absolutes, heightened arousal for high-stakes liars (Ekman, 1992), as measured in voice pitch, would probably be greatest when presenting a complete fabrication, because strong cognitive effort would be required to remember and replicate completely false propositions presented to an interrogator, for example. The task of creating a complete fabrication may be more cognitively complex than telling a truthful message, even in everyday life (Zuckerman et al., 1981). Yet when a person tells the literal truth but merely changes the time that the truthful instance occurred (temporal displacement), the liar must remember only one global deceptive proposition: that of the new temporal framing of the truthful instance. Arguably, temporal displacement is not more complex than delivering a truthful statement, and requires an insignificant amount of extra memory storage and retrieval in order to keep temporal details in the story straight. Spatial/setting displacement, likewise, although slightly more laborious in terms of keeping details straight, should not be significantly different than telling a truthful story. The propositions that must be held in mind are those that frame the context, which is deceptive, although the truth remains the same. The deceiver may be concerned with being found out, which might heighten internal anxiety, but the mental processes and operations required to carry out the temporal and spatial/setting displacements draw minimally on cognitive resources when compared to a complete fabrication, where several propositions must be simultaneously held in working memory and processed, in order to avoid discrepancies and ultimate discovery of the deception. Affective displacement might be more complex to carry out effectively than temporal and spatial/setting displacement, since liars tend to produce more negative statements when lying (Bond & Lee, 2005; DePaulo et al., 2003; Horvath, 1973), if they were to try to hide a positive feeling for another person. If they were expressing positive statements about a person they disliked, it would be more difficult to maintain those positive expressions, since negative affect might leak (Ekman & Friesen, 1969) during the description.

We measured voice pitch using Avaaz Timed Frequency Representation (TFR; Avaaz, Innovations, Inc.) software, by averaging fundamental frequency (F_o) of the voice over the duration of each statement. F_o (voice pitch) has been found to be elevated in deceptive statements when compared to truthful statements in a number of studies (e. g., Anolli & Ciceri, 1997; Ekman, 1985; Scherer, 1981; Streeter et al., 1977).

Method

Participants

Sixteen paroled felons, ages 20–49, participated in one group. Six Caucasian (3 males, 3 females), 7 Hispanic (3 males, 4 females), and 3 African American (2 males, 1 female) participants acted as message presenters. Previous convictions included murder, robbery, child abuse, assault, and burglary. Time on parole ranged from 1 week to 4 years. Each participant received $40. Sixteen university students participated as message presenters in another group for partial course credit. One Caucasian (1 male), 1 Hispanic (1 male), and 14 African Americans (6 males, 8 females), ages 18–44, participated. Experiments lasted 3 hours with breaks. Interrogators and job interviewers were undergraduate and graduate students.

Procedure

Paroled felon participants reported age, years of education, ethnicity, convictions, sentence length, length of prison term(s) served, and time since latest release from prison. Students reported age, years of education, and ethnicity. Experimenters read instructions to participants before each of the interrogation, interview, and person description sessions. Participants produced statements in the three procedural conditions.

Interrogation Session   Participants were instructed to go to a professor's office. Participants were asked to wait in a hallway until all people in the professor's office left to take a break. Participants were told to enter

Table 3.1 *Reality Monitoring Algorithm Results: Paroled Felon and Student Groups*

Statement Type	Group	
	Paroled Felons M (SD)	University Students M (SD)
Absolute Truth	1.51 (6.7)	7.76 (4.9)
Complete Fabrication	1.36 (5.8)	5.51 (8.7)
Temporal Displacement	1.42 (7.1)	6.38 (8.9)
Spatial/Setting Displacement	1.49 (9.4)	5.97 (8.5)
Affective Truth	1.97 (7.1)	7.99 (7.0)
Affective Displacement	1.21 (7.5)	7.72 (7.8)

Notes. A repeated measures analysis of variance showed no differences within groups (paroled felons, students), with Greenhouse-Geisser corrected estimates, $F(4.34, 130.29) = 0.22, p = .94$. Mauchly's test indicated that the assumption of sphericity had not been violated, $X^2(14) = 10.63, p = .72$. Between groups, there were statistically significant differences in algorithm values, $F(1, 30) = 17.51, p = .0001$.

the office, take a specific book from a bookshelf, and hide it under the professor's desk. Participants were told to tell the complete truth about what he or she did in an interrogation, and were told to make up a complete fabrication about the book removal. They also were told to create an alibi by describing a true event which took place before they reported for the experiment, and to report that the event occurred during the time the alleged book removal took place (temporal displacement). In a fourth condition, they were told to create an alibi by saying that they were in a different setting during the time that the alleged book removal took place (spatial/setting displacement). All conditions were counterbalanced.

Interview   Participants filled out a generic employment application and were told that they would be interviewed for a mock position. In counterbalanced orders, participants were told to tell the truth and completely fabricate their job history to the interviewer. They were also told to tell the literal truth about their past work history, but only to change time details (e. g., "I worked at Vic's Landscaping Service from Feb., 1999 to March, 2001"; temporal displacement). In a fourth interview, they were told to change the cities in which they worked (spatial/setting displacement).

Affective Displacement   Participants were asked to talk about a person that they truly liked in a truthful and in a deceptive way. They also spoke truthfully and deceptively about a person that they disliked. Each participant produced four statements (two truthful, two deceptive) in the affective displacement condition.

Participant Statement Videotaping   Participants were videotaped with a Sony Digital Handycam mounted on a tripod. Audio from the video was converted to .wav files using GoldWave digital audio editing software (GoldWave, Inc.), so that language could be transcribed and processed in LIWC, and so that voice pitch could be analyzed using Avaaz TFR.

Results

Message Details: LIWC

An algorithm was constructed to determine whether the Reality Monitoring framework would discriminate truthful from deceptive messages, and also to determine how gray area messages would compare to those "absolutes." The algorithm was set up as follows:

sensory + time + space + affect − cognitive mechanism words

Proportions of words recognized and coded by LIWC were used in the algorithm. A repeated measures analysis of variance revealed that the algorithm did not discriminate displacements from either truth or lies within the paroled felon or student groups. However, there were expected differences between groups on all message types. Paroled felons provided fewer RM details in their messages overall than students. Table 3.1 shows means and standard deviations of the paroled felon and student groups, and the repeated measures analysis of variance test results.

Arousal Analysis: Voice Pitch

Within groups, t-tests showed no significant differences in the paroled felon group in voice pitch except between affective displacement and affective truth statements, $t(15) = 3.19$, $p = .006$. Interestingly, complete fabrications were not more arousing for felons when compared to their truthful statements, although lying about an important person was more arousing than telling the truth about an important person. In the student group, mirroring results in past research studies, voice pitch was higher in complete fabrications when compared to truth, $t(15) = 6.61$, $p = .0001$. Temporal displacements were not as arousing as complete fabrications, $t(15) = 3.06$, $p = .008$, but were significantly more arousing than telling the truth, $t(15) = 6.56$, $p = .0001$. Table 3.2 depicts descriptive statistics and t-test results for both groups.

Table 3.2 Voice Pitch Results: Paroled Felon and Student Groups

	Group	
Statement Type	*Paroled Felons* *M (SD)*	*University Students* *M (SD)*
Absolute Truth	161.57 (65.8)	154.41 (52.1)[2,3,4,5]
Complete Fabrication	159.03 (65.6)	184.52 (51.1)[6,7]
Temporal Displacement	160.57 (54.2)	169.21 (47.7)[3,6,8]
Spatial/Setting Displacement	154.68 (63.7)	179.02 (66.1)[2]
Affective Truth	147.23 (64.8)[1]	184.38 (55.8)[5,8]
Affective Displacement	176.61 (61.4)[1]	175.39 (47.2)[4,7]

Note. Within-groups t-tests identified by numbers in superscripts.
[1]-$t(15) = 3.19$, $p = .006$
[2]-$t(15) = 3.84$, $p = .002$
[3]-$t(15) = 6.56$, $p = .0001$
[4]-$t(15) = 4.38$, $p = .001$
[5]-$t(15) = -6.66$, $p = .0001$
[6]-$t(15) = 3.06$, $p = .008$
[7]-$t(15) = 2.32$, $p = .04$

Discussion

Telling the literal truth to deceive is effective only to the extent that a change in a critical temporal detail does not betray the speaker's temporal displacement. However, when a speaker tells the literal truth with deceptive intent, heightened arousal, at least in the noncriminal population, does betray the speaker as evidenced in elevated voice pitch. Knowing that the truth is being presented in a different time frame seems to create enough of an autonomic response "leakage" (Ekman, Friesen, & Scherer, 1976) through the acoustic channel. Based on findings from our limited study, a temporal displacement does lie in the gray area between truth and complete fabrication, since this type of message is more arousing than truth but less arousing than producing a completely fabricated statement. This finding is localized to the noncriminal population, however.

Paroled felons in this experiment either held extensive practice in lying, or the experimental manipulation was not strong enough to elucidate differences between experimental conditions. Message details and voice pitch measures did not differentiate when paroled felons told the truth, lied, or made temporal or spatial/setting displacements. However, the fascinating finding in this population concerned talking about important people in their lives—telling lies about a loved one created heightened arousal in this group. If we think about people who have been in trouble with the law, we might consider that their families are sometimes devastated by their loved one's arrest, conviction, and incarceration. The lawbreaker probably spends months or years thinking about how he or she has negatively impacted loved ones, and so when he or she speaks about important people in an opposite way (an affective displacement), there might be strong feelings of guilt when talking negatively about the loved ones whom he or she has already hurt. Likewise, if they speak about a judge for whom they hold strong negative feelings, for example, providing an affective displacement in the positive direction results in heightened arousal. We believe that their heightened arousal was due to specific emotions felt (guilt, anger) when making affective displacements, rather than due to a generalized, undifferentiated arousal (Zuckerman et al., 1981).

Do displacements lack critical verbal details when compared to truth and complete fabrications? Our findings were inconclusive. The RM algorithm used in some previous research did not apply to statements in this small experiment. However, when noncriminal and criminal populations were compared, the criminal population showed few sensory, temporal, spatial, affective, and cognitive operations in their statements. Further research is necessary with a larger number of participants to replicate this finding and if replicated, to determine why paroled felons do not provide many RM details in their statements.

Are the gray area statements we tested closer to the absolute truth, or are they closer to completely-fabricated statements? The findings from this study indicate that in noncriminal populations, gray area messages are different from absolutes. All of the displacements we tested were more emotionally arousing than telling the truth, and temporal and affective displacements were less arousing than telling a complete fabrication. However, we believe that by artificially stimulating people to create absolute messages (what really happened in the professor's office with that book?; what is your true job history?), and displacements, we are not creating conditions that mimic the real world. In the real world, as we have suggested, the absolutes are completely steeped in fog, and the gray areas between the absolutes—truth and complete fabrication—are quite extensive.

References

Aertsen, J. A. (1988). *Nature and creature: Thomas Aquinas's way of thought.* Boston, MA: Brill Academic.

Anolli, L., & Ciceri, R. (1997). The voice of deception: Vocal strategies of naïve and able liars. *Journal of Nonverbal Behavior, 21,* 259–284.

Augustine. (395/1887). De mendacio (On lying). In P. Schaff (Ed.), *A select library of the nicene and post-nicene fathers of the Christian church* (Vol. 3, pp. 457–477). Buffalo, NY: The Christian Literature Company.

Bartlett, F. C. (1932). *Remembering: A study in experimental and social psychology.* Cambridge, England: Cambridge University Press.

Bavelas, J. B., Black, A., Chovil, N., & Mullett, J. (1990). *Equivocal communication.* Newbury Park, CA: Sage.

Bond, G. D. (2008). Deception detection expertise. *Law and Human Behavior, 32,* 339–351.

Bond, G. D., & Lee, A. Y. (2005). Language of lies in prison: Classification of prisoners' truthful and deceptive natural language. *Applied Cognitive Psychology, 19,* 313–329.

Bond, G. D., Malloy, D. M., Arias, E. A., Nunn, S. N., & Thompson, L. A. (2004). Post-probe decision making in a prison context. *Communication Monographs, 71,* 269–285.

Bond, G. D., Thompson, L. A., & Malloy, D. M. (2005). Lifespan differences in the social networks of prison inmates. *The International Journal of Aging and Human Development, 61,* 161–178.

Buller, D. B., & Burgoon, J. K. (1994). Deception: Strategic and nonstrategic communication. In J. A. Daly & J. M. Wiemann (Eds.), *Strategic interpersonal communication* (pp. 191–223). Hillsdale, NJ: Erlbaum.

Conway, M. A., & Pleydell-Pearce, C. W. (2000). The construction of autobiographical memories in the self-memory system. *Psychological Review, 107,* 261–288.

DePaulo, B. M. (1992). Nonverbal behavior and self-presentation. *Psychological Bulletin, 111,* 203–243.

DePaulo, B. M., Kashy, D. A., Kirkendol, S. E., Wyer, M. M., & Epstein, J. A. (1996). Lying in everyday life. *Journal of Personality and Social Psychology, 70,* 979–995.

DePaulo, B. M., Lindsay, J. J., Malone, B. E., Muhlenbruck, L., Charlton, K., & Cooper, H. (2003). Cues to deception. *Psychological Bulletin, 129,* 74–118.

DePaulo, B. M., & Rosenthal, R. (1979). Telling lies. *Journal of Personality and Social Psychology, 37,* 1713–1722.

Ekman, P. (1985). *Telling lies: Clues to deceit in the marketplace, marriage, and politics.* New York: Norton.

Ekman, P. (1992). *Telling lies: Clues to deceit in the marketplace, marriage, and politics* (2nd ed.). New York: Norton.

Ekman, P. (2001). *Telling lies: Clues to deceit in the marketplace, marriage, and politics* (3rd ed.). New York: Norton.

Ekman, P., & Friesen, W. V. (1969). Nonverbal leakage and clues to deception. *Psychiatry, 32,* 88–106.

Ekman, P., Friesen, W. V., & Scherer, K. R. (1976). Body movement and voice pitch in deceptive interaction. *Semiotica, 16,* 23–27.

Ekman, P., & O'Sullivan, M. (2006). From flawed self-assessment to blatant whoppers: The utility of voluntary and involuntary behavior in detecting deception. *Behavioral Sciences and the Law, 24,* 673–686.

Feldman, R. S., Forrest, J. A., & Happ, B. R. (2002). Self-presentation and verbal deception: Do self-presenters lie more? *Basic and Applied Social Psychology, 24,* 163–170.

Godfrey, D. K., Jones, E. E., & Lord, C. G. (1986). Self-promotion is not ingratiating. *Journal of Personality and Social Psychology, 50,* 106–115.

Grice, H. P. (1989). *Studies in the ways of words.* Cambridge, MA: Harvard University Press.

Horvath, F. S. (1973). Verbal and nonverbal clues to truth and deception during polygraph examinations. *Journal of Police Science and Administration, 1,* 138–152.

Johnson, M. K. (1988). Reality monitoring: An experimental phenomenological approach. *Journal of Experimental Psychology: General, 117,* 390–394.

Johnson, M. K., Foley, M. A., Suengas, A. G., & Raye, C. L. (1988). Phenomenal characteristics of memories for perceived and imagined autobiographical events. *Journal of Experimental Psychology: General, 117,* 371–376.

Johnson, M. K., Hashtroudi, S., & Lindsay, D. S. (1993). Source monitoring. *Psychological Bulletin, 114,* 3–28.

Johnson, M. K., & Raye, C. L. (1981). Reality monitoring. *Psychological Review, 88,* 67–85.

Lee, A. Y., Bond, G. D., Scarbrough, P. S., Gillan, D. J., & Cooke, N. J. (2007). Team training and transfer in differing contexts. *International Journal of Cognitive Technology, 12,* 17–28.

Malone, B. E., Adams, R. B., Anderson, D. E., Ansfield, M. E., & DePaulo, B. M. (1997, May). *Strategies of deception and their correlates over the course of friendship.* Poster presented at the annual meeting of the American Psychological Society, Washington, DC.

Masip, J., Sporer, S. L., Garrido, E., & Herrero, C. (2005). The detection of deception with the reality monitoring approach: A review of the empirical evidence. *Psychology, Crime, & Law, 11*, 99–122.

McCornack, S. A. (1988, November). *The logic of lying: A rational approach to the production of deceptive messages*. Paper presented at the annual meeting of the Speech Communication Association, New Orleans, LA.

McCornack, S. A. (1992). Information manipulation theory. *Communication Monographs, 59*, 1–16.

McCornack, S. A. (1997). The generation of deceptive messages: Laying the groundwork for a viable theory of interpersonal deception. In J. O. Greene (Ed.), *Message production: Advances in communication theory* (pp. 91–126). Mahwah, NJ: Erlbaum.

Newman, M. L., Pennebaker, J. W., Berry, D. S., & Richards, J. M. (2003). Lying words: Predicting deception from linguistic styles. *Personality and Social Psychology Bulletin, 29*, 665–675.

O'Sullivan, M., & Ekman, P. (2004). The wizards of deception detection. In P. A. Granhag & L. Stromwell (Eds.), *The detection of deception in forensic contexts* (pp. 269–286). Cambridge, England: Cambridge University Press.

Pennebaker, J. W., Francis, M. E., & Booth, R. J. (2001). *Linguistic inquiry and word count: LIWC* (2nd ed.) [Computer software]. Mahwah, NJ: Erlbaum.

Perry, Jr., W. G. (1999). *Forms of intellectual and ethical development in the college years: A scheme*. San Francisco: Jossey-Bass.

Pontari, B. A., & Schlenker, B. R. (2000). The influence of cognitive load on self-presentation: Can cognitive busyness help as well as harm social performance? *Journal of Personality and Social Psychology, 78*, 1092–1108.

Scherer, K. R. (1981). Vocal indicators of stress. In J. Darby (Ed.), *Speech evaluation in psychiatry* (pp. 171–187). New York: Grune and Stratton.

Schlenker, B. R. (1982). Translating actions into attitudes: An identity-analytic approach to the explanation of social conduct. *Advances in Experimental Social Psychology, 15*, 193–247.

Schlenker, B. R. (2002). Self-presentation. In M. R. Leary & J. P. Tangney (Eds.), *Handbook of self and identity* (pp. 492–518). New York: Guilford.

Sporer, S. L. (1997). The less traveled road to truth: Verbal cues in deception detection in accounts of fabricated and self-experienced events. *Applied Cognitive Psychology, 11*, 373–397.

Streeter, L. A., Krauss, R. M., Geller, V., Olson, C., & Apple, W. (1977). Pitch changes during attempted deception. *Journal of Personality and Social Psychology, 35*, 345–350.

Taylor, M., Lussier, G. L., & Maring, B. L. (2003). The distinction between lying and pretending. *Journal of Cognition and Development, 4*, 299–323.

Vrij, A., Akehurst, L., Soukara, S., & Bull, R. (2004). Let me inform you how to tell a convincing story: CBCA and reality monitoring scores as a function of age, coaching and deception. *Canadian Journal of Behavioral Science, 36*, 113–126.

Vrij, A., Edward, K., Roberts, K. P., & Bull, R. (2000). Detecting deceit via analysis of verbal and nonverbal behavior. *Journal of Nonverbal Behavior, 24*, 239–263.

Zuckerman, M., DeFrank, R. S., Hall, J. A., Larrance, D. T., & Rosenthal, R.

(1979). Facial and vocal cues of deception and honesty. *Journal of Experimental Social Psychology, 15,* 378–396.

Zuckerman, M., DePaulo, B. M., & Rosenthal, R. (1981). Verbal and nonverbal communication of deception. In L. Berkowitz (Ed.), *Advances in experimental social psychology* (Vol. 14, pp. 1–59). New York: Academic.

Chapter 4

Deception by Selective Quotation

Matthew S. McGlone

Quotations are the evidence upon which journalists build stories about public figures, and readers in turn form impressions of these figures. Their presumed status as fact is symbolized by separating them from other text constituents via inverted commas, a stylistic convention originally used to herald sententious remarks (Culbertson & Somerick, 1976; Garber, 1999), but now universally recognized in nonfiction as signaling an exact replication of a source's words. However, empirical analyses of direct quotations suggest they are often far from faithful reproductions. In conversation, quotations are less likely to duplicate speech word-for-word than to selectively depict certain speech aspects while omitting or distorting others (Clark & Gerrig, 1990). For example, one might recount an ironic comment overheard about the weather (e.g., "Nothing but blue skies, just like the weatherman said!" uttered in a downpour) by reconstructing the intonation and illocutionary force of the comment (e.g., "She said 'Um, isn't this great weather?' in this totally sarcastic tone..."), but not the exact wording nor the target of derisive intent. Such reconstructions fail to meet the strict verbatim criterion we expect of passages portrayed as direct quotations, but do succeed as demonstrations of a source's intentions (Wade & Clark, 1993).

Although the standards of reproduction accuracy are higher in journalism than in casual conversation, it is not uncommon for quotations in news stories to be at variance with what was actually said (Blankenburg, 1970; Lehrer, 1989). The least objectionable modifications occur when writers tidy up the grammar, replace unheralded pronouns with proper names, or remove expletives from a statement, all practices recommended by many journalism educators (e.g., Leslie, 1986). Slightly more problematic is the substitution of synonyms for words the author deems too obscure for the target audience to understand. Revising content words increases the potential for semantic drift from the original testimony; however, writers can keep it in check if they obtain second opinions from their sources and peers regarding any differences in meaning between the original and revised statements. At the other extreme are cases in which authors attribute entirely fabricated quotes to sources that misrepresent their attitudes or beliefs. In one infamous case, psychoanalyst Jeffrey Masson accused reporter Janet Malcolm (1983) of concocting several quotes in a *New Yorker* profile in which he came across as crass and egotistical. Malcolm denied the charge, insisting that Masson had actually used provocative phrases such as "intellectual gigolo" to describe himself, although the disputed phrases did not appear in her audiotape or written records of their conversations. At the end of a drawn out libel lawsuit, the U.S. Supreme Court found in the reporter's favor, ruling that the quotes in her article were protected by the First Amendment even if they had been concocted. The *Masson v. Malcolm* ruling generated considerable debate among journalists about ethical standards in quotation. While most agree that inventing quotes is an unacceptable practice, few journalists endorse pre-publication review or other measures that might reduce its occurrence at the expense of ceding creative control of their work.

In light of the potential for distortion, forgoing any alteration of a source's words might seem the only sure-fire way to avoid misrepresentation. However, verbatim replication in no way guarantees that a quote accurately represents the source's intended meaning or beliefs. Consider the common complaint of public figures cited in news media that although their words were accurately reproduced in a story, the words were nonetheless quoted "out of context." Taken literally, the charge is absurd, as there is no contextual void in which a sound bite can exist in isolation. The article or broadcast in which a quote appears is its current context, albeit one different from the context in which the words were originally uttered. If the charge is modified to reflect this fact— i.e., one instead says the words were "quoted out of their original context"— it becomes merely banal, in that all quotes entail extracting some portion of a source's words from their original context. The real objection often is not to removing a quote from its original context (as all quotes are), but to the quoter's decision to exclude from the excerpt certain nearby phrases or sentences (which thereby become "context" simply by virtue of the exclusion) that serve to clarify the intentions behind the selected words. Comparing this practice to surgical excision, historian Milton Mayer coined the term "contextomy" to describe its use by Julius Streicher, editor of the infamous Nazi broadsheet *Der Stürmer* in Weimar-era Germany. One of the early tactics Streicher used to arouse anti-semitic sentiments among the weekly's working-class Christian readership was to publish truncated quotations from Talmudic texts that, in their shortened form, appear to advocate greed, slavery, and ritualistic murder (Mayer, 1966). In a similar vein, U.S. clergyman and radio propagandist Father Charles Coughlin cited highly circumscribed quotations from the New Testament to persuade American Catholics that the Bible endorsed persecution of the Jewish people. Coughlin often invited his radio audience to consult the verses he had so brazenly abridged to prove for themselves that Jews are held in divine contempt (Warren & Warren, 1996; see also Hill & Cheadle, 1996). Although rarely employed to the malicious extremes of the Nazis or their sympathizers, contextomy is a common method of misrepresentation in contemporary mass media.

One of the most familiar examples of contextomy is the ubiquitous "review blurb" used in film advertising. To create these blurbs, studio promoters dissect multiple reviews of a film and then select the most positive comments for use in advertisements. The lure of media exposure associated with being "blurbed" by a major studio undoubtedly encourages some critics to write positive reviews of mediocre movies. However, even when a review is negative overall, studios have few reservations about excerpting it in a way that misrepresents the critic's opinion (Broydo, 1997). For example, the ad copy for Dreamworks SKG's 2007 comedy *Norbit* contained a quote from *Chicago Tribune* critic Michael Wilmington praising the film's star—"Eddie Murphy's comic skills are immense" (Wilmington, 2007). One might infer from the quote that Wilmington's review of the film was positive. At best, it was lukewarm. Turned off by film's crude humor, which he describes early in the review as "an often awful parade of flatulent gags about big butts, sadistic relationships and sexual idiocy" and later as "a weird nightmare of rampaging femininity and gross gags," Wilmington gave it only a mediocre two stars out of four in his rating system. Why then did he refer to Murphy's comic skills in the review? Not because he saw them on display in the movie, but instead to question why a comedian of such high caliber would waste his talents on such a clunker:

> *Murphy's comic skills are immense* [italics added], and "Dreamgirls" shows he's a fine straight dramatic actor too. So why does he want to make these huge, belching spectaculars, movies as swollen, monstrous and full of hot air as Rasputia [the lead female role, played by Murphy in a fat suit] herself—here misdirected by Brian Robbins of "Good Burger," "Varsity Blues" and that lousy" "Shaggy Dog" remake?"

Similarly, Twentieth Century Fox contextomized critic Jeff Vice's (2005) review of its forgettable screen adaptation of the *Fantastic Four* comic book, including just one word from it—"fun"—in the film's ad copy. The word appears only once in the review, and its sentential context leaves little doubt that Vice did not think the movie was much fun (and certainly not fantastic):

> Too often the film shows the limitations of its budget, which was reportedly between $60 million and $70 million (pretty small for

this type of production). Several of the effects look unfinished and chintzy. Mark Frost and Michael France's script also borrows heavily from other superhero films, including material taken directly from the first "Spider-Man" film and "Superman II." And the romance between Alba and Gruffudd's character is groan-inducing (both actors give stunningly awful performances). Where it works best is when it's trying to be more light-hearted. The verbal sparring between Johnny and Ben is easily the highlight of the film. (Thanks to Evans and Chiklis, who seem to be the only ones having *fun* [italics added] here).

Many critics have become so fed up with having their opinions misrepresented via selective quotation that they have changed the way they write reviews. Instead of producing the punchy prose that has long been characteristic of the genre, these critics deliberately avoid one-liners, colorful similes, and effusive adjectives to thwart promotional excerpting. Howard Movshovitz, film critic for the *Denver Post,* succinctly described this logic when he quipped, "If I ever write a line I think can be quoted, I change it" (Reiner, 1996, p. 123).

Contextomy is also a common spin tactic among unscrupulous political journalists. For example, consider the yew tree controversy that plagued former U.S. Vice President Al Gore in the late 1990s. The trouble began when David Ridenour, a columnist for the Texas newspaper *Austin American-Statesman,* wrote a piece criticizing the vice president's environmental policy agenda. Ridenour specifically criticized Gore's willingness to put "environmental politics before people" as a moral failure and cited a passage from his 1992 book *Earth in the Balance* as evidence of this willingness. In the passage, Gore (1992) describes his stance on the preservation of the Pacific yew, a tree with potentially important medicinal uses:

> The Pacific Yew can be cut down and processed to produce a potent chemical, Taxol, which offers some promise of curing certain forms of lung, breast and ovarian cancer in patients who would otherwise quickly die. It seems an easy choice—sacrifice the tree for a human life—until one learns that three trees must be destroyed for each patient treated. (p. 119)

Proceeding from this quotation, Ridenour (1998) argued that the vice president would rather sacrifice people than deplete the Pacific yew population, and thus lacked human compassion. Following the publication of the article, numerous references to the quotation appeared in conservative op-ed columns, magazines, radio, and television shows across the country. A year later, it even surfaced in a discussion of environmental policy on the floor of the U.S. House of Representatives. After reading the excerpt to his House colleagues, Rep. David McIntosh (R-Indiana) took issue with the vice president's apparent preference for trees over human lives: "Three trees versus a human life, three trees versus the ability to prolong someone's life who is suffering from cancer? I would pick the individual, the person, the human being who is a cancer patient and suffering from that dreaded disease and say it is clear three trees are worth it. We can sacrifice three trees to save one human life. But the Vice President apparently does not think that is so clear" (109th Congress., 2nd Session, 145 *Cong. Rec.* H3376, 1999). If it were merely the ratio of trees to human lives that had bothered the vice president, Rep. McIntosh's outrage might be justified. However, a very different picture of Gore's concerns emerges when the excerpt is examined in the context of the words immediately preceding and following it in his book (Ridenour's excerpt is in italics):

> Most of the [tree] species unique to the rain forests are in imminent danger, partly because there is no one to speak up for them. In contrast, consider the recent controversy over the yew tree, a temperate forest species, one variety of which now grows only in the Pacific Northwest. *The Pacific Yew can be cut down and processed to produce a potent chemical, Taxol, which offers some promise of curing certain forms of lung, breast, and ovarian cancer in patients who would otherwise quickly die. It seems an easy choice — sacrifice the tree for a human life — until one learns that three trees must be destroyed for each patient treated,* that only specimens more than a hundred years old contain the potent chemical, and that there are very few of these Yews remaining on earth. Suddenly we must confront some very tough questions. How important are the medical needs of future generations? Are those of us alive today entitled to cut down all of those trees to extend the lives of a few of us, even if it means that this unique form of life will disappear forever, thus making it impossible to save human lives in the future? (p.119)

In its original context, Gore's expression of reluctance to cut down yews does not, as his critics alleged, appear to be motivated by a fanatical pro-flora platform. Rather, it is based on the decidedly pro-person concern that toppling too many now would limit the supply available to benefit cancer patients of future generations. By strategically omitting this and other legitimate reasons Gore offered for preserving the yew, Ridenour reduced the vice president's sober assessment of the dilemma to an embarrassing blurb confirming his reputation among conservatives as a "radical" environmentalist.

As the preceding examples illustrate, contextomy can be used to create a false impression of a source's attitudes in the service of motives as harmless as selling movie tickets or as harmful as character assassination. Yet, even when it is put to malicious extremes, repairing the attributional damage would seem a straightforward matter. If an audience forms a false impression based on a contextomized quote, then "recontextualizing" it—i.e., presenting the quote with enough of its original context to make the source's true intention transparent—should correct the error. There are, however, problems with this strategy. One serious problem is the paucity of means by which to bring the recontextualized quote to the attention of the audience that has been misled. It would, of course, be ideal to transmit the correction via the same media vehicles (newspapers, news broadcasts, etc.) by which the contextomized version was disseminated in the first place. But mainstream news media rarely own up to quotation distortions, and highly partisan vehicles almost never do. Moreover, the errors that are corrected are primarily "objective" errors such as misidentifying the source, not "subjective" errors like quoting out of context (Ryan & Owen, 1977; Lehrer, 1989). There are currently few incentives for journalists to come clean about committing contextomy, regardless of whether they did it accidentally or on purpose. A recent survey of senior journalists by the *Columbia Journalism Review* found that more than half think major news organizations lack proper internal guidelines for correcting errors, and almost 4 in 10 believe that reporting errors are rarely corrected because reporters and editors try to hide them (Hickey, 1999). The organizational climate of news media is simply not conducive to admitting mistakes, let alone giving them prominent display. Unfortunately, the handful of media vehicles that do put a spotlight on journalistic errors and distortions— e.g., *EXTRA*, the magazine of the media watch group FAIR (Fairness & Accuracy in Reporting), CNN's *Reliable Sources,* NPR's *On the Media*—draw small audiences. Ironically, these "watchdog" vehicles tend to attract people who already have a deep distrust of news media and, consequently, are among those least likely to be misled by reporting inaccuracies in the first place.

Many media critics (as well as some crusading insiders) have called on news organizations to do a better job of informing the public about reporting errors. If these calls are heeded, reporters might someday be required to routinely disclose cases in which a source accuses them of quoting out of context, and would also be obliged to provide audiences with enough of the quote's original context to judge for themselves whether the accusation is justified. Under these optimal conditions, will recontextualization dispel the false impression created by a contextomized quote? There is reason to be skeptical. People are quick to infer character traits from inadequate linguistic and behavioral evidence, a bias so pervasive and misguided that social psychologists often refer to it as the "fundamental attribution error" (e.g., Ross, 1977). These dispositional snap judgments not only discount the influence of context (social or otherwise) on behavior, but also persist when people are made aware of how poor an indicator of character or attitudes the behavioral evidence is. Jones and Harris (1967) demonstrated this bias in a classic psychological experiment. Participants read one of two student essays praising or criticizing Cuban leader Fidel Castro. Some were told that the student had been free to determine the content of the essay, while others were told the student had been randomly assigned the task of writing a positive or negative position by his debate coach. Participants inferred that the positive or negative comments in the essay reflected the writer's true beliefs, even when they believed the student had not freely chosen his position. Remarkably, similar effects have been observed in this experimental paradigm when the participants themselves are in charge of randomly assigning writers to affirmative or negative positions (Gilbert & Jones, 1986). A bias towards dispositional attributions works against the repair of contextomy, which entails revising a dispositional attribution of verbal behavior (e.g., "the quote from Al Gore *indicates that* he puts the environment before people") to yield a contextual attribution ("the quote from Al Gore <u>was</u> *edited to make it appear as if* he puts the environment before people"). While dispositional attributions are typically simple and reflexive, contextual attributions are complex and effortful (Gilbert & Malone, 1995). People may be reluctant to exchange a straightforward (albeit erroneous) dispositional interpretation of a quote for a more complicated contextual interpretation, especially when the inferred disposition coheres with other characteristics attributed to the target individual (e.g., "Al Gore is a liberal").

Dispositional coherence of this sort provided the foundation for perhaps the most startling and effective display of contextomy in recent memory. Opponents of U.S. "affirmative action" policies in the 1990s recruited a highly credible, yet improbable spokesman for their cause—the late Dr. Martin Luther King, Jr. Conservatives argued that the policy ignores the civil rights leader's contention that merit, not race, should determine the distribution of educational and employment resources, and thereby promotes the color consciousness King had sought to eliminate. This portrayal of King's philosophy was based almost entirely on a single comment from one of his speeches, albeit the most famous comment from his most celebrated speech at the 1963 March on Washington: "I have a dream, that my four little children will one day live in a nation where they will not be judged by the color of their skin, but by the content of their character." Through misappropriation and manipulation of this sentence, King was transformed from a left-wing activist into a right-wing muse. Thus, in a discussion on CNN's *Crossfire*, conservative author David Horowitz (1994) proudly noted the alignment he perceived between the civil rights leader's political leanings and his own: "Martin Luther King, in my view, was a conservative because he stood up for, you know, belief in the content of your character—the value that conservatives defend today." California Governor Pete Wilson routinely quoted King in his successful campaign to pass Proposition 209, the 1996 ballot initiative that ended all public-sector affirmative action programs in the state. Characterizing these programs as an obstacle to King's dream comparable to the segregation he had fought in his lifetime, Wilson (1996) asserted "we won't achieve that dream until we also end the system of preferential treatment that, in fact, judges people by the color of their skin rather than by the content of their character" (p. 171). Governor Mike Foster advanced a similar argument to defend his executive order eliminating affirmative action in Louisiana. "I can't find anywhere in King's writings," Foster claimed, "that King wanted reverse discrimination [referring to affirmative action]. He just wanted to end all discrimination based on color" (Sterngold, 1996).

King's family members, former colleagues, biographers, and admirers have on several occasions pointed out the portions of his writings that Governor Foster and others apparently overlooked (e.g., Aronson, 1997; Lempinen, 1997; Dyson, 2000). The anti-affirmative action spin on King's famous quotation is incompatible with the overall message of his 1963 speech or any other work in his considerable oeuvre. Frequent excerpting from the speech's "dream sequence" has overshadowed the equally powerful but disheartening comments he made about the government's failure to improve the lot of Black Americans after emancipation:

> Instead of honoring this sacred obligation, America has given the Negro people a bad check—a check which has come back marked "insufficient funds." But we refuse to believe that the bank of justice is bankrupt. We refuse to believe that there are insufficient funds in the great vaults of opportunity of this nation. So we have come to cash this check—a check that will give us upon demand the riches of freedom and the security of justice. (1964, p. 218)

King clearly contended here that the federal government owes something to its Black citizens, but at no point in the speech does he demand that it be a race-based allocation of jobs and resources. Nevertheless, interpreting his "bad check" metaphor as evidence that he favored such reparations is no more of an inferential leap than concluding that his "dream" prohibited it. One need not, however, rely solely on his metaphors to infer his attitude toward affirmative action. In *Why We Can't Wait* (1964), he addressed the issue quite literally:

No amount of gold could provide an adequate compensation for the exploitation and humiliation of the Negro in America down through the centuries. Not all the wealth of this affluent society could meet the bill. Yet a price can be placed on unpaid wages. The ancient common law has always provided a remedy for the appropriation of the labor of one human being by another. This law should be made to apply for American Negroes. *The payment should be in the form of a massive program by the government of special, compensatory measures which could be regarded as a settlement in accordance with the accepted practice of common law. Such measures would certainly be less expensive than any computation based on two centuries of unpaid wages and accumulated interest* [italics added]. I am proposing, therefore, that, just as we granted a GI Bill of Rights to war veterans, America launch a broad-based and gigantic Bill of Rights for the Disadvantaged, our veterans of the long siege of denial. (p. 137)

Here King expressed not only a desire for a government program of compensatory measures for African Americans, but also a vision of reparations more radical than most affirmative action advocates endorse. Several sentences later, he anticipated objections that such measures constitute discrimination against disadvantaged whites, countering that "the moral justification for special measures for Negroes is rooted in the robberies inherent in the institution of slavery" (p. 138). The aptness of this rationale might be a matter of debate, but the fact that King espoused it incontestably refutes suggestions that he opposed race-based compensation.

Numerous other passages in King's speeches and writings convey with equal clarity his belief that long-term government assistance was necessary to achieve racial equality. His family and followers referred to many of these passages in op-ed pieces, open letters, television interviews, and other media events intended to publicly reclaim his misappropriated "dream" rhetoric. Yet the de-radicalized, anti-intervention image of King—an image based largely on a single contextomized sentence from his vast body of writings—persists in political discourse and prevails as a tactic for maligning minority assistance programs. Distressed by its increasing credibility among non-Black constituencies, biographer Michael Dyson (2000) nevertheless expressed great skepticism that the image could be corrected by reminding people of the comments King made that are incompatible with it. The alarming alternative strategy Dyson proposed was a 10-year moratorium on public readings, broadcasts, or excerpting of the "I Have A Dream" speech. Suspending the speech would not only take away anti-affirmative action forces' most effective (and deceptive) sound bite, Dyson argued, but also would encourage people to study King's other powerful but less familiar orations and writings. Many critics ridiculed Dyson's logic, contending that a speech so successful in drawing people to the cause of civil rights in the first place is an essential reference for addressing rhetorical challenges to this cause (e.g., Ramos, 1999). Although a moratorium is inadvisable (and infeasible) for many reasons, Dyson's reasoning is not as weak— nor is the rebuttal value of King's speech necessarily as strong—as these critics contend.

Contextomy yields two negative consequences for a quoted source: Initially, a false impression of the source's attitude(s) and subsequently, a residual distortion after the misleading quote is restored to its original context. The residual distortion reflects a very common process in interpersonal perception whereby people spontaneously form simplistic, stable impressions of others from complex, variable behavior. The phenomenon social psychologists refer to as the "fundamental attribution error" amounts to a chronic disregard of context when interpreting the behavior of others (Jones & Harris, 1967; Gilbert & Malone, 1995). From this perspective, it is not surprising that recounting the context of King's oft-quoted dream comments has failed to dispel the myth that he considered the dream attainable without government intervention. Despite his towering status as a moral authority and his numerous other significant writings, most Americans' conception of King's teachings is derived mainly or entirely from these comments. Thus reminders of the pragmatic view of race relations he actually held conflict not only with cynical portrayals of affirmative action as "reverse discrimination," but also the notion of "color blindness" people erroneously associate with King based on his famous color-character contrast. In this regard, the fundamental attribution error poses a major obstacle for civil rights leaders' efforts to rhetorically reclaim his contextomized comments.

The notion of contextomy developed here is a curious incarnation of a more general problem in interpersonal communication—how to determine the extent to which verbal behavior reflects sources' enduring beliefs rather than variables operating in the communicative context (Brown, 1958; Quine, 1960). This determination is never trivial and people often err. Various cognitive, cultural, and motivational factors tilt people toward dispositional rather than contextual explanations of others' messages (Ross, 1977; Sperber & Wilson, 1986). Contextomy exploits this tendency in advertising, journalism, and political debate by violating an assumption of intertextual discourse audiences rarely question—that words portrayed as a direct quotation constitute not only a verbatim replication of the source's comments, but also faithfully represent the source's beliefs and attitudes. Transcripts, recordings, and "earwitness" testimony enable us to confidently assess whether the former condition has been satisfied, but the latter is harder to evaluate. Even a seemingly transparent declaration (e.g., "I did not have sexual relations with that woman...Miss Lewinsky") can permit murky accounts of its derivation (e.g., "By 'sexual relations,' I was referring to coitus only") when socially or politically expedient. The degree to which we resonate with the new spin on an old quote may depend less on the supporting evidence than on our attributional investment in the quote, as the King case study indicates. It also depends on our knowledge of the social, cultural, and historical context in which the words were originally uttered, not merely their linguistic context (McGlone & Tofighbakhsh, 2000). Without this knowledge, a quotation may persuade us of propositions that its source would never endorse.

References

Aronson, R. C. (1997, September 18). Affirmative action opponents twist King's vision. *Cleveland Plain Dealer,* p. 10B.

Blankenburg, W. B. (1970). News accuracy: Some findings on the meaning of errors. *Journal of Communication, 20,* 375–386.

Brown, R. (1958). *Words and things.* New York: Free Press.

Broydo, L. (1997). (Not such a) Thriller! *Mother Jones, 22*(6), 17.

Clark, H. H., & Gerrig, R. (1990). Quotations as demonstrations. *Language, 66,* 764–805.

Culbertson, H. M., & Somerick, N. (1976). Quotation marks and bylines – what do they mean to readers? *Journalism Quarterly, 53,* 463–469.

Dyson, M. E. (2000). *I may not get there with you: The true Martin Luther King, Jr.* New York: The Free Press.

Garber, M. (1999). Quotation marks. *Critical Inquiry, 25,* 653–664.

Gilbert, D. T., & Jones, E. E. (1986). Perceiver-induced constraint: Interpretation of self-generated reality. *Journal of Personality and Social Psychology, 50,* 269–280.

Gilbert, D. T., & Malone, P. S. (1995). The correspondence bias. *Psychological Bulletin 117,* 21–38.

Gore, A. (1992). *Earth in the balance.* New York: Houghton Mifflin.

Hickey, N. (1999). Handling corrections. *Columbia Journalism Review, 38*(2), 42–3.

Hill, J., & Cheadle, R. (1996). *The Bible tells me so: Uses and abuses of holy scripture.* New York: Anchor Doubleday.

Horowitz, D. (1994, September 5). *Crossfire* [Television broadcast]. Washington, DC: CNN.

Jones, E. E., & Harris, V. A. (1967). The attribution of attitudes. *Journal of Experimental Social Psychology, 3,* 1–24.

King, M. L., Jr. (1964). *Why we can't wait.* New York: Signet.

Lehrer, A. (1989). Between quotation marks. *Journalism Quarterly, 66,* 902–906.

Lempinen, E. W. (1997, January 18). Pro-affirmative action coalition is taking shape; Martin Luther King Jr.'s son expected to lead it. *San Francisco Chronicle,* p. A13.

Leslie, J. (1986). The pros and cons of cleaning up quotes. *Washington Journalism Review, 31,* 44–46.

Looking at the record of the Vice-President, 109th Congress, 2d Sess., 145 Cong. Rec. H3376 (1999) (testimony of Rep. David McIntosh, R.-Indiana).

Malcolm, J. (1983, December 5). Trouble in the archives – I. *The New Yorker, 59*(1), 59–152.

Mayer, M. (1966). *They thought they were free: The Germans, 1933–45.* Chicago: University of Chicago Press.

McGlone, M. S., & Tofighbakhsh, J. (2000). Birds of a feather flock conjointly (?): Rhyme as reason in aphorisms. *Psychological Science, 11,* 424–428.

Quine, R. (1960). *Word and object.* Cambridge, MA: Harvard University Press.

Ramos, D. (1999, December 24). Review of "I may not get there with you: The true Martin Luther King" by Michael Eric Dyson. *Salon.* Retrieved May 30, 2008, from http://www.salon.com/books/review/1999/12/24/dyson/index.html

Reiner, L. (1996). Why movie blurbs avoid newspapers. *Editor and Publisher: The Fourth Estate, 129,* 123.

Ridenour, D. (1998, August 16). How would Gore fare if he were called on to serve? *Austin American-Statesman,* p. A15.

Ross, L. (1977). The intuitive psychologist and his shortcomings: Distortions in the attribution process. In L. Berkowitz (Ed.), *Advances in experimental social psychology* (Vol. 10, pp. 174–221). New York: Academic Press.

Ryan, M., & Owen, D. (1977). An accuracy survey of metropolitan newspaper coverage of social issues. *Journalism Quarterly, 54,* 27–32.

Sperber, D., & Wilson, D. (1986). *Relevance: Communication and cognition.* New York: Oxford University Press.

Sterngold, J. (1996, January 12). A new governor acts to halt affirmative action. *New York Times,* A21.

Vice, J. (2005, July 8). Fantastic four [Movie Review]. *Deseret Morning News.* Salt Lake City, UT. Retrieved May 30, 2008, from http://deseretnews.com/movies/view/ 1,1257,405000619,00.html

Wade, E., & Clark, H. H. (1993). Reproduction and demonstration in quotations. *Journal of Memory and Language, 32,* 805–819.

Warren, D., & Warren, D. (1996). *Radio priest: Charles Coughlin, the father of hate radio.* New York: Free Press.

Wilson, P. (1996). The minority-majority society. In G. Curry (Ed.), *The affirmative action debate* (pp. 167–174). Reading, NY: Addison Wesley.

Wilmington, D. (2007). *Movie review: Norbit. Chicago Tribune.* Retrieved May 5, 2008, from http://chicago.metromix.com/movies/review/movie-review-norbit/163050/content

Chapter 5

Truth Telling as a Journalistic Imperative

Seow Ting Lee

In mass communication, truth telling is a fundamental given. To communicate, one has to be believed. In journalism, with its emphasis on pursuing and publishing the truth, truth telling is a core professional value. When journalists lie and deceive, they violate a basic journalistic principle that requires journalists to be honest in gathering, reporting, and interpreting information. Although the opposite of truth telling—deception—may be necessary for realizing the media's watchdog role, bringing journalists closer to the truth, and facilitating the public's right to know, deceptive techniques undermine media credibility—an important consideration in today's climate of public distrust of journalists. Poll after public poll show an abysmally low regard for journalists. Journalists consistently rank near bottom—outperforming only used car salesmen—in Gallup's Annual National Survey on the Honesty and Ethical Standards of 21 professions (Gallup, 2008).

This chapter focuses on exploring the moral and professional antecedents of truth telling as a journalistic imperative, and understanding the ethical reasoning of journalists in managing the concept of truth. Is deception acceptable, and if so, to what extent and under which conditions? How do journalists defend acts of deception and lying? If truth telling is a universal value, albeit a flawed one, a better understanding of the tensions between truth telling and professional demands is particularly important in the increasingly challenging and competitive environment that journalists operate today. Patterson and Wilkins (2004) describe truth telling as one of two central responsibilities of journalism, in that journalists have "a greater responsibility to tell the truth than most professions," in addition to fostering political participation (p. 74). According to Lambeth (1992), truth telling is one of five moral journalistic values that include freedom, stewardship, humaneness, and justice. Christians, Fackler, Rotzoll, and McKee (2005), who noted that the press's commitment to truth telling is part of its rhetoric, observed that virtually every code of ethics begins with the newsperson's duty to tell the truth under all conditions. Truth telling is etched into the Hutchins

Commission's (1947) prescriptions; a free, effective press should provide a truthful account of the day's events. Journalists are expected to tell the truth but paradoxically, they may have to deceive to get at the truth. Although the broader picture of truth in Western thought can be traced to Milton (1644), who argued in *Areopagitica* that truth can emerge only through a free exchange of information, and to J. S. Mill (1854/1989) who advanced the notion of a marketplace of ideas, truth telling appears to be a universal as well as a core journalistic value across cultures. Cooper, Clifford, Plude, and White (1989), who examined 100 media ethics codes from around the world, found non-Western media systems are also committed to truth telling. Laitila's (1995) study of 31 European journalistic codes found a high agreement on truthfulness. According to Mieth (1997), truthfulness is a protonorm. When confronted by the many transgressions against truth telling in journalism, one may be tempted to question journalists' reverence for truth telling but the descriptive reality that some people do not tell the truth does not imply truth telling is not a universal value. Both nature and culture are necessary for individual expression of values. A renewed interest in globalization has lead scholars to revisit global media ethics, especially focusing on truth telling as a core journalistic value (Herrscher, 2002; Strentz, 2002; Rao & Lee, 2005). Scholars and journalists continue to see truth telling as a core journalistic value although they disagree on the conditions that justify deception. The next section traces the history of deception in journalism and discusses examples of journalistic violations of truth telling.

Truth Telling in Journalism

Truth telling is a complex concept. It may be a universal value but at least a quarter of all human conversations involve deception, or a message knowingly transmitted by a sender to foster a false belief in the receiver (Buller & Burgoon, 1996; DePaulo, Kashy, Kirkendol, Wyer, & Epstein, 1996). Deception is widely acknowledged to be a contravention and yet it is a systemic occurrence in human relationships, from little white lies perpetuated in the niceties of social intercourse to the more capacious deception in politics and warfare. As Mieth (1997) observed, truth telling is a basic norm, but people often "invoke at one moment the norm of truthfulness and at the next moment, the right to lie, depending on circumstances and context" (p. 87). Truth telling is an important theme underlying many ethical conundrums confronted by journalists— not only in their treatment of news sources but also of news audiences. Of the 10 questionable practices discussed by Weaver, Beam, Brownlee, Voakes, and Wilhoit (2007), at least four—false identification, undercover reporting, hidden cameras, and recreation of news events—involve deception. Journalists knowingly resort to deception because it makes getting a story easier and more objective; may be the only way to acquire vital information; is viewed as just treatment for sources who have engaged in illegal or unethical behavior; and is essential for a reporter's safety. However, lying, regardless of benefits, always damages trust that is essential to a society's functioning.

But what is truth? The answer is far from simple. The definition of truth changes with shifting worldviews—from the pre-Socratic Greek conception based on human memory and oral traditions to the pragmatic notion of what is filtered through individual perception. The journalistic concept of objective reporting was influenced by the Enlightenment view of truth as verifiable, replicable facts that are perceivable by human senses and do not vary according to cultural and individual differences. To understand truth telling in journalism, we must view truth beyond the facts-only perspective. When we say that we expect journalists to tell the truth, the theoretical conceptualization of truth is often confined to factual accuracy at the newswriting stage, but within the field, there is an implicit understanding that journalists are expected to tell the truth to *news audiences* but paradoxically, they may have to deceive *news sources and newsmakers* to get at the truth. Christians et al. (2005) suggested that one way to understand truthfulness in journalism is to broaden our scope to consider "the antonym of truthfulness and to account for newsgathering as well as newswriting" (p. 54). With these perspectives in mind, we focus on *journalistic deception*, which takes many forms, from outright lying to deceiving or misleading, misrepresenting, or merely less than forthright behavior with the intention to cause a reader/viewer or a source/newsmaker to believe what is untrue. Many examples are found in the history of journalism, from 18th century media hoaxes and 19th century impersonations by muckrakers, to more recent cases of hidden cameras and plagiarism. One of America's first great hoaxers was Benjamin Franklin, who fabricated stories in a well-meaning attempt to educate readers. One such story is "A Witch Trial at Mount Holly," published in his *Pennsylvania Gazette* on October 22, 1730. The hoax, appearing as a news story filed from New Jersey about a witchery trial, was aimed at ridiculing Americans who believed in witchcraft (Fedler, 1989, pp. 7–9). Today, few journalists and members of the public would tolerate fabrication, even for the purpose of educating readers. The *Washington Post's* Janet Cooke was fired and had to return her Pulitzer in 1981 when it was found that her story about 8-year-old heroin user, Jimmy, was fabricated. In 2003, in a scandal that rocked American journalism, *New York Times* reporter Jayson Blair was fired for fabrication in what the paper described as "profound betrayal of trust and a low point in the 152-year history of the newspaper." Fabrication is but one aspect of journalistic deception. A more passive version involves withholding information. It is not uncommon to find journalists withholding information to avoid interfering with police investigations. During the 1991 Gulf War, some American papers knowingly reported an amphibious training manoeuver that turned out to be a case of strategic deception by the U.S. military, luring Iraqi forces into erroneous positions. The media played a compliant role when the CIA planted a false story about the defection of 60 Iraqi tanks to dampen Iraqi morale (Harris, 1999). The temptations for breaching truth telling in times of wars have led Knightley (1975), paraphrasing Senator Joseph Hiram, to suggest that in war, truth is the first casualty.

While public and professional condemnation of deception in the newswriting phase is mostly loud and clear, the same cannot be said for deception in newsgathering. Many media scholars consider a little deception indispensable in newsgathering. As Kieran (1997) notes: "Paradoxically, we demand that journalists tell the truth and yet, to get at the truth, they may have to lie" (p. 66). According to Meyer (1987), "the news business is following an unconscious rule that offhand, casual deception is okay, but elaborate and carefully planned deceptions are wicked" (p. 81). Christians et al. (2005) observed that outright deception rarely occurs in the newswriting phase but deception in newsgathering is a persistent temptation because it facilitates information gathering. Although some forms of deception are condoned by journalists, checklists such as the Poynter Institute's guidelines for justifying deception and codes of ethics created by professional journalists' associations and news organizations do reflect an understanding within the field that deception is a prima facie wrong (Black, Steele, & Barney, 1997). While the checklists and codes differ in clarity, specificity and depth in addressing deception, some common themes are discernable:

1. *Justification*: Deception must be justified and pass the test of publicity. It should be used as a last resort for a story that is of profound importance, when the benefits accruing to society outweigh the harm to individuals—in a utilitarian calculus;
2. *Deliberation*: Any decision to use deception must have been made at the highest editorial level, with ample discussion about the short- and long-term consequences;
3. *Disclosure*: Journalists must disclose to the audience the method used;
4. *Legality*: Deceptive methods must be used within legal boundaries;
5. *Method*: Hidden cameras are permissible in some cases but falsification of information is absolutely prohibited, with impersonation falling somewhere in between.

The term "deception" in codes of ethics seems to refer exclusively to impersonations and hidden cameras although many codes discussed photo manipulation and fabrication. There are few references to lying to sources, withholding of information from the audience, false attribution, staging, and misrepresentation of motives. Not surprisingly, the literature on journalistic deception has focused on undercover work, impersonation, or hidden cameras (e.g., Bivins, 2003; Black, Steele, & Barney, 1997; Goodwin & Smith, 2003; Lambeth, 1992; Rivers & Mathews, 1988). The preoccupation with deception as a newsgathering rather than a newswriting concern can be traced to the belief that journalists are less likely to fabricate their work than to deceive to get information. For more than 100 years, journalists have resorted to deception in pursuit of news. In 1887, *New York World* reporter Elizabeth Conran ("Nellie Bly") faked insanity to enter a mental asylum to report the shocking conditions (Olasky, 1988). Although Bly is often credited as the first journalist to use deception in newsgathering, in 1871, the *New York Times'* Augustus St. Clair, with a female friend, posed as a couple in need of an abortion (illegal at that time). St. Clair's article, "The Evil of the Age" published on August 23, 1871 exposed a Dr. Rosenzweig, who tried to kill St. Clair (who saved himself by drawing his revolver) (Olasky, 1988). The story took another twist when a patient St. Clair met at the clinic was found dead in a trunk at a railway station four days later from complications from an abortion. Dr. Rosenzweig was charged and found guilty. St. Clair and his editor Louis Jennings justified their use of deception by alluding to a noble end, as the article led to stricter anti-abortion laws and increased news coverage of abortionists.

A more recent example of journalists breaching the truth telling principle in pursuit of the "noble end" or information deemed to be of public interest, is the Mirage Bar case. In 1977, the *Chicago Sun-Times* bought a tavern, rigged it with plumbing and electrical problems, and set up reporters as bartenders and placed photographers in hidden rooms to document pay-offs to city inspectors. Despite winning some acclaim, the series lost the Pulitzer because judges objected to the deception. In the 1992 Food Lion case, *ABC PrimeTime Live* reporters went undercover as meat-handlers to obtain evidence of unhygienic meat processing, by falsifying resumes and using hidden cameras to record footage that was later aired on television. Food Lion, which sued ABC for fraud, did not dispute the truthfulness of the report but instead focused on the way ABC gathered information. Carl Bernstein and Bob Woodward described in their book *All the President's Men* (1974) how they lied to Watergate's Deep Throat to get him to confirm a story.

Clearly, the discussion of journalistic deception should not be confined to investigative newsgathering methods. The focus on investigative newsgathering methods in the literature (Rivers & Matthews, 1988;

Lambeth, 1992; Black et al., 1997; Kieran, 1997; Weaver & Wilhoit; 1996; Weaver et al., 2007) ignores violations of truth telling inherent in situations arising from the journalist-source relationship, and in plagiarism, photo manipulation, quote tampering, staging, false attribution, or outright fabrication of information—acts that do initiate or sustain false beliefs. The rhetoric of truth telling in journalism is even less convincing unless we also dissect the implications of journalists deceiving their audiences, newsmakers, and news sources.

Defining Journalistic Deception

Definitions of journalistic deception generally concur on the elements of intent and goal, in that deception is a deliberate attempt to lead someone to believe in what is untrue. Goodwin and Smith (2003) outlined three types of journalistic deception:

- *Active deception*: Reporters staging events to expose wrongdoing, as in the *Chicago Sun-Times* Mirage Bar or using audio-visual recording devices surreptitiously.
- *Misrepresentation*: Reporters impersonating non-reporters such as policemen, doctors, or victims' kin. Before the advent of cellular phones, journalists have been known to resort to the simple trick of calling from phone booths at the police station and declaring: "I am calling from police headquarters."
- *Passive deception*: Reporters, by not identifying themselves, allow themselves to be taken for members of the public to observe people without their realizing a reporter is present. An example is the restaurant critic who does not tell servers he is a journalist.

However, Goodwin and Smith's (2003) definition of journalistic deception does not consider the deceptive element inherent in the withholding of information from news audiences in cases of fabrication or staging, consistent with the slant in the literature toward covert information-gathering (hidden cameras and microphones) and undercover techniques such as impersonation and sting operations—newsgathering methods typically associated with investigative reporting.

Bok (1989) in *Lying* defines a lie as any intentional deceptive message that is *stated* and classified lies employed by journalists as a category of "lies for the public good" (p.165)—thus viewing journalistic deception as a newsgathering device. Deception is a broader concept: "When we undertake to deceive others intentionally, we communicate messages meant to mislead them, meant to make them believe what we ourselves do not believe" (p. 13). Bok concedes that people can deceive through gesture, disguise, action or inaction, and even silence.

A more comprehensive theoretical discussion of journalistic deception is seen in the work of Elliot and Culver (1992), who defined it as an act of communicating messages, verbally (lie) or nonverbally through the withholding of information with the intention to initiate or sustain a false belief. This definition not only covered deceptive practices in newsgathering but also potential for deception in relationships between journalists and their audiences (e.g., fabrication), as well as the omission-commission distinction. Elliot and Culver contended that deception is a prima facie wrong, and any deceptive act that lacks adequate justification by the perpetrator is unethical. They offered three "conditions" for journalistic deception: Intent, verbal or non-verbal action, and withholding of information. Elliot and Culver's definition offered much richness by capturing the omission-commission distinction (that can be traced to St. Thomas Aquinas (1225?–1274) who argued in *Summa Theologica* that not telling the truth is less sinful than uttering a lie). Disagreeing with Aquinas and philosophers who suggest that deception by omission is less egregious than deception by commission (e.g., Chisholm & Freehan, 1977; Freid, 1978), Elliot and Culver observed that some forms of deception by omission may be more problematic than lies, although lies contain a property of assertion not found in deception through omission. They classified journalistic deception into three categories:

- *Investigative deception* occurs when journalists lie (or via a non-verbal equivalent) and withhold information while collecting data. Examples include a reporter who pushes through a crowd and police barricade declaring, "I'm a doctor."
- *Interrogative deception* pertains to journalists' responsibilities to provide truthful information about interview procedures, including telling a source that an interview is taking place, how it is being recorded, and what the potential harm is.
- *Informative deception* involves making false statements in a news story or intentionally withholding information, staging in television news, and withholding or skewing a source's identification that may bias a story.

Based on Elliot and Culver's (1992) definition, journalistic deception includes hidden cameras and microphones; impersonation; non-identification; recreation of news events (staging); fabrication; plagiarism; photo manipulation; false attributions, quote tampering; lying to sources including putting a positive spin on an interview topic; lying to protect a source, and flattering a source or showing insincere empathy. Even flattery is deceptive because "[t]he reporter is going out of his/her way to elicit trust that goes beyond normal social interchange" (p.145).

The antecedents of journalistic deception can be traced to its roots in philosophy. Two philosophical schools that best illustrate the every-day tensions in truth telling are utilitarianism and Kantian theory. The former, with its teleological perspective of focusing on consequences diverges from the latter's deontological perspective viewing truth telling as a duty without exception.

Utilitarianism and Kantian Theory

Utilitarianism, the dominant ethical view in North American society, is an influential force shaping journalists' reasoning about truth telling and providing a justification for violation of the truth telling principle. Utilitarianism, often described as "the greatest happiness for the great-est number," originated with English philosophers Jeremy Bentham and J. S. Mill. As a teleological theory concerned with maximizing good and minimizing evil, utilitarianism suggests that the consequences of an action determine whether the action is right or wrong. Hence, there are conditions under which deception is morally acceptable, or even obliga-tory. Unlike Utilitarians, those who prohibit lies struggle with decep-tion's precise definition as seen in the definitional differences that form St. Augustine's arguments against lying; in *De Mendacio*, he used an eight-fold distinction, beginning with lies uttered in the teaching of reli-gion (the worst sin), and ending with harmless lies that could save some-one from harm (Hoose, 1998).

Bok (1989) discussed the concept of "lying to liars"—an idea that can be traced to Protestant thinker Hugo Grotius who suggested it is more acceptable to lie to people who have lied. This reasoning is seen in the way many journalists justify the use of deceptive methods as a reasonable means of going after the "bad guys." When Food Lion sued, an indignant Ira Rosen, *ABC PrimeTime's* senior producer for investiga-tions, asked: "Who are the bad guys here? Food Lion was putting out out-of-date food out there. We were just covering the story. And for that we get put on trial?" (Baker, 1997, p. 112). Grotius argued that a false-hood is a lie in the strict sense of the word only if it conflicts with a right of the person addressed (Bok, 1989). Based on this, a journalist may believe that a criminal or a terrorist has no right to the truth. To lie or deceive him or her is therefore not wrong. The right in question is that of liberty of judgment, which is implied in all speech but can be lost if the listener has evil intentions, or not yet acquired as in the case of children or the mentally impaired, or when freely given up, as in a poker game.

The strongest objection to lying comes from German philosopher Immanuel Kant, who devoted considerable energy to the topic in his seminal work, *Grounding for the Metaphysics of Morals: On a Supposed Right to Lie Because of Philanthropic Concerns*. Kant (1785/1993), who defined a lie as any intentional statement that is untrue, considered lying to be an affront to human dignity. Through a deontological perspective, the moral rightness of an action depends on the act rather than the consequences. Truth telling is thus a duty without exception. If a person tells the truth, he is not accountable for the consequences, good or bad.

> If by telling a lie you have in fact hindered someone who was even now planning a murder, then you are legally responsible for all the consequences that might result therefrom. But if you have adhered strictly to the truth, then public justice cannot lay a hand on you, whatever the unforeseen consequences might be. (p. 427)

To Kant, fabrication or deception to gather news, no matter how important, is indefensible. His ban on lying is so austere that he does not even believe in lying to save a life. These two philosophical viewpoints—utilitarianism and Kantianism—shape journalists' approaches to truth telling but they do not fully explain the dynamics of journalistic deception, especially when viewed from the perspective of professional conduct subject to external and organizational pressures.

Research in Journalistic Deception

Most of the literature on journalistic deception is philosophical and normative (e.g., Elliot & Culver, 1992; Kieran, 1997). One of the few empirical studies of journalistic deception is Luljak's (2000) participant observation study at an unnamed television station in the Midwest. Luljak found that deception in newsgathering was casual and routine, to the extent that journalists did not even think of it as deception. Only a few cases involved newsroom-wide deliberation, for example concealing an intern's identity to gain student seating in a university stadium. Routine practices include suppressing information that would be embarrassing to subjects, bantering insincerely with sources, and broadcasting interviews containing false information as a favor to law-enforcement authorities. Luljak (2000) found six types of journalistic deception: broadcasting misleading information, misrepresentation of motives, concealment of one's role as reporter, surreptitious recording, misleading sources, and staging.

Lasorsa and Dai (2007), in a content analysis, examined 10 high-profile fabrication cases, including the *New York Times'* Jayson Blair and *Boston Globe*'s Mike Barnicle stories. The study found that newsroom organizational culture contributes to journalistic deception. Prior to revelation of a deception, there was an incubation period during which a "first flag" related to the reporter's earliest work that gives rise to suspicion—is overlooked. The study also identified patterns in deceptive news. They are more likely to be filed from a remote location, to be on a story topic conducive to source secrecy, to be on the front page (or magazine cover), to contain more sources, more "diverse" sources and more hard-to-trace sources. Few studies, however, have examined journalists' attitudes toward deception in its many forms (impersonation, nonidentification, hidden cameras and microphones, lying to sources, fabrication, staging and false attribution, etc.) or explored the variables influencing tolerance for deception. Lee (2004, 2005) was one of the first few to operationalize journalistic deception and examine the factors influencing journalists' attitudes. The next section will discuss the findings in greater detail.

What Journalists Say about Deception

The following discussion of journalistic deception is based on a Web-based survey and depth interviews I conducted with journalists from the IRE (Investigative Reporters and Editors, Inc.). The survey generated 740 responses, or a response rate of 19.4%. The respondents were 42.3% females and 57.7% males, with a mean age of 40 and a median of 39. They are not journalism neophytes. Their demographic profile shows a sample of experienced journalists from large news organizations. The news careers of survey participants ranged from 1 to 49 years, with a mean of 15.8 years and a median of 15. More than half (59.5%) worked for newspapers followed by television (14.2%). The rest worked for magazines, radio, Web-based media, and wire services, and "other" media (research departments, alternative weeklies, and media outlets in journalism schools). They worked for news organizations employing a mean of 230 full-time journalists, and a median of 100. More than half (57.6%) of the news organizations had codes of ethics, and 17.3% employed full-time or part-time ombudsmen. Nearly half of the respondents had a bachelor's degree, and 43% had a bachelor's degree and higher. About 41% had an undergraduate degree in journalism/mass communication, and 14% had a double major that included journalism/mass communication. About 70% had completed a college-level class in journalism/media ethics.

Depth interviews were conducted with 20 journalists who volunteered through the survey. Interviews are useful for understanding a journalist's perspective of journalistic deception, and for probing accounts of deceptive behavior, which is difficult to observe directly due to the associated stigma. The 20 journalists come from newspapers of all sizes, magazines, weeklies, wire services, local television stations and networks, and Web-based media. The longest news career for interviewees is 30 years and the shortest is 4.

Assessing Journalistic Deception: Sixteen Deceptive Practices

My survey with IRE members evaluated 16 deceptive practices on a scale from "not at all justified" to "very justified" based on the question, "Given an important story that is of vital public interest, would the following be justified?" The results show that the journalists considered some practices more deceptive than others, suggesting that journalistic deception is a continuum. The practice of "making a statement that is untrue to readers/viewers" garnered the highest rejection, with an overwhelming 99% of respondents rating it as "not at all justified" (711) or "mostly not justified" (19). The least rejected practice was "withholding information from sources," with only 9.8% of respondents indicating that the practice was "not at all justified" (33) and "mostly not justified" (39). In summary, the 16 deceptive practices were rejected in the following order:

1. Making an untrue statement to readers/viewers;
2. Using nonexistent characters or quotes in a story;
3. Altering quotes;
4. Altering photographs;
5. Publishing or airing information that you have no access to or cannot verify yet;
6. Recreating a news event (staging);
7. Making an untrue statement to sources;
8. Providing misleading or false attribution to protect a source;
9. Claiming to be someone else;
10. Putting a positive spin on a story to make it more interesting;
11. Withholding information from readers/viewers;
12. Recording sound or image without the interviewee/newsmaker's knowledge;
13. Getting employed in a firm or organization to get inside information;
14. Misrepresenting motives by flattering a source or showing empathy;
15. Using hidden cameras and microphones;
16. Withholding information from sources.

Two patterns were evident. First, the journalists reacted more favorably to deceptive practices targeting *news sources* than those targeting *news audiences*. Second, the journalists were more tolerant of deceptive practices that involved *omission* (withholding information; surreptitious recording) than practices involving *commission* (impersonation; lying; tampering with or falsifying information). As the 16 practices were presented sans context, five scenario questions were used to bridge the con-

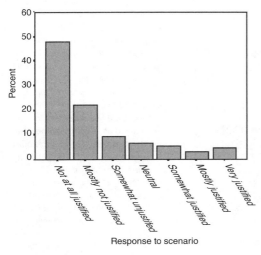

Reporter Jane Smith receives a tip-off that a popular local steakhouse is serving old meat. Although there have been no cases of food poisoning so far, the old meat is a potential public health hazard. To get evidence of wrongdoing, Smith applies for the position of assistant to the chef, by creating a fake resume claiming extensive experience working in restaurants. Is it justifiable for Smith to go undercover and impersonate a steakhouse employee?

Figure 5.1 Steakhouse.

textual gap by inserting into each a deceptive practice: (1) impersonation (steakhouse), (2) lying to a source (campaign finance), (3) hidden cameras (nursing home), (4) fabricating a story (FBI), and (5) withholding a story (Special Forces).

Five Scenario Questions

A direct comparison among the scenarios is difficult considering the qualitative differences posed by the contextual details in each scenario,

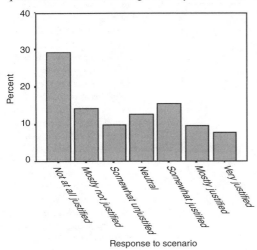

Newspaper reporter Alan Meyer gets an anonymous phone call from a person who claims newly elected Governor Shawn Williams received illegal contributions amounting to $400,000 from a large real-estate company. The caller refuses to meet Meyer but suggests he talks to a local businessman who helped launder the money. At first, the businessman denies the allegations. However, when Meyer tells him he has witnesses and documents to prove the case (when in fact he doesn't), the person agrees to cooperate if he is not identified in the story. Is it justifiable for Meyer to lie to the businessman?

Figure 5.2 Campaign finance.

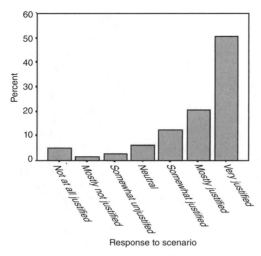

TV reporter Lauren Gray is investigating patient abuse by home health providers—private agencies that send health workers into homes to do everything from housecleaning to semi-skilled nursing. The Better Business Bureau has lodged multiple complaints and so has the state nursing home board, but they lack the authority to act. District Attorney Paul Johnson tells Gray that while his office has begun a criminal investigation, it has been stymied by a lack of evidence or by frail or elderly witnesses who may be unconvincing in court. Gray is urged to pursue the story, the official involved agreeing to release public documents and go on the record. Seven people receiving in-home care agree to let Gray place hidden cameras in their homes. Should wrongdoing occur, Gray plans to speak to the provider, show the tape and ask for an on-the-record response. If no wrongdoing occurs, Gray plans to report this as well. Is it acceptable to use hidden cameras?

Figure 5.3 Nursing home.

but the results are consistent with the pattern of responses to the 16 deceptive practices.

The journalists were more approving of hidden cameras in the nursing home than impersonation in the steakhouse. Impersonation, according to Elliot (1989), is the most insidious of all deceptive newsgathering

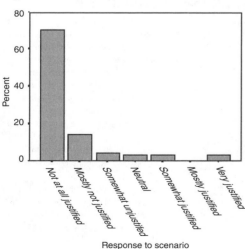

The editors at Big Moon Times have information that the FBI has traced a group of suspects to their town. These suspects are believed to have sent a letter that contained anthrax spores to a network TV station in New York City. It is also believed the suspects may have biological weapons at their disposal and may use them if confronted. Rumors of the FBI's arrival in town are circulating. To buy time and divert the suspects' attention, the FBI requests the newspaper's assistance in planting a fake story to say the town is not being targeted and that FBI agents are searching other distant towns and are already moving to adjacent states looking for the suspects. Is it justifiable for the editors to publish the story?

Figure 5.4 FBI.

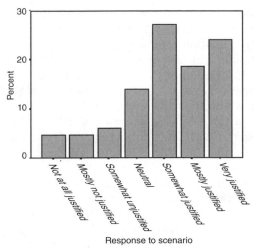

Newspaper reporter Richard Flink has information that U.S. Special Forces have left their base in North Carolina for a secret mission to nab members of a terrorist network and its leader hiding in Somalia. When Flink approaches Major General Bill Davidson to verify the information, the Major General denies the plan exists. However, Flink has sources domestic and abroad that confirm U.S. Special Forces officers have been spotted in neighboring Kenya. When Fink decides to write a story, the Major General and the Assistant Defense Secretary call the paper to tell Flink the operation is actually in place but they ask him to withhold the story for the safety of the U.S. military personnel involved in the mission. Is it justifiable for the newspaper to withhold the story?

Figure 5.5 Special forces.

methods because the journalist is pretending to be someone she is not for the sole purpose of getting a story. The illegality of impersonating certain public officials is an added complication. Inherent in impersonation is deception by commission. In contrast, this element is weaker in hidden cameras, which many journalists consider to be a guileless, objective tool of information gathering. Conceivably, the nature of the information—wrongdoing against defenseless victims in the nursing home scenario—is another persuasive factor.

Compared to the other scenarios, the campaign finance scenario, which involved a journalist lying to a crooked source, shows the least distinctive pattern of response. Respondents, although showing some disapproval, were more divided. This question is an attempt to test Bok's concept of "lying to liars." Depth interviews with the journalists also showed that many believed it is more acceptable to deceive someone who is a bad person, especially in justifying deception. From the journalists' accounts, it is more acceptable "to lie to Osama bin Laden than to a

Figure 5.6 Journalistic deception as a continuum.

Sunday school teacher," consistent with Bok's notion of "lying to liars." As explained by one of the journalists interviewed: "When you get down and deal with pigs, you get a little mud on you."

Comparing the responses to the FBI and Special Forces scenarios, it is clear that respondents considered that the act of withholding a story less egregious than fabricating a story. The FBI scenario, which involved journalists fabricating a story to mislead terrorists and aid law enforcement activities, generated the strongest disapproval among the five scenarios. To the journalists, the act of withholding a story is an omission that is less problematic morally than publishing a false story, notwithstanding the good that can be achieved by both. The omission-commission distinction is supported by responses to the 16 deceptive practices and the depth interviews that showed more tolerance of practices based on omission than those based on commission. Some journalists interviewed maintained that only acts involving outright falsification of information could be viewed as "lying" and "deception"; it is not deceptive to withhold a reporter's identity as no lie was spoken. It was natural for the journalists to offer non-identification as a morally sound alternative to impersonation and fake resumes. As one journalist put it, "It's okay if you don't tell people who you are, but you cannot put on a doctor's jacket and pose as a doctor, or tell people, 'Hey, I am a lawyer.'" In summary, the journalists' responses to the 16 deceptive acts and five scenarios in the survey, as well as depth interviews, revealed a scheme of moral reasoning based on three domains:

1. Who is being deceived: news audiences or newsmakers/sources?
2. What is the perceived moral character of the person deceived: good or bad?
3. What is the nature of the deceptive act: commission or omission?

Fabricating a story is considered a deviant act without exception while hidden cameras and lying to sources are acceptable in some circumstances, and may even be desirable. Flattering a source was not only highly tolerated but also appreciated, as journalists expressed admiration for colleagues who could charm their way to a good story. A journalist has this to say: "A credible journalist would never in a million years think of fabricating a story. That's the cardinal—you just don't do that. But everyone flatters sources, or they should be!"

The journalists carefully distinguish between deception aimed at news *audiences* and news s*ources*, considering the latter to be less deserving of the truth. When the person being deceived is a newsmaker or a person instrumental to a story, the journalists were less inclined to object. Few journalists are willing to breach the implicit contract between journalists and their audiences, consistent with an understanding of journalism as an impartial and truthful purveyor of information. In applying utilitarian reasoning, journalists view newsmakers and news sources are a means to an end, the end being the fulfillment of a duty to news audiences. The differential treatment of audiences and newsmakers is a flawed one; in the minds of journalists, these two groups are mutually exclusive, but by viewing audiences and newsmakers as separate, journalists risk alienating all.

Second, the journalists were more tolerant of deception aimed at wrongdoers, thereby supporting Bok's (1989) notion of lying to liars, in viewing deception as just treatment for unethical persons. Journalism's moral authority was expressed in a sense of reciprocity or "an eye for an eye" justification. Deception is often viewed as an appropriate strategy for dealing with difficult newsmakers, especially the "crooks" and the "bad guys," as a way to extract information that would have been impossible to obtain otherwise. One journalist declared she would not lose too much sleep over deceiving "someone who is intentionally hurting other people." Clearly, moral judgment is an integral aspect of newswork. In assessing the moral character of the newsmaker or news source, these journalists exercised a moral authority for retaliation and for leveling a perceived power imbalance. In interviews, they revealed a preconceived notion of who is bad and who is good: politicians, judges, executives have a smaller claim to the truth than the single mother, the blue-collar worker, or the less powerful and the less media-savvy—a notion shaped by journalism's social surveillance function and an innate distrust of institutions and officials. An overdependence, however, on preconceived notions can be dangerous. People consider others to be less ethical than themselves, and there is no evidence to suggest that journalists are better than others in judging moral character. Journalists may deploy deception as an act of reciprocity but few people perform better than chance in judging whether they have been deceived (Ekman, 2001). The double standard is remarkable; when dealing with newsmakers, the journalists relied on a utilitarian calculus of harm and benefit, but when it came to news audiences, they were guided by a Kantian perspective rejecting all deception.

Third, the journalists considered deception by commission more egregious than deception by omission, consistent with general assessment of deception. Ekman (2001) offers several explanations for people's higher tolerance of deception by omission. It is easier to conceal than to falsify; and harder to get caught because the deceiver does not need to work out a fictional story in advance. Concealment is passive, and hence involves less guilt. If caught, a person can rely on a number of excuses: ignorance, memory lapse, or an intention to reveal the information later.

Variables Shaping Tolerance of Deception

Some studies have linked journalists' individual traits, such as education, journalism training, professional experience, age, and gender, etc., with patterns of moral decision making (e.g., Singletary, Caudill, Caudill, & White, 1990; Voakes, 1997; Weaver & Wilhoit, 1996; Weaver et al, 2007) but most found that external influences (e.g., organizational pressures, professional values, and routines of work) outweigh individual variables (Borden, 2000; Breed, 1955; Graber, 1997; Valenti, 1998; Voakes, 1997; Weaver et al., 2007; Wulfemeyer, 1990). As noted by Weaver et al. (2007), journalists' tolerance of questionable ethical situations is not linked to situational or personal characteristics. Thirty-eight variables from the survey were considered as potential factors influencing tolerance of journalistic deception. They range from age, gender, journalism experience, attendance of religious services, political learning, and education to medium, supervisory role, organization size, and chain ownership. A regression analysis shows that, in general, external factors are better predictors of tolerance of journalistic deception than individual-level variables. In essence, tolerance of deception is shaped mainly on the job, as a function of organizational factors and newsroom pressures consistent with the literature.

Competition and Medium

Competition and medium are the two most salient predictors of tolerance of deception, underscoring the importance of organizational influences. Journalists who rated higher the importance of competition as a consideration in ethical judgment were more likely to tolerate journalistic deception. The salience of competition supports a large body of literature describing how business pressures shape journalists' work (e.g., Bagdikian, 2000; Borden, 2000; McChesney, 1997). In interviews, competition emerged as a key motivation for deception. Although journalists assigned an instrumental value to journalistic deception (as a strategy for getting important information when all means have been exhausted, handling difficult newsmakers, protecting news sources, facilitating objectivity, or self defense), many conceded that deception was motivated by "pure laziness." Convenience, cost, deadlines, and a desire to get a competitive edge push journalists to use hidden cameras, tamper with quotes, fabricate characters and quotes, manipulate photographs, hide their identities, or impersonate non-journalists. As noted by one of the journalists interviewed:

> The primary focus from above our bosses is not, 'Let's talk about ethical and journalistic considerations.' The focus is we need to do a

compelling story that is going to get lots of attention and grab viewers. A whole lot of the time, the two things conflict—a lot.

Journalistic deception is inspired by a desire to gain the largest audience share but over time, it erodes public confidence in a media outlet, to the extent of reducing its audience size.

Medium is another important predictor. TV journalists were more tolerant of deception than their print colleagues. Not only were the TV journalists more tolerant of hidden cameras, they were also more tolerant of other deceptive practices. As a medium low in interactivity, TV is driven by visual impact. Weinberg (1997) and Paterno (1997) observed that TV journalists, due to their heavy reliance on visuals to tell a story, are more likely than print journalists to use undercover, deceptive methods. One method rarely works alone. The demands for visuals may push journalists to use hidden cameras but to work well, cameras typically are accompanied by impersonation and lying to sources. The trend toward surreptitious recording is likely to continue with advances in technology and availability of smaller and less intrusive gadgets.

The Chilling Effect

Those who rated higher the importance of legality were less tolerant of journalistic deception, consistent with the notion that legal concerns may have a chilling effect (Borden & Pritchard, 1997; Kirtley, 2000; and Voakes, 1998). Many journalists interviewed were also concerned about the legality of deceptive practices but quickly connected them to the bottom line. Not surprisingly, the journalists who were more concerned about legal issues were also more cautious about deceptive practices, many of which push at the boundaries of legality.

Gender and Organization Size

The male journalists were more tolerant of journalistic deception than the female journalists. Thoma (1986) found that women consistently scored higher in the Defining Issues Test (Rest, 1983, 1986) that measures an individual's moral development, but a more plausible explanation comes from Gilligan (1982), who suggested that women's moral reasoning differs from men's. Women apply a care perspective—preserving relationships, compassion, and minimizing harm—unlike men who use principles of justice, equality, impartiality, and rights. Possibly these male-centered elements, intrinsic in the concept of journalistic deception and its retaliatory and instrumental utility, appealed less to female journalists. Journalists from larger news organizations were more likely to reject journalistic deception. Larger news organizations tend to have larger pools of resources that facilitate a stronger commitment to ethics training and hence a stronger awareness of ethical issues.

Education and Codes of Ethics: Lost Causes?

Some variables such as journalism experience, journalism education, media ethics education, codes of ethics, and ombudsmen—which appear intuitive—were not salient predictors of tolerance of deception. Some studies have found that age and life experience significantly shape moral decision-making (e.g., Rest, 1983, 1986; Weaver & Wilhoit, 1996; Weaver et al., 2007). According to Weaver and Wilhoit (1996), older and more experienced journalists were more cautious using questionable reporting practices. In my study, age and experience do not appear to be important, and contrary to common wisdom—and perhaps of some disappointment to journalism educators—my survey found no relationship between tolerance of deception and media ethics instruction, college-level journalism class, or journalism major, or ombudsmen. Similarly, whether an organization has an official code of ethics is not a predictor of a journalist's tolerance of journalistic deception. In interviews, journalists questioned the effectiveness of codes, likening them to "pieces of paper" that few journalists pay attention to, consistent with the literature critical of ethics codes. As noted by Black (1985), codes of ethics will be obeyed when journalists willingly subject themselves to ethical standards above and beyond their own personal beliefs or when the code has clear enforcement provisions. From interviews with journalists, these two ingredients were missing. There was a strong conviction that "personal" ethics or "intuition" will prevail. With experience comes the knack of knowing what is right and what is wrong. Many journalists felt their codes of ethics were too general to be useful. As many as 15% of survey respondents did not know whether their organizations have codes. Those who had codes could not verbalize their content, and the few who were aware of their codes' enforcement provisions had difficulties articulating them.

Genuine moral development occurs only when people develop beyond a stage of being other-directed by rules to an inner-directed stage of internalized rules. The progression from heteronomy where right and wrong are defined externally to an autonomous stage of reflective judgment allows journalists to find meaning in and relevance of a rule, and to defend it. Perhaps the rejection of codes of ethics is indicative of this growth. As observed by the journalists, codes are useful for a young reporter but less so for a veteran journalist. However, legality, another rule-based approach, appears to be a more salient deterrent. Journalists may have rejected codes of ethics but they view laws to be more binding.

Conclusion

Journalistic deception is shaped by a set of independent variables that include competition, medium, and legality as well as motivations of public interest, objectivity, last resort, self-defense, convenience, etc. In an ethical filtering process, journalists consider whether the deceptive act is targeted at newsmakers or audiences, the moral character of the person deceived, and the omission-commission distinction. Although the journalists considered some deceptive acts to be more problematic than others, they clearly see journalistic deception as a prima facie wrong. Their attempts to justify, normalize, and classify journalistic deception reflect an understanding that any form of journalistic deception is a departure from the norm. The journalists were guided by a distinctive set of tacit rules and subtleties consistent with the notion of journalistic deception as an occupational construct. Shaped by a complex interplay of values and norms central to journalism and its culture as well as organizational pressures and the contours of a broader moral framework, journalistic deception should not be confused with the generic interpretation of deception that occurs in everyday life, for example, lying about the price of one's laptop, cheating on one's spouse, or occupational lies deployed by the police to fight crime. Unfortunately, these subtleties and tacit rules are easily lost on non-journalists, and inevitably escalate into a source of friction between journalists and the people they want to serve.

Journalistic deception is common, just as deception is common in human interaction. One may then ask: If deception is a common occurrence in human interaction, must journalists be vilified for using it? Clearly, the "everyone is doing it" argument is unacceptable. Some, especially non-journalists, may lament journalism's spiritual schizophrenia and over-reliance on situational ethics, but if and when performed correctly, journalistic deception is defendable. Rather than urge journalists never to deceive, the focus should be on how to deceive ethically. Rules exist, and conscience prevails. The inevitability of deception in human communication should not discourage the continued exploration of journalistic deception as an area of study and journalistic growth. Journalists can deceive or not deceive—it is a choice, not a certainty.

References

Aquinas, T. (1981). *Summa theologica*. London: Christian Classics.

Bagdikian, B. (2000). *The media monopoly* (6th ed). Boston: Preston Press.

Baker, R. (1997, March/April). In Greensboro: Damning undercover tactics as "fraud." *Columbia Journalism Review, 19*, 23–26

Bernstein, C., & Woodward, B. (1974). *All the president's men*. New York: Simon & Schuster.

Bivins, T. (2003). *Mixed media: Moral distinctions in journalism, advertising, and public relations*. Mahwah, NJ: Erlbaum.

Black, J. (1985, Fall/Winter). The case against mass media codes of ethics. *Journal of Mass Media Ethics, 1*(1), 14–21.

Black, J., Steele, B., & Barney, R. (1997). *Doing ethics in journalism: A handbook with case studies.* Boston: Allyn & Bacon.

Bok, S. (1989). *Lying: Moral choice in public and private life* (2nd ed.). New York: Random House. (Original work published in 1978)

Borden, S. L. (2000). A model for evaluating journalist resistance to business constraints. *Journal of Mass Media Ethics, 15,* 159–166.

Borden, S. L., & Pritchard, M. (1997). News sources and deception. In E. D. Cohen & D. Elliot (Eds.), *Journalism ethics: A handbook* (pp. 102–106). Santa Barbara, CA: ABC-CLIO.

Breed, W. (1955). Social control in the newsroom. *Social Forces, 33,* 326–335.

Buller, D. B., & Burgoon, J. K. (1996). Interpersonal deception theory. *Communication Theory, 6,* 203–242.

Chisholm, R., & Freehan, T. (1977). The intent to deceive. *Journal of Philosophy, 74,* 143–159.

Christians, C. G., Fackler, M., Rotzoll, K. B., & McKee, K. (2005). *Media ethics: Cases and moral reasoning* (7th ed.). New York: Longman.

Cooper, T. W., Clifford, G. C., Plude, F. F., & White, R. A. (1989). *Communication ethics and global change.* New York: Longman.

DePaulo, B. M., Kashy, D. A., Kirkendol, S. E., Wyer, M. M., & Epstein, J. A. (1996). Lying in everyday life. *Journal of Personality and Social Psychology, 70,* 979–995.

Ekman, P. (2001). *Telling lies.* New York: Norton.

Elliot, D. (1989). Journalistic deception. In P. Y. Windt, P. C. Appleby, M. P. Battin, L. P. Francis, & B. M. Landesman (Eds.), *Ethical issues in the professions* (pp. 144–146). Englewood Cliffs. NJ: Prentice-Hall.

Elliot, D., & Culver, C. (1992). Defining and analyzing journalistic deception. *Journal of Mass Media Ethics, 7,* 69–84.

Fedler, F. (1989). *Media hoaxes.* Ames: Iowa University Press.

Freid, C. (1978). *Right and wrong.* Cambridge: Harvard University Press.

Gallup. (1998). Nurses shine, bankers slump in ethics rating, 2008. Retrieved Feb 11, 2009, from http://www.gallup.com/poll/112264/Nurses-Shine-While-Bankers-Slump-Ethics-Ratings.aspx

Gilligan, C. (1982). *In a different voice: Psychological theory and women's development.* Cambridge, MA: Harvard University Press.

Goodwin, G., & Smith, R. F. (2003). *Groping for ethics in journalism* (3rd ed.). Ames: Iowa State University Press.

Harris, R. J. (1999). *A cognitive psychology of mass communication* (3rd ed.). Mahwah, NJ: Erlbaum.

Herrscher, R. (2002). A universal code of journalism ethics: Problems, limitiations, and proposals. *Journal of Mass Media Ethics, 17,* 227–289.

Hutchins Commission. (1947). *A free and responsible press.* Chicago: University of Chicago Press.

Hoose, B. (1998). *Christian ethics: An introduction.* Wilmington, DE: Michael Glazier Books.

Kant, I. (1993). *Grounding for the metaphysics of morals* (2nd ed.). J. W. Ellington (Trans). Indianapolis, IN: Hackett. (Original work published 1785)

Kieran, M. (1997). *Media ethics: A philosophical approach.* Westport, CT: Praeger.

Kirtley, J. (2000). Is it a crime? An overview of recent legal actions stemming from investigative reports. In M. Greenwald & J. Bernt (Eds.), *The big chill: Investigative reporting in the current media environment* (pp. 137–156). Ames: Iowa State University Press.

Knightley, P. (1975). *The first casualty: From the Crimea to Vietnam, the war correspondent as hero, propagandist, and myth maker.* New York: Harcourt Brace Jovanovich.

Laitila, T. (1995). Journalistic codes of ethics in Europe. *European Journal of Communication, 10,* 513–526.

Lambeth, E. (1992). *Committed journalism: An ethic for the profession* (2nd ed.). Bloomington: Indiana University Press.

Lasorsa, D. L., & Dai, J. (2007). Newsroom's normal accident. An exploratory study of 10 cases of journalistic deception. *Journalism Practice, 1,* 159–174.

Lee, S. T. (2004). Lying to tell the truth: Journalists and the social context of deception. *Mass Communication & Society, 7,* 97–120.

Lee, S. T. (2005). Predicting tolerance of journalistic deception. *Journal of Mass Media Ethics, 20,* 22–42.

Luljak, T. (2000). The routine nature of journalistic deception. In D. Pritchard (Ed.), *Holding the media accountable: Citizens, ethics, and the law* (pp. 11–26). Bloomington: Indiana University Press.

McChesney, R. W. (1997). *Corporate media and the threat to democracy.* New York: Seven Stories.

Meyer, P. (1987). *Ethical journalism.* Lanham, MD: University Press of America.

Mieth, D. (1997). The basic norm of truthfulness: Its ethical justification and universality. In C. Christians & M. Traber (Eds.), *Communication ethics and universal values* (pp. 87–104). Thousand Oaks, CA: Sage.

Mill, J. S. (1989). *J. S. Mill: On liberty and other writings.* Cambridge University Press. (Original work published 1854)

Milton, J. (2006). *Areopagitica: A speech of Mr. John Milton for the liberty Of unlicensed printing.* New York: Lawbook Exchange. (Original work published 1644)

Olasky, M. (1988). *The press and abortion, 1838–1988.* Hillsdale, NJ: Erlbaum.

Paterno, S. (1997, May). The lying game. *American Journalism Review,* 40–45.

Patterson, P. & Wilkins, L. (2004). *Media ethics: Issues and cases* (5th ed). McGraw-Hill: Boston, MA.

Rao, S., & Lee, S. T. (2005). Globalizing media ethics? An assessment of universal ethics among international political journalists. *Journal of Mass Media Ethics, 20,* 99–120.

Rest, J. R. (1983). Morality. In P. H. Mussen (Ed.), *Handbook of child psychology, Vol III Cognitive development* (pp. 556–629). New York: Wiley.

Rest, J. R. (1986). *Moral development: Advances in research and theory.* New York: Praeger.

Rivers, W. L., & Mathews, C. (1988). *Ethics for the media.* Upper Saddle River, NJ: Prentice-Hall.

Singletary, M. W., Caudill, S., E. Caudill, & White, A. (1990). Motives for ethical decision-making. *Journalism Quarterly, 67,* 964–972.

Strentz, H. (2002). Universal ethical standards? *Journal of Mass Media Ethics, 17,* 263–276.

Thoma, S. (1986). Estimating gender differences in the comprehension and preference of moral issues. *Developmental Review, 6,* 165–180.

Valenti, J. M. (1998). Ethical decision making in environmental communication. *Journal of Mass Media Ethics, 13,* 219–231.

Voakes, P. S. (1997). Social influences on journalists' decision-making in ethical situations. *Journal of Mass Media Ethics, 12,* 18–35.

Voakes, P. S. (1998, Summer). What were you thinking? A survey of journalists who were sued for invasion of privacy. *Journalism and Mass Communication Quarterly, 75,* 378–393.

Weaver, D. H., Beam, R. A., Brownlee B. J., Voakes, P S., & Wilhoit, G. C. (2007). *The American journalist in the 21st century: U.S. news people at the dawn of a new millennium.* Mahwah, NJ: Erlbaum.

Weaver, D. H., & Wilhoit, C. G. (1996). *The American journalist in the 1990s: US newspeople at the end of an era.* Mahwah, NJ: Erlbaum.

Weinberg, S. (1997). Undercover investigations. In E. D. Cohen & D. Elliot (Eds.), *Journalism ethics: A handbook* (pp. 107–109). Santa Barbara, CA: ABC-CLIO.

Wulfemeyer, K. (1990). Defining ethics in electronic journalism: Perceptions of news directors. *Journalism Quarterly, 67,* 984–991.

Chapter 6

The Sin in Sincere
Deception and Cheating in the Visual Media

Paul Martin Lester

> Beauty is truth, truth beauty, that is all ye know on earth, and all ye
> need to know.
>
> John Keats (1819), *Ode on a Grecian Urn*

The controversial French cultural theorist, Jean Baudrillard, rumored to
have died March 11, 2007, argued in his seminal work "Simulacra and
Simulations" that modern society is a reality constructed with imitated
scenes based on the symbolism of signs. For Baudrillard (1988), what
is real to humans is, in truth, a reproduction of reality. Although that
statement is literally true, as external information gathered by our senses
is filtered and reproduced inside the mind, Baudrillard adds an anti-cor-
porate message in which this modern construct is controlled and propa-
gated by the media. This unprecedented media power is ceded freely by
a collectively agreed upon pact between the media and those who are a
part of the consumer culture.

Baudrillard defines the relationship between what the media sell—
from consumer goods, services, and particular lifestyles to political
persuasive arguments—and what we become through this synergetic,
symbolic process. In this way he goes beyond the impressions of the
semiotic pioneers de Saussure, Peirce, and Barthes with their collections
of iconic and indexical signs and their chains of symbolic associations,
towards a more fundamental cultural inherency of the mind—a perfect
solipsistic state of being that negates any notion of a "true life" and its
inevitable misunderstood meanings.

Plato's famous cave shadow metaphor that helped define how citizens
are influenced by messages they come to believe as real gets a new technological update, "Cave 2.0," when every person is conveniently provided with a high-definition "WebTV" screen and near instantaneously
connection with surround sound speakers hidden within the walls of
their home "cave." Plato's famous metaphor helped explain for ancient
Greeks and others the nature of illusion and reality where all citizens
were bound together watching the same shadow dance on the same cave

wall. For Baudrillard, the difference between Plato's and today's version is one of degree and not kind. For we each live within our own, self-created skull caves watching in darkness the movie that is our lives. For Baudrillard, there is no difference between the worlds outside and inside our heads, between the concrete and the symbolic, between what the media show and what we become by its consumption, and between the commercial and its inherent deception.

Consumerism and its doppelgänger manipulation almost always combine when discussing examples of visual deception. The cover of *Newsweek* magazine's extra edition immediately following the attack on 9/11 is an apt example.[1] Although, at first glance, the word and picture choices seem in line with the most ethical traditions associated with documentary news photojournalism, an unethical manipulation is clearly evident, but only for those trained to notice. The image of the World Trade Center's south tower seconds after the moment of impact is a frightening combination of fire, smoke, and debris. But the picture is highly manipulated for purely commercial reasons. Through digital manipulation, the sky around and above the top of the tower was removed so that the building would appear to jut from the page in front of the *Newsweek* name. Creating this three-dimensional effect, common with most magazine covers vying for a customer's attention on a crowded news rack, is especially reprehensible given the important historical nature of the photograph. When an average viewer reads the cover as a subconscious symbol of consumerist culture instead of a representation of a reality as true as possible, the fakery illustrates the worst fears of Baudrillard.

The ethical collapse evident in the image of the twin tower is a visual metaphor for the collapse of truth through the media manipulation of images. Either through persuasive, educational, journalistic, entertainment, or commercial purposes, the media are extremely well positioned by history, technology, and public reliance to create manipulated images that deceive the public.

Philosopher Bernard Gert (2004) in his little book *Common Morality* identifies "The ten general rules ... [that] account for all the kinds of actions that are morally prohibited and required." Gert's 10 moral rules of do not kill, do not cause pain, do not disable, do not deprive of freedom, do not deprive of pleasure, do not deceive, keep your promises, do not cheat, obey the law, and do your duty, comprise a moral system that should be followed under typical conditions. Gert acknowledges that each of the rules may be violated, but the violation can only be acceptable if there is sufficient justification to warrant the harm that may occur (p. 20). For this chapter, the moral laws "do not deceive" and "do not cheat" directly apply to a discussion of manipulation in the mass media. As will be explored in the examples below, some manipulations are deceptive while others are considered a form of cheating.

Deception is defined as "a deliberate attempt to mislead others" (DeP-aulo et al., 2003, p. 74). The deception can be in the form of a direct action or in a nonaction. Deception can also be verbal or nonverbal. For Gert (2004), "Any behavior that a person knows or should know will significantly increase the chances that someone will have false beliefs can count as violating this rule" (p. 41). Cheating is a more serious moral violation. It is defined "When an individual intentionally violates a rule or social convention that others reasonably believe that person to be following" (Elliott & Culver, 1992, p. 70). With Gert, "The one respect in which cheating seems different from all of the other moral rules is that it does not seem possible to violate this rule unintentionally" (p. 46).

Deception and cheating are deliberate perversions of the truth and are only justified if "all impartial rational persons would estimate that less evil would be suffered if that kind of violation were publicly allowed" and never justified "if more would suffer if that violation were publicly allowed" (Elliott, 1998, p. 9). It is the group, the community, that ultimately determines what action or nonaction is ethical or not. Dr. Frans B. M. de Waal, an Emory University primatologist remarks, "The moral system is one that revolves the tension between individual and group interests in a way that seems best for the most members of the group" (Wade, 2007, p. D6). Ethical dilemmas only occur when there is a conflict within or between groups concerned with their individual or shared values and loyalties. Having a body of reasonable individuals determine whether an action is morally justified or not is a concept that helped early humans progress from individual nomads to a community of groups living together. Perseverance of individuals within a group has always been a vital component to human interaction. But when deception and cheating are allowed within a society, group conciliation can degrade into suspicion and division.

Throughout the history of visual production and presentation, such diverse practitioners and consumers as magicians, artists, advertisers, movie producers, journalists, and average users have employed techniques to deceive others. In most cases, the deceptive effects have been happily accepted by willing patrons, but in other cases, they amount to cheating and have caused scorn from professionals and the public.

Magic is a form of stagecraft that relies on deception. Jean Eugène Robert-Houdin thrilled 19th century Parisian audiences with his elaborately constructed mechanical robots that appeared to move as if they were actually alive. The contemporary humor-based magician duo of Penn Jillete and Teller (he was born Raymond, but legally changed to his last name only) make audiences slightly uncomfortable with their props that can include spikes, straitjackets, bear-traps, and knives. Magic, whether up-close sleight-of-hand tricks to elaborate disappearing illusions that can span a city block, relies on an audience member's suspension of their disbelief. In order to fully enjoy magic, one must be willing to play along with the skilled performers. Such deception is not only acceptable it is mandatory.

With its roots in the techniques employed by magicians, spirit photography is also a tradition steeped in deception, but with a commercial purpose. An early 20th century popular fad based on Spiritualism, the belief that one can communicate with the deceased, spirit photographs supposedly captured the likeness of a dead person on photographic paper. The famous magician and escape artist, Harry Houdini made it part of his life's mission to root out fraudulent mediums who provided spirit photographs through double exposure techniques. Usually, a psychic medium would make an appointment with a customer and ask for a picture of the deceased. This portrait, it was told, was necessary in order to communicate more easily with the spirit body. The spirit photographer would then expose part of a negative plate with the image. Using that same negative during a portrait sitting, the photographer simply developed the image and showed the print to the amazed and grateful customer (Lester, 1991, pp. 102–103). Spirit photographic customers were deceived because they were unsophisticated about how photography worked and because they wanted to believe in the truth of spirit pictures.[2] With spirit photographs, the printed deceptions amounted to fraud, the same as cheating as naïve customers were thought to believe in the photographic fakes and pay for the privilege.

The early history of photography has its share of phony images. Although he is seldom given credit, Frenchman Hippolyte Bayard discovered a unique photographic process independent of popular photography pioneers Joseph Niépce, Louis Daguerre, and Henry Fox Talbot. Frustrated by the lack of recognition, Bayard made the first faked picture and caption combination in 1840.[3] He posed as a corpse and wrote on the back of the print, "The Government, which has supported Daguerre more than is necessary, declared itself unable to do anything for M. Bayard, and the unhappy man threw himself into the water in despair." Two years later, the *Societe d'Encouragement pour l'Industrie Nationale* gave Bayard a prize of 3,000 francs (adjusted for inflation, the amount is the equivalent to about $12,500 US dollars) (Lester, 1991, pp. 91–92). Since most knew that Bayard had not drowned and was only protesting his government's slight, his photograph was deceptive, not cheating.

In 1857, Oscar Rejlander produced a deceptive picture with a documentary quality. Captioned, "Street urchins tossing chestnuts," the photograph shows a young boy in ragged clothes delightfully looking up at a chestnut he has presumably just tossed into the air. But stopping a moving object in mid-air was a technical feat impossible with the slow film and lenses in use at that time. Rejlander produced the effect through the deceptive use of a fine thread that dangled the nut in front of the boy.[4] In that same year, he also made the controversial, "The Two Ways of Life," an elaborate story of a young man's decision to follow the good or evil way of life.[5] Since it would have been nearly impossible to photograph the 20 or so models portrayed in the entire image at once with the equipment of the day, Rejlander made 32 separate exposures and combined them to produce the single photograph (Lester, 1991, pp. 92–93). Since the photographs were meant to be illustrations, and he used tricks that were considered ethical for that time, the fact that viewers were deceived by their production is of minor consequence.

The genre of art known as *trompe l'oeil*, to "mislead the eye," exploits one of the four key visual cues of the human brain, depth (the other three are color, form, and movement). Humans are generally fascinated with paintings, prints, and motion pictures in which the images seemingly extend out of the substrate and toward the viewer. As discussed earlier, the popularity of the technique for magazine covers is based on this principle of visual awareness. The 19th century Catalan artist Pere Borrell del Caso is most known for his striking work, *Escapando de la Crítica*, "Escaping the Critic," in which a startled boy tentatively explores the world outside his frame.[6] Taking up del Caso's style is the English contemporary artist Julian Beever who also plays with the depth visual cue by his elaborate yet temporary chalk drawings on city sidewalks or buildings.[7] The interesting fact of Beever's work is that passersby cannot see the three-dimensional effect. It is only after being photographed that his drawings are admired. With del Caso's and Beever's work, viewers enjoy being deceived and are not cheated.

The French painter, Georges-Pierre Seurat, founder of the art movement known as neo-impressionism, is most famous for his pointillist masterpiece, *Un Dimanche Après-midi à L'Ile de la Grande Jatte* painted between 1884 and 1886.[8] Because of the pointillist technique, the content of his work of art can only be fully appreciated within the mind of the gallery patron. By using a series of small, colored dots on a canvas, Seurat used a procedure that resulted in a picture that is meaningless if viewed inches away. All a person will see up close is an, albeit, exquisite collection of filled-in painted circles without substance. But if one stands away, the relaxing scene of French citizens enjoying a sunny Sunday afternoon on a Seine river island northwest of central Paris are in full view.

Contemporary Seattle-based photographer Chris Jordan is an artist who manipulates objects to create elaborate informational graphics—a form of graphic design that most often translates words into pictures to help explain complex concepts visually. In one of his pieces, Jordan recreates Seurat's scene but with different colored and shaded aluminum soft drink cans instead of paint blots. In *Cans Seurat*, Jordan uses, 106,000 cans that represent the number of sugar-water drinks consumed within the United States every 30 seconds.[9] However, Jordan's image is misleading.

The viewer naturally has the impression that the photographer stacked the cans in high columns corresponding with the colors and tones of the Seurat painting. In truth, Jordan takes individual photographs of single cans and combines them on his computer. As such, his pictures do not exist as physical objects in reality, but as two-dimensional printed photographs. Unlike the Seurat painting, the meaning of Jordan's work is only made clear after a viewer gets closer and closer to the photographic print. But as with the original Seurat work, there is no harm in the deception as viewers are intrigued and educated by the process.

Advertising producers also use deceptive techniques to various degrees of subtly in advertisements and commercials and with television shows and in motion pictures in order to promote their products and services. "Jezebel," a blog that includes critical discussions of celebrities and their public images, featured 11 alterations to the face and body of singer Faith Hill for her cover portrait for *Redbook* magazine. The art director of *Redbook* thought that these computer-generated manipulations were necessary so Hill would "skew younger" and attract more persons to buy the publication ("Here's Our Winner," 2007). In its "PhotoShop of Horrors" page, Jezebel offers other examples of digital tricks used by the fashion industry ("Photoshop of Horrors," 2008). "The Dove Self-Esteem Fund," started by the makers of Dove products and the Ogilvy advertising agency, shows the extent of advertising manipulation in their ground-breaking anti-stereotype advertising. One short film, *Evolution* shows how a woman is transformed into a supermodel through hair, make-up, lighting, and software deceptive tricks.[10] For Dove, deception that educates is acceptable. Deception that makes potential customers feel bad about their bodies is cheating.

In a world of TiVo time shifting, Internet downloads, and heavy competition for advertising dollars, product placement is a form of deception that most advertisers and some customers will admit is a necessary part of media viewing. As with many television shows and motion pictures, producers are willing to charge advertisers a substantial fee to have a character use a product. When an episode of NBC's popular situation comedy, *The Office* called for a restaurant setting, a Chili's restaurant was selected. The result was a subtle advertisement for the chain. Furthermore, with the high cost of movie production and marketing, motion pictures are also filled with advertisements. The 2004 Ben Stiller comedy *Dodgeball*, for example, included product placements for Under Armour, Nike, Vitaminwater, Fiji Water, Pepsi, Budweiser, Bud Light, ESPN, Fox Sports, and Nautilus (Lester, 2006, p. 77). Although most sophisticated visual consumers can spot the obvious placement of a product in a program, untrained and uneducated consumers do not have such knowledge. For them, such placement is a form of cheating.

Since the earliest history of motion pictures, directors have employed

deceptive techniques that have ranged from stage-managing to sophisticated computer-generated images. One of the first short films was the
1902 classic, *Le Voyage dans la Lune*, conceived and directed by the
French magician, Georges Méliès. In the charming motion picture heavily influenced by stage magic tricks learned over the years, Méliès visually delights viewers with a spacecraft hitting the eye of the complaining
"man in the moon," professorially clad astronomers who vanquish moon
beasts with a slap of their umbrellas, and dive under water for further
adventures. With *Voyage*, Méliès inaugurated the science fiction genre
and the use of special effects. Twenty years later, a different sort of film
was introduced, the serious, anthropological documentary, Great Britain's Robert Flaherty's *Nanook of the North*. Supposedly an untainted
look at Eskimo life in the Canadian arctic, the movie nevertheless used
several staged and scripted scenes composed by Flaherty to add dramatic
interest. Modern-day documentary filmmakers such as Ken Burns, Wer-
ner Herzog, Michael Moore, and Errol Morris, have also been criticized
for what they leave in and what they omit from their films. Consequently,
the Academy Award competition recently added stipulations for documentary directors when they submit their films for consideration to detail
such methods as "reenactments, scripted sequences, and the use of actors,
stop-motion photography, computer imagery, and specially trained or
bred animals" in order to render as true as possible film documents (Piccalo, 2007, p. E5). Of course, docudramas and bio-flicks are known for
compressing time sequences, combining characters, and straying from
the truth if a bit of fiction is more interesting. The extent of the stage-
managing and special effects within a documentary determine whether
a director is guilty of mere deception or outright cheating, but when a
purely fictional movie employs the documentary language of "based on a
true story" in order to create additional interest in the drama, the public
can feel cheated as with such films as Joel and Ethan Coen's 1996 movie
Fargo and the 1999 box office phenomenon from the minds of Daniel
Myrick and Eduardo Sánchez, *The Blair Witch Project*.

Since the first computer-generated motion picture produced by
Edward E. Zajac of AT&T Bell Laboratories in 1963 that showed how
a communications satellite circling the globe might function, the movie
industry has consistently improved the extent and quality of the digital
production of images.[11] By and large, viewers have been willing to believe
in their creations and support their efforts through box office sales.
Five years after Zajac's crude animated experiment, Stanley Kubrick
employed simple computer graphic monitor displays in his classic *2001:
A Space Odyssey*. About 20 years after Zajac, Walt Disney Company's
science fiction effort, *Tron*, sparked cover magazine stories and television news publicity because of the 20 minutes of computer-generated
images. Unfortunately, the film was a box office disappointment. But 30

years after the first computer film, directors such as James Cameron and Steven Spielberg were astounding audiences with their digital creations in such motion pictures as *Terminator 2* and *Jurassic Park*. Of course, moviegoers do not believe in time-traveling killer robots or that cloned dinosaurs walk the earth on a remote island. However, the computer images appeared so real that viewers were happy to be momentarily deceived. Fifty years after Zajac, Cameron will have released his science fiction adventure *Avatar* that will contain about 60% computer-generated images with such a high degree of production skills that audiences will not be able to tell the difference between live-action and computer programs ("FAQ for Avatar," 2008). When provided within the context of a fictionalized motion picture, such deception is acceptable.

Journalism deception and cheating has a long history. But with its professional role-related responsibility to tell the truth in a fair and balanced way, journalism manipulation, when discovered, more often skews toward cheating rather than simple deception.

The Scottish-born photographer Alexander Gardner was hired by American Mathew Brady to take pictures for him during the American Civil War. Although Gardner's photographic portfolio is filled with treasured moments captured on film including a portrait of President Abraham Lincoln taken 4 days before his assassination, Gardner's career is tarnished somewhat by a blatant manipulation.

Gardner made a series of pictures of the body of 18-year-old Pvt. Andrew Hoge of the 4th Virginia Infantry in Gettysburg as a Confederate and then as a Union soldier. In one, the photograph shows Hoge lying on his back, his face turned toward the camera, and his rifle propped up against one of the rocks in a picture titled, "The Home of a Rebel Sharpshooter, Gettysburg."[12] But in another picture by Gardner the same soldier is in a different location. This photograph is a closer view of the young man still lying on his back, but his face is turned away from the camera and his rifle lies on the ground by his side.[13] Although one noted historian viewed Gardner's stage-managing as "nothing serious," when a photographer fakes a picture, all the work produced by that artist is put into question (Lester, 1991, pp. 95–96). Although Gardner's reputation is slightly damaged by his direct manipulation of the body and the false caption accompaniments, his actions do not rise to the level of cheating.

During the depressed economic times in America during the 1930s, President Franklin D. Roosevelt's administration set up the Resettlement Administration, later named the Farm Security Administration (FSA) to help those who had lost their jobs in the agricultural field. Another purpose of the FSA was to produce films and still photographs to document the dire conditions of the land and its people to be used as publicity so that public support would rally behind controversial legislation. One of the FSA photographers, Dorothea Lange, made what has been called the greatest single photograph in the history of the medium, a portrait of Florence Thompson with three of her seven children. The picture is also known simply as "The Migrant Mother."[14] The six images that Lange made of the desperate family living in a crude, canvas, three-sided lean-to tent show a photographer knowingly moving in closer for a better composition and actively stage managing the Thompson family members (Sprague, n.d.). Stage managing, as with the theatre phrase from which it comes, is a term used to describe the act of controlling what the subjects of a photograph or moving image say and do. In today's media environment, if a photojournalist for a newspaper stage-managed a news event without telling her editor, that act and its omission are grounds for immediate dismissal.

In the first photograph taken by Lange, 14-year-old Viola faces the camera while sitting on a rocking chair outside the tent. Standing within the tent can be seen Ruby, 5, wearing a knit cap and Katherine, 4. Florence is seated holding 1-year-old Norma. All except the baby look at the camera. For the second image, Viola has moved the chair inside the tent "in hopes her photo can not be taken." Katherine stands next to Florence looking at the camera. Florence is turned "talking to Ruby, who is hiding behind her mother." The third image is a closer portrait of Florence and the baby. The fourth picture shows Ruby's chin propped on Florence's shoulder while holding the baby. Ruby no longer wears the knit cap. The fifth photograph is a slightly different version of the fourth. Florence looks more towards the camera. Finally, the last image, the one that would become an icon for many regarding the unsure future of America, shows Florence with her right hand touching her face and holding baby Norma with Katherine and Ruby on either side of Florence with their faces turned away from the camera. In the original photograph, Viola's finger and hand can be clearly seen at the lower right of the frame holding back the tent flap. In subsequent versions of the famous print, the finger, thought of as a distraction or clear evidence of Lange's stage direction, was removed from the composition. Dorothea Lange knew that children looking into the camera and smiling would not be as strong an image as having them turn away. The six images reveal how Lange "worked the situation" to create the best possible moment. It is clear that Lange's stage managing is a form of deception because most viewers assume photographers take pictures of events that happen before their cameras without overt manipulation. However, the actions of Lange do not rise to cheating since few were harmed and this powerful portrait helped many.

Another documentary photographer for the FSA was Arthur Rothstein who made a photograph of a sun-bleached steer's skull on a dry patch of ground that almost derailed his career.[15] When it was discovered that Rothstein had moved the skull to a better position, Republican politicians used the picture to attack the credibility of all the FSA photographs and particularly the Democratic Roosevelt administration. Rothstein was accused of traveling around the country with his suitcase, his camera, and his skull. Although he claims to have only moved the skull 10 feet, Rothstein regretted the controversy for the rest of his career (Lester, 1991, p. 112–114). Nevertheless, Rothstein cheated the public with his manipulation of the skull because he did so deliberately in order to create a more strikingly propagandistic image.

The February 1982 cover of *National Geographic* magazine was a milestone in computer digital manipulation. *Geographic*, long known for its well-earned reputation of journalism excellence with words and pictures, used one of the first digital scanners, a Scitex, and altered the image on its cover. The original horizontal picture of the Great Pyramids of Giza by Gordon Gahan would not fit on the vertical cover format used by the magazine. No worries. The pyramids were simply digitally moved closer together to accommodate the layout.[16] Unfortunately, the director of photography at the time did not tell readers that the image should have been called an illustration and not an accurate representation. Because readers who had been to Egypt called and wrote the magazine to question the position of the two pyramids, the editor was forced to admit that the image was faked. Little known about this situation is also the fact that Gahan paid the three men on the camels to repeatedly ride across the frame so he could get the separation he wanted between them. Sadly, Gahan died in a helicopter accident the year after the issue was published (Lester, 1991, pp. 123–124). Nevertheless, photographs used for a respected magazine known for its high standard of credibility should be manipulated only to aid in the publishing process. By moving pyramids and camel jockeys, *National Geographic* was guilty of cheating.

Patrick Schneider and Rick Loomis are Pulitzer Prize winning photographers with portfolios that are the envy of photojournalists around the world. But even though they both committed essentially the same picture manipulation, one was suspended from his newspaper while the other remains in high regard. In 2002 Patrick Schneider of *The Charlotte Observer* was stripped of three awards in the North Carolina Press Photographers contest and suspended from his job for 3 days when it was learned that he used PhotoShop to darken the background of several images. One picture that stood out was an emotionally charged picture of firefighters during a comrade's funeral. The background was completely eliminated and turned black (Meyer, 2003). On the other hand, Rick Loomis of the *Los Angeles Times* won the 2003 Newspaper Photographer of the Year award with a striking portfolio of images from Afghanistan. Ten of his pictures had their backgrounds blackened with a more traditional technique than Schneider used—a black cloth was held behind the subjects.[17] Schneider had to return his awards and lost 3 days of pay while Loomis received nothing but accolades (Lester & Elliott, 2004, pp.

12–13). The difference between the two results was that in today's professional environment procedures that capture "what the camera saw," even if heavily stage-managed, are considered more ethical while manipulations that are imposed later using software and a computer are considered more deceptive. Both techniques impose the photographer's ego upon their subjects, rob viewers of possibly valuable background content and context, and are better reserved for obviously posed studio assignments. Sadly, Schneider did not learn a lesson from his suspension. About 4 years after his public embarrassment, he was fired from the *Observer* for once again manipulating the background color in a picture of a firefighter on a ladder to make the image more dramatic (Winslow, 2006).

Brian Walski, a staff photographer for the *Los Angeles Times*, was fired on April 1, 2003, when his editors discovered that he had combined two images into one that were taken in Basra during the first month of the Iraqi war. No joke. In one image a man with a child in his arms is moving toward a British soldier while other men are seated on the ground nearby. In another image the man is distracted and looking to his left while the soldier is gesturing with his left arm motioning him to sit down. What was obvious to Walski is that the moment would have much more impact if the part of the picture of the man looking at the soldier and the part from the other image of the soldier gesturing were combined into one photograph. Sure enough, the result was a better picture and one that ran on the front pages of the *Times* and the *Hartford Courant*. But as with the pyramid manipulation, someone noticed the deception. Walski had mistakenly left multiple remnants of the same seated men in the composite photograph. In his defense, Walski admitted that he might have performed this bit of digital magic because "this was after an extremely long, hot and stressful day" (Van Riper, 2003).

A journalist, especially when covering a war, has one of the most stressful occupations one can imagine. Besides worrying about being injured or killed, a journalist must also be concerned about getting enough water, food, and sleep. Also adding to the stresses are pressures from editors to get the best words and pictures possible from these extreme situations because of competition from other news sources, in print and on television. David Callahan writes of the pressures for fame and fortune that can lead to cheating from business to sports professional settings. With a more competitive economy, Callahan writes, "success and job security can't be taken for granted" (Callahan, 2004, p. 20). Nevertheless, Walski's act of PhotoShop alteration goes down as one of the most notorious examples of picture manipulation in recent years. However slight the actual content within the two images were changed, to perform such an alteration is a cheat on the unfortunately dwindling members of the public who still believe what they see in the news.

Despite the many examples of cheating from established media, deception is a natural component among online gamers and social network users. Photographer Robbie Cooper made real-world and virtual-world portraits of persons along with their self-created online avatars for his book with Tracy Spaight, *Alter Ego: Avatars and Their Creators*. With online games such as *World of Warcraft*[18] and alternative lifestyle programs such as *Second Life*,[19] users employ the software tools available within the program to create avatars, online graphic entities that represent themselves either realistically or as fantasy beings. Interaction with other users through text, voice, or body language within the elaborate virtual environments is a key element that drives interest in the programs. Role-playing, a phrase that implies a certain degree of deception, is a part of the online experience. As Cooper explains, "People really throw themselves into the role play element, or consider their avatar to be an extension of their real world selves" (Cawston, 2007). But as the famous cartoon by Peter Steiner published in 1993 in the *New Yorker* magazine of a dog on a computer explaining to another dog why he is online, "On the Internet, nobody knows you're a dog," sometimes deception and cheating can be one and the same.[20]

A male member of *Second Life* confessed to the author that he enjoyed being a woman entity. The "game" for him, and thus the deception, was being able to pass among other female avatars as one of the gals (of course, he was assuming he was in the company of other females). But he put an end to that avatar after he felt threatened and uncomfortable by not being able to initiate female-related conversation topics and fool his fellow players. However, he was quite able to engage in personal relationships as a male avatar with female entities despite his real-world marital status. Does it count as cheating if you are married and have sex with someone online without the knowledge or consent of your real life spouse? The short answer is, yes. Despite the claim that "what happens online stays online," the experience is still embedded in the real world. In the end, it is two (or more) users sitting in front of a computer and typing on a keyboard or speaking into a microphone that is as real as it sometimes gets.

Given these sins of admission along with the sins of omission, deception and cheating are prevalent in the media because they simply reflect society's values of the day. The Josephson Institute of Ethics located in Marina Del Rey, California, conducts numerous surveys to middle school, high school, and college students. Not surprisingly, almost all of the young respondents said that they were satisfied with their own ethical behavior and character. But disturbingly, three quarters of those respondents also admitted that they considered themselves to be "serial liars" willing to say anything "to save money [or] to get a good job." In another study, it was found that an average adult tells 13 lies a week and in another it was found that "some form of deception occurs in nearly two-thirds of all conversations" (Keyes, 2004, p. 7). As Dan Zak (2007) of the *Los Angeles Times* reports, "Lying is a necessary, near involuntary practice that keeps the fabric of society from unraveling" (p. E12).

Why do we lie? The social psychologist Paul Ekman explains, "We lie to avoid punishment, to get a reward, to protect others, to escape awkward social situations, to enhance our egos, to control information, and to fulfill our job descriptions" (Zak, 2007, p. E12). But ethicist Ralph Keyes (2004) warns that all of this deception and cheating indicates "a declining sense of community and eroding ethics. This means we must live among semi-strangers, with little assurance of their verisimilitude, and with no reliable way to detect their lies" (p. 42). No matter. Whether personally or seen in the mass media, it seems we are all liars willing to tolerate a little deception if we are amused and to tolerate a little cheating if we are not involved. But every personal or public lie creates a simulated representation of the truth that generates the same sort of deviousness that Baudrillard alludes to in the corporate/media sphere. In that way, a lie causes each of us, as Baudrillard might posit, *pour mourir un peu* [to die a little].

As the lovely liar Kurt Vonnegut might say, "And so it goes."

Notes

1. See http://emc.elte.hu/~hargitai/wtcmemorial/newsweek.jpg
2. See http://www.prairieghosts.com/doyle11.jpg
3. See http://photo.box.sk/design/camera001.jpg
4. See http://commfaculty.fullerton.edu/lester/writings/urchins.html
5. See http://www.passionedigitale.org/public/The%20two%20ways%20of%20life.jpg
6. See http://lagataaranya.blogspot.com/2006/05/pere-borrell-del-caso.html
7. See http://users.skynet.be/J.Beever/pave.htm
8. See http://en.wikipedia.org/wiki/Image:Georges_Seurat_-_Un_dimanche_après-midi_à_l%27Île_de_la_Grande_Jatte.jpg
9. See http://www.chrisjordan.com/images/current2/1178132066.jpg
10. See http://www.campaignforrealbeauty.com/flat4.asp?id=6909
11. See http://econ.arizona.edu/zajac/ZajacVideoPage.htm
12. See http://www.britannica.com/ebc/art/print?id=10942&articleTypeId=1
13. See http://college.hmco.com/history/us/resources/shared/primary/source/images/gettysburg2.jpg
14. See http://memory.loc.gov/service/pnp/ppmsca/12800/12883r.jpg
15. See http://www.nocaptionneeded.com/wp-content/uploads/2007/10/bleached-skull-steer.jpg
16. See http://www.frankwbaker.com/isbmag.htm
17. See http://www.poynterextra.org/NPPA2003PJ/pictures/NPY1st.swf. Specifically, image numbers 27–36 in the slide presentation.
18. See http://www.worldofwarcraft.com/
19. See http://secondlife.com
20. See http://www.unc.edu/depts/jomc/academics/dri/idog.html

References

Baudrillard, J. (1988). *Simulacra and simulations*. Stanford University Web site. Retrieved January 25, 2008, from http://www.stanford.edu/dept/HPS/Baudrillard/Baudrillard_Simulacra.html

Callahan, D. (2004). *The cheating culture: Why more Americans are doing wrong to get ahead.* Orlando, FL: A Harvest Book.

Cawston, R. (2007, May 15). Alter ego: Avatars and their creators, Robbie Cooper. Open Democracy Web site. Retrieved January 25, 2008, from http://www.opendemocracy.net/arts/alterego_4620.jsp

DePaulo, B. M., Lindsay, J. J., Malone, B. E., Muhlenbruck, L., Charlton, K., & Cooper, H. (2003). Cues to deception. *Psychological Bulletin, 129,* 74–118.

Elliott, D. (1998). On deceiving one's source. *International Journal of Applied Psychology, 6,* 1–9.

Elliott, D. & Culver C. (1992). Defining and analyzing journalistic deception. *Journal of Mass Media Ethics, 7,* 69–84.

FAQ for Avatar. (2008). Internet Movie Database Web site. Retrieved January 25, 2008, from http://imdb.com/title/tt0499549/faq2008

Gert, B. (2004). *Common morality: Deciding what to do.* Oxford: Oxford University Press.

Here's our winner! 'Redbook' shatters our 'Faith' in well, not publishing, but maybe god. (2007). Jezebel Web site. Retrieved January 25, 2008, from http://jezebel.com/gossip/photoshop-of-horrors/heres-our-winner-redbook-shatters-our-faith-in-well-not-publishing-but-maybe-god-278919.php

Keats, J. (1819). *Ode on a Grecian Urn.* The English History Web site. Retrieved January 25, 2008, from http://englishhistory.net/keats/poetry/odeonagrecianurn.html

Keyes, R. (2004). *The post-truth era: Dishonesty and deception in contemporary life.* New York: St. Martin's Press.

Lester, P.M. (1991). *Photojournalism: An ethical approach.* Hillsdale, NJ: Erlbaum.

Lester, P. M. (2006). *Visual communication: Images with messages.* Belmont, CA: Wadsworth.

Lester, P. M., & Elliott, D. (2004). Fade to black: Ethical practices a matter of what the camera saw. *News Photographer, 59*(4), 12–13.

Meyer, P. (2003). In defense of photographer Patrick Schneider and the fictions of a "code of ethics" Zone Zero Web site. Retrieved January 25, 2008, from http://zonezero.com/editorial/octubre03/october.html

Photoshop of horrors. (2008). Jezebel Web site. Retrieved January 25, 2008, from http://jezebel.com/tag/photoshop-of-horrors/

Piccalo, G. (2007, August 5). Negotiating the slippery slope of nonfiction. *Los Angeles Times,* pp. E1, E5.

Sprague, R. (n. d.). *Migrant mother: The story as told by her grandson.* Migrant Grandson Web page. Retrieved January 25, 2008, from http://www.migrantgrandson.com/galary.htm

Van Riper, F. (2003). Manipulating truth, losing credibility. *Washington Post* Web site. Retrieved January 25, 2008, from http://www.washingtonpost.com/wp-srv/photo/essays/vanRiper/030409.htm

Wade, N. (2007, September 18). Is 'do unto others' written into our genes? *New York Times*, pp. D1, D6–D7.

Winslow, D. R. (2006, August 2). A question of truth: Photojournalism and visual ethics. National Press Photographers Association Web site. Retrieved January 25, 2008, from http://www.nppa.org/news_and_events/news/2006/08/ethics.html

Zak, D. (2007, December 27). Telling lies is part of life, and that's the truth. *Los Angeles Times*, p. E12.

Chapter 7

Sincerity and Hypocrisy

Clancy Martin

In his *Truth and Truthfulness* (2002), Bernard Williams recently argued that there is a tension, in contemporary society generally and academic society in particular, between the belief that truthfulness is an important virtue, and the seemingly contradictory doubt that truth is the sort of thing we can hope to access. Williams thinks he can resolve this tension by showing us that the truth is not as elusive as we have come to believe, and that, when it is difficult to find, it is nevertheless crucial that we continue to search for it. He insists that we cannot do without Truth-with-a-capital-T. His goal is to stabilize the notions of truth and truthfulness, in such a way that what we understand about truth and our chances of arriving at it can be made to fit with our need for truthfulness (Williams, 2002, p. 3). Williams' concerns are pressing for those of us who are interested in the intersections of truth and deception; crucial to his account is what he calls the virtue of sincerity. Without a robust virtue of sincerity, he thinks, our usual way of understanding the virtue of truthfulness will fall apart. And without truthfulness, we lose the truth. We will be abandoned to a morass of self-deceptions, half-truths, and lies.

I will not contest Williams' claim that there is a deep connection between truthfulness and the truth. But he fails to see deep connections between truthfulness and various forms of falsehood. My work here is part of a larger project that attempts to develop a robust account of the relationship between truthfulness and deceptiveness (Martin, in press). Narrowly considered, Williams is obviously right: It does seem that we cannot make sense of a virtue of truthfulness if we cannot give a plausible account of the true. Indeed, this is why the contemporary failure by philosophers to give an adequate and uncontroversial account of the true should be deeply troubling. Even the best leading minds on the subject agree that there is no consensus among philosophers on the subject of truth (Rorty & Engel, 2007).

If we take deception seriously, we can make some headway on the notorious problem of the truth. My thesis—and, I take it, the thesis of the book in which this chapter appears—is that truthfulness and deceptiveness, and ultimately, the true and the false, are much more interdependent than they are usually taken to be. My goal in this chapter is to look at just one part of that larger story: the virtue of sincerity, and how it relates to the vice of hypocrisy. I try to show how complex the virtue of sincerity is—if it is indeed a virtue—and how easily sincerity may be turned to the supposedly hypocritical purposes of deception and self-deception. Using some speculative psychological analyses offered by the German philosopher Friedrich Nietzsche, I suggest that we may find that we cannot successfully practice what most people consider to be one of the basest vices of deception—the vice of hypocrisy—without also practicing the virtue of sincerity. As part of my story, we will look at various other ways in which truth and deception mix in vicious and virtuous ways, such as vanity, self-deception, and Harry Frankfurt's notorious activity of bullshitting (Frankfurt, 2005). Whether truthfulness, deception, self-deception, and the vices and virtues that accompany these practices, turn out to be harmful or helpful, and when, is the most interesting part of the tale.

Bernard Williams, Truthfulness, and Sincerity

Let us begin with Williams' analysis (2002) of the connection between truthfulness and the truth. Briefly, his argument for the interconnectedness of truthfulness and truth goes like this: (a) we cannot get along without trust, because human flourishing requires mutual cooperation, (b) but trust and successful communication requires truthfulness, and (c) truthfulness presupposes that there are truths.

It is silly to disagree with Williams when he argues that we all recognize that there are some "plain truths," truths like "my computer is presently resting on the coffee shop table" or "I am presently writing this sentence" (these statements are no longer true, but they were true, at least, when I wrote them). In "The State of Nature," an explanatory philosophical fiction Williams envisions to reveal the connections between truth and truthfulness, he asks us to imagine "a small society of human beings sharing a common language, with no elaborate technology and no form of writing"(Williams 2002, p. 41). In this society plain truths are of the "Look out! Here comes a tiger!" or "Wait, those are the bad berries!" variety. We are not supposed to bring a great deal of philosophical baggage to this account: these truths are supposed to wear their truthfulness, so to speak, on their face. Any philosophically naïve person (and here being philosophically naïve is to be recommended) would recognize these plain truths as true.

Williams identifies two virtues of truthfulness that must emerge in such a society: accuracy and sincerity. Accuracy is the virtue of thoughtfully and thoroughly investigating and deliberating over the evidence for and against a belief before assenting to it. Accuracy is performing due diligence over one's own beliefs (and it is plausible that one might perform this duty that much more diligently when one is considering the good not only of oneself, but of one's family, or entire community). Sincerity is the virtue of genuinely expressing to others what one in fact believes (whether one securely knows what one in fact believes, especially when it comes to beliefs about oneself, will turn out to complicate this considerably). In the state of nature Williams imagines, the accurate and sincere reporting of truths between persons certainly seems to be necessary to the development of trust between persons, and facilitates human flourishing. Truthfulness, on this account, is instrumentally valuable.

We should notice that it does not follow from the instrumental value of truthfulness that there are truths. When we are sincere and accurate, so this story goes, we arrive at truths about the way the world really is. But a State of Nature pragmatist might respond: suppose every time I call out "Watch out! Here comes a tiger," what, in fact, approaches is a murderous enemy disguised in a tiger-suit. It is easy enough to imagine experiences suffered by our State of Nature pragmatist that reliably substantiated such a mistaken belief. The statement, though false, is sincere. So far as the pragmatist can prudently ascertain, it is accurate: accuracy is a human and approximate virtue, it is merely an epistemological "doing-one's-best," so we cannot ask of our truth-seeker to actually peek under the tiger skin. Moreover, we cannot make truth a requirement for accuracy: We cannot say that a belief must be true to be accurate, or we will be arguing in a circle. So, the belief is sincere, it is accurate, and thus on Williams' standards it is truthful. It serves the purposes of trust and human flourishing. It is a justified, working pragmatic belief, and yet it is also obviously false. The virtues of truthfulness can provide increasingly good justifications for a belief, but it does not look as though these virtues will provide the truth.

Williams (2002) also claims that truthfulness is intrinsically valuable—that truthfulness is a good in and of itself, independent of any other goods it might confer—and though we might like to agree with him, it is hard to see how his or any other State of Nature story can provide truthfulness with more than instrumental value. If truthfulness were intrinsically valuable sincerity would seem, other things being equal, to carry the mark of goodness around with it, since sincerity at the very least seeks to be a mode of truthfulness (at least, at this stage of our analysis: things will get much messier for sincerity presently). But truthfulness in this primitive society serves the purely functional role of promoting human flourishing. The state of nature account is interesting because it make plausible the notion that, for purely natural reasons, truthfulness is likely to emerge as a human virtue. But the fact that a virtue promotes certain goods clearly does not make that virtue good in itself. The functional state of nature story shows that truthfulness may at times be useful, but it does not show that it is anything more than useful.

One reason to worry about an account of truthfulness that makes it instrumentally valuable—and the reason, no doubt, that Bernard Williams would like to provide an account of its intrinsic value—is that it is easy to give an account of deception that makes its practice instrumentally valuable. Machiavelli notoriously argued that, most of the time, falsehood is instrumentally much more valuable for the Prince than the truth, and that thus for instrumental reasons the Prince must be a virtuoso of deception (Machiavelli, 2005). And Machiavelli is writing in a long tradition of great thinkers who have recognized the instrumental benefits of deception. Plato's *gennaion pseudos* in *The Republic* (1961) is justified specifically in terms of its instrumental benefits, and later thinkers such as Grotius (1925) and, in our own day, Arthur Sylvester (1967), have insisted that deception is justified and even necessary to produce certain goods of human flourishing. Most of us will agree that at least some deceptive practices—such as the lie of a physician to a dying child—can be justified instrumentally. The physician Joseph Collins (1999) has argued that good medical practice is inseparable from the recognition that at least sometimes one must lie to one patient.

One imagines that deception is most often practiced precisely because the deceiver recognizes that here the truth will not do the job we need it to: whether it is a simple matter of politeness about a friend's appearance, or a complex question about the relationship between the governed and the governing. (Cases of deception being practiced just for the malicious fun of it, or out of habit, are in the literature as early as Aristotle [1962, pp. 38–44], but Aristotle plausibly suggests that such cases are the exception and not the rule.) It looks as though there are some purposes to which the truth is better suited, and some that better fit with deception. Or it may be that when and how the truth or a lie will do the necessary instrumental work is a function of who is using the truth or the falsehood. Still another possibility is that any complex purpose involves a similarly complex mix of truths, half-truths, half-lies and out-and-out deceptions. We will not settle the issue here; these questions may well in the end be settled by psychological experimentation rather than through armchair philosophical speculation. But the point, of course, is that truthfulness—and its sometime partner, sincerity—is not obviously better or worse suited to accomplishing specific ends than is the tactic of being deceptive. And insofar as the virtue of truthfulness is therefore undermined as a virtue (as a thing which uniquely creates or seeks value), sincerity is similarly undermined, and even when it is operating in the way we normally suppose sincerity ought to operate. When we consider how knotty the operations of sincerity actually are, however, the problem of whether or not sincerity is a virtue gets still worse.

The Interconnectedness of Truthfulness and Deception: Nietzsche

The most comprehensive and insightful analyst of the intersections of truthfulness and deception in the philosophical literature is Friedrich Nietzsche. Especially in *Human, All-too-Human* (1996) and *Daybreak* (1997), his two early works on moral psychology, Nietzsche offered a comprehensive examination of the motives, techniques and purposes people share for lying to one another, believing one another's lies, and lying to themselves. Nietzsche's central theme is how sincerity and hypocrisy work together, especially within the context of truthfulness and deception. Nietzsche argues that on almost no subject are people so thoroughly self-deceived as in the lies they tell. As he once put it: "People lie unspeakably often, but afterwards they do not remember it and on the whole do not believe it" (Nietzsche, 1997, p. 155).

Nietzsche was particularly interested in the parallels between believing the lies others tell us and believing the lies we tell ourselves (he called self-deception "the unclean art of self-duping" [Nietzsche, 1996, p. 52]). Nietzsche's insight was that, in many communicative contexts and practices, deception of others and deception of self go hand-in-hand.

Consider the following two aphorisms, which are concerned with the practice of vanity: "We are like shop windows in which we are continually arranging, concealing or illuminating the supposed qualities others ascribe to us: in order to deceive ourselves" (Nietzsche, 1997, p. 172). "Vanity: Interest in oneself, the desire to feel pleasure, attains in the vain person to such an intensity that he seduces others to a false, much too high assessment of himself, yet then submits to the authority of these others: that is to say, he induces error and then believes in this error" (Nietzsche, 1996, p. 59).

Here deception both depends upon and reinforces self-deception, and vice versa. The vain person knows that he will not satisfy the cognitive needs he has without the opinion of another. He cannot persuade himself of his own virtues, because he does not believe in those virtues. Nonetheless, he has the need to believe in himself. So he deceives another: he manipulates, through words or actions, another into holding a higher estimation of him than he, the deceiver, knows that person ought to hold. But he is not a mere flatterer or boaster who lies merely to control the behavior of the other person (the familiar deceptive types of flatterer and boaster first enter the literature in Aristotle [1962, pp. 38–44]); rather, Nietzsche insisted that the person to whom he lies must change the other's opinion of himself, because only through that other can he change his self-estimation. Once the vain person sees that the deceived has, in fact, changed his opinion, does hold him in high regard, he allows himself to accept the other's new opinion as good evidence—indeed, as sufficient evidence—for revising his belief. He no longer asks himself, "Why does this person hold me in high regard?" because that question naturally would interfere with the process of acquiring the belief he is determined to hold. (Throughout our analysis of sincerity we will see that avoiding the wrong sorts of questions is crucial to the strategizing of the sincere person. Sincerity and dogmatism go hand-in-hand, here). Now he simply asks, "Does this person esteem me? For if so, I must be estimable." Seeing that the deceived individual does esteem him, forgetting entirely that she is deceived, forgetting that he himself has practiced the deception, he esteems himself. Not only has he believed his own press; he is himself the author of it! Moreover, the deceiver depends upon the sincerity of the deceived individual: He can see that she really does believe in her elevated estimation of him, and he takes that sincerity as further evidence for the revision of his own belief. Consequently, once he has convinced himself of her sincerity, in short order he can himself be sincere. Now the self-estimation he professes is the self-estimation he possesses.

I have lingered for a few pages on vanity because it operates in a manner very similar to the vice I am most interested in: hypocrisy. Here is Nietzsche's brief, famous analysis:

> The hypocrite who always plays one and the same role finally ceases to be a hypocrite; for example priests, who as young men are usually conscious or unconscious hypocrites, finally become natural and then really are priests without any affectation. If someone obstinately and for a long time wants to appear something it is in the end hard for him to be anything else. The profession of almost every man, even that of the artist, begins with hypocrisy, with an imitation from, with a copying of what is most effective. (Nietzsche, 1996, p. 51)

The hypocrite practices his deception by acting, by "playing a role," by pretending to be something he is not. Thus hypocrisy begins as a particular kind of insincerity: rather than saying something that does not reflect his beliefs, the hypocrite does something that does not reflect his beliefs. Unlike the deceptive strategy of the vain person, however, the hypocrite's deception may not necessarily be motivated at first by the acknowledged need for self-deception. He may expect that the maintenance of his position, given his abilities, will always require this unhappy pretending to be something that he knows he is not: a life as a poseur. This would be a life lived in the manner of what Eve Sedgwick (1991) calls an "open secret": a regime of knowledge and ignorance that helps us to maneuver through everyday life, though not without danger for those who challenge it publicly. It is a widely, albeit tacitly, accepted understanding that a hypocrisy—a kind of mutual deception about self-deception—is necessary to developing one's capacities, be they personal or professional.

In a marvelous meditation on Shakespeare's "Sonnet 138," Harry Frankfurt (2006, pp. 57–63) argues that, indeed, falling in love and staying in love may, at least in some instances, involve precisely this kind of cooperative hypocrisy. We cannot fall in love without lying to one another a little bit, without allowing ourselves to be lied to, without believing the lies we are being told and are telling, without pretending, without trying to be more in love than at first we "truly" are. But this need not be covert: Both lovers may understand that this is part of the process and engage in it with just the same eagerness, and delight; one is tempted to say, with the same sincerity.

In his marvelous study *Faking It* (2003) William Miller argues that we are surrounded with lies, hypocrisies, insincerities, and open secrets that allow us to do important things we otherwise could not do in everyday life: They leave us the elbow room necessary to become what we are, without which we would forever be stuck in the state in which we were born. Indeed, Miller (2003) goes further, and argues that it is a condition of modernity that individuals must seem to be what they are trying to become, if they are to change at all, for modernity is contingent upon a changing self and society (pp. 121–132). What holds in a culture or context of self-deception is also true for the particular individual who does not consider himself to be a part of deception en masse. Even if the hypocrite has no intention of deceiving himself, the continued practice of the deception of others results, over time, in the deception of oneself. A habit of self-deception typically results in the self-deception becoming a truth. As Miller (2003) puts it, echoing Nietzsche's point, we are all engaged in "becoming what [we] pretend to be" (p. 118). Like the vain person, then, the hypocrite, over time, becomes sincere. But the state of sincerity was only achievable through the strategic practice of hypocrisy; and it is a strange practice of truthfulness that must begin with this (superficially odious, though now perhaps not so odious as we first supposed) practice of deception.

Nietzsche also warned us against believing too readily the "sincere deceiver." In a brief passage that strikingly illustrates the kind of intersection between truth, truthfulness, sincerity and self-deception that I am interested in, he writes: "One of the commonest false conclusions is this: because someone is true and honest towards us, he speaks the truth" (Nietzsche, 1996, p. 53). Here the dupe believes the deceiver because he is comforted by the apparent attitude of the deceiver toward the dupe; the dupe believes what the liar says about him, because the deceiver offers him an image of what he himself would have us suspect that such normative categories are themselves examples of the vice of hypocrisy. In this passage there need be no other deception than the self-deception of the dupe: the true and honest speaker who does not speak the truth may not deliberately deceive his auditor. It could well be that, while speaking in error, the deceiver supposes himself to be speaking truthfully. In this case we would not say that the deceiver was lying: he was merely misleading, while misled himself.

Nevertheless, and fascinatingly, the communicative act of the deceiver becomes a kind of lie, because the dupe understands the message of the speaker in a deliberately deceptive way. That is to say, it is not just the potential deceiver who does the work here: the dupe is essential to the creation of the false effect. To be sure, we could consider the grounds of the speaker's message, which would involve the kind of ordinary "fact-checking" (in Bernard Williams' sense of ordinary factual truths) to ascertain the truthfulness of a report. Yet, the dupe chooses to accept the message on epistemologically illegitimate grounds, grounds like "I want to believe him," or "I believe him because I like him" or "I believe him because I like what he is saying" or "I will believe him, because he has been true and honest towards me." As with the vain person's use of the other's sincerity as a criterion for accomplishing his own transformation of deception into sincerity, so here the goodness of the other becomes the criterion for the truthfulness of the other. It is not truth that confers value, but value confers truth: or, as in this case, it confers the appearance of truth, while in fact masking a deception. This is not to suggest that we should not trust others, and believe what they tell us, especially when they have proven themselves trustworthy. Williams is right to argue that communication cannot proceed without some measure of mutual trust (Williams, 2002, p. 90). But it is to insist that we can self-deceptively use our trust in the service of our desire to hold certain beliefs. We can, in the old phrase, "turn a blind eye," and in so doing lead ourselves willfully into falsehood.

All of our arguments thus far have been more or less informed by an intuition that, at least in many cases, the truth is valuable and falsehood is not. And it is an astonishingly difficult intuition to overcome. No matter how much evidence we are presented with to the contrary, it is hard to convince ourselves that there isn't something "well, just plain good" about the truth and "well, just plain bad" about falsehood. But Nietzsche argues that our belief in goodness itself, our belief in the very possibility of value, stands at the intersection of these complex forces for falsehood and truth. That is to say, we should not see truth and falsehood in terms of their value, because our very notions of value are created by complementary powers of truth and falsehood. Turning Frankfurt's argument about the instrumental value of truth and trust on its head, he writes: "Goodness has mostly been developed by the protracted dissimulation which sought to appear as goodness: wherever great power existed men saw the need for precisely this kind of dissimulation: it inspired a feeling of trust and security." And this is done, he says, out of the "duty to dissimulate" (Nietzsche, 1997, p. 143). Here the impious fraud becomes a Platonic *pius veritas* such that goodness is not identified with truth but depends on deception. We let great power lie to us, so that we will not feel doubt and insecurity.

And how does great power practice its dissimulation? How do the best liars lie? Here Nietzsche makes an armchair observation that it is hard not to agree with, and which offers the very heart of my thesis:

> With all great deceivers there is a noteworthy occurrence to which they owe their power. In the actual act of deception, with all its preparations, its enthralling in voice, expression and gesture, in the midst of the scenery designed to give it effect, they are overcome by belief in themselves....Self-deception has to exist if a grand effect is to be produced. For men believe in the truth of that which is plainly strongly believed. (Nietzsche, 1996, p. 53)

And, once more, but succinctly: "The evil moment: Lively natures lie only for a moment: immediately afterwards they lie to themselves and are convinced and honest" (Nietzsche, 1997, p. 173). Nietzsche probably had Wagner in mind, here: *Daybreak* was written not long after the end of Nietzsche's friendship with Wagner, and many of his unsympathetic remarks about lying and liars are targeted at the notoriously meretricious composer. Yet, the psychological point goes well beyond individual examples. It illustrates what is perhaps the most effective way of lying to others, especially when those others want to be lied to: hypocritically and yet sincerely.

The epistemological process here is now, I think, familiar, but nevertheless astonishing. It calls to mind a cover that the European edition of *The Economist* magazine ran a few years ago with the header, "Sincere Deceivers," and a photo of George W. Bush and Tony Blair arm-in-arm. The point is that to effectively practice the hypocrisy of believing one thing and doing another, one must first engage in a process of self-deception so that one can practice the hypocrisy sincerely. Once sincerity is displayed, the public, who self-deceptively uses the sincerity of its leaders as a measure of their truthfulness, can enthusiastically embrace the lie that is being told.

It is commonplace that individuals engage in self-deceptions to convince themselves of something in order to achieve or acquire something otherwise out of reach. (In her *The Life of the Mind* [1971, pp. 36–41], Hannah Arendt has a particularly nice description of how this process occurs in self-creation, in the context of a brief discussion of how hypocrisy contributes to self-formation.) In a more sophisticated form, such as we have just considered, individuals lie to themselves or others in order to facilitate someone else's successful self-deception. The former is an individual matter, while the latter implicates liar and dupe in a disturbing kind of social contract of mutual deception. That social contract is fostered by a social context, and as a result, the individual lie almost never exists in its pure form. (This is an interesting practical fact that is too often ignored. It may be that we suppose we lie only infrequently because so many of our lies—both the ones we believe and the ones we tell—are already deeply embedded in communicative practices.) Once even the simplest self-deception is enacted, it reshapes the social context into one more conducive for the liar to achieve his self-deception; that in turn begins to implicate others in the same lie. To take an example from literature, when, in the story of "The Emperor's New Clothes," the Emperor insisted on lying to himself about his new clothes, he created a circumstance in which his subjects would be more willing to be duped: for instance, by holding a parade. He "placed all bets" on the lie, believed it in every aspect of his daily life, in the hopes that he might just get away with the deception. In the process, he altered the nature of the public sphere: his ministers, his subjects, even plucky tailors who did not wish to be duped felt the pressure to adopt the small lie, not realizing that it would then be easier to continue the lie than to reflect critically and publicly on it.

The real danger seems to be the way that self-deceivers willfully, even gratefully, subordinate their critical reason to the deceptions of authority figures: not least because of the tremendous latitude for criminal policy it gives over to those great deceivers. In an aphorism entitled "Being deceived" Nietzsche writes: "If you want to act you have to close the door on doubt: said a man of action. And aren't you afraid of thus being deceived? replied a man of contemplation" (Nietzsche, 1997, p. 208). In the case of "The Emperor's New Clothes," the dupe is the very powerful person who, in general, Nietzsche described as likely to be the liar, though from these many examples we can see that there is a great variety of possible social permutations, with either dupe or liar being in positions of authority, or even dupe and liar being one and the same person. At its core, however, we see a motivated irrationality creating a social contract of deception: when two or more persons agree to abandon their critical reason in favor of a set of mutual, reciprocal deceptions. And the Nietzschean response to Williams is Machiavellian and clear: In the real pragmatics of the ordinary world, in a State of Nature that takes how human beings actually conduct themselves into account, it is not truthfulness alone but a complex web of truth- and falsehood-seeking strategies that allow us to flourish.

Nietzsche identifies fear as a key motivator for the lies we choose or allow ourselves to believe and makes the ordinary person out to be the dupe of lying authorities. This was also the model he later applied to his analysis of the success of Christianity in history: We experienced fear, especially the fear of our own cruel natures, and, in an attempt to escape that fear, we accepted the deceptions told to us by a class of lying priests. We would rather be secure than know the truth. As we have seen, Nietzsche thought that our drive for truth is also motivated by the need for security. The origin of our desire for truth, he sometimes argued, is in a kind of evolutionary advantage which the truth provides: As it is in an antelope's advantage to know whether or not a tiger truly lies in wait beyond the next hill, so it is in our advantage to know whether or not an antelope is hiding in the grasses (Nietzsche, 1997, p. 27). The value is security and success: Truth has no value "in itself," and similarly lies are neither valuable nor vicious except insofar as they contribute to that security or success. One class of lies—lies about the world, promise-breaking sorts of lies, and so on—are in most instances the kind of lies that will make us less secure, particularly when they encourage us to fight wars or commit genocides, creating irreparable wounds; we should avoid being duped by them. (It is hard to read Nietzsche's pronouncements about great deceivers and not see him as presciently anticipating the terrible lies told by Hitler—and indeed, the unmistakable and deplorable sincerity of Hitler evident to anyone who watches film of his speeches was part of the original inspiration for this chapter.)

When lying, Nietzsche seems to be suggesting, do so willfully, critically, even consciously—especially when lying to oneself. Certain kinds of experience and activity require deception and self-deception. The mistake is not in allowing those kinds of experiences, but in further insisting, in duping ourselves and others to believe, that some of those experiences are in a strong sense true. We can lie and allow ourselves to be lied to: but we must do so in a spirit of playful skepticism—what Frankfurt (2006) is after in his discussion of the lies of love in "Sonnet 138"—above all we must not be dogmatists in our lies. One might say that, therefore, we must never be sincere (or at least, never too sincere).

Frankfurt and the Vice (or Virtue?) of Bullshit

But surely we should be worried about an account of communication and communicative practices that does not emphasize care for the truth. We want to believe what people tell us, and we want to believe that they themselves believe what they are telling us. (This is why it is often said that a liar tells two lies: the first about the subject of his lie, and the second that he himself believes it.) An interesting account of a communicative practice that disregards the truth has recently (and resoundingly) entered the literature on truthfulness and lies: Harry Frankfurt's (2005) *On Bullshit.*

Like Williams, Frankfurt insists on the philosophical importance of distinguishing truthful from other-than-truthful kinds of talk. But, unlike Williams, Frankfurt observes that one cannot distinguish truthful talk from the other sorts until one is good and clear about how the other-than-truthful kinds of talk operate. He believes, following Nietzsche (and announcing the theme and the method that orients both this chapter and the book of which it is a part), that philosophers and other thinkers have worried a lot about truthfulness, but perhaps all of us should think a little more about deception. His hope is that by thinking more intelligently about falsehood, we may make greater progress then we have, as yet, towards truthfulness and truth.

The key to bullshit is its epistemological carelessness. Bullshit depends on a "lack of connection to a concern with truth . . . [an] indifference to how things really are" (Frankfurt, 2005, pp. 33–34). (For an attack on this characterization of bullshit as carelessness see Thomas Carson, in press.) This carelessness distinguishes bullshit from other kinds of talk we are considering here. A truthful claim conscientiously seeks the facts; a lie equally conscientiously avoids them; but bullshit, frankly, does not give a damn. Nevertheless, bullshit may or may not contain elements of the truth. According to Frankfurt, there are instances of bullshit that are entirely true. This is due to the fact that, he argues, one recognizes bullshit not by its relation to the truth, but by the way in which it is made. Both truthful statements and lies must be made with care, and with a close eye on the facts; bullshit, however, is usually sloppily made and is always made with an active disregard for the way things really are. It is for this reason that he is led to his now-infamous claim that "bullshit is a greater enemy of truth than lies are" (2005, p. 61): A lie is still epistemologically responsible insofar as it is, if it will succeed as a lie, not true. A lie that turns out to be true—such as, say, the lie told by the liar at the crossroads who accidentally sent you down the right road because he is bad at directions, or the more famous "lie" told by Galileo in the 17th century that the earth revolves around the sun (Galileo was denounced as both a heretic and a liar)—is somehow or other indicted as a lie: It is, at the very least, not as successful an example of a lie as the lie that turns out to be false. Bullshit, on the other hand, may be true, false, or (as is commonly the case) a bewildering mix of the two. It is a special kind of talk that is made independent of our usual desire to match (or mismatch) our talk with the true and the false.

It is for this reason that bullshitters, as a type, are characterized by their lack of concern for the truth. Again, both truthful speakers and liars are concerned to know the truth—the former, so that they can feel confident of their reports; the latter, so that they can feel confident that their lies succeed. A liar who does not know where the truth is will have a difficult time feeling sure that he has guided his dupe away from it. Similarly, both our sincere speaker and our hypocrite are engaged in truth-seeking or truth-avoiding activities: The truth acts as a regulative norm for their speech and action. Indeed, in some cases the hypocrite would not practice his hypocrisies if he did not feel assured that eventually the hypocrisy would be overcome, that his practice of falsehood would become a practice of truth. But the bullshitter, in bullshitting, opts altogether out of the "truth-talk" or "aim at the truth" game.

Nevertheless, the bullshitter is indeed trying to get away with something: He is, at the very least, wanting to incline you toward his tale, his bullshit. Whether or not he wants his audience to believe the yarn he is spinning is less certain: It may be that he is trying merely to divert and entertain, or it may be that—as in the bullshit we see evident in many kinds of advertising—the bullshitter actually wants to influence our behavior. In this latter case, we might worry that the bullshitter is attempting to deceive us about his enterprise, and that, therefore, in a certain way, he misrepresents what he is up to: That is, the bullshitter may be concerned to hide the fact that he is bullshitting. But one would like to think that the bullshitter is trying to accomplish more with his bullshitting than just merely disguising the act itself. Otherwise, why bullshit at all? It would be easier to accomplish the same end by simply keeping one's mouth shut.

Bullshit is certainly a way of saying what you do not mean, and, on this ground, it looks as though it may fall prey to the same criticism as a lie. But the difference that makes bullshit innocuous and lies blameworthy is that bullshit need not pretend to be truthful speech. A lie only works with truth as its pretense. But bullshit can allow that it is not after the facts. Much of our talk enjoys this same epistemological "get out jail free" card: When we are polite, for example, we are not lying, nor are we undermining communication, yet we are certainly often doing something other than telling the truth. We are engaged in a different kind of talk than the sort that is involved in getting at the way things really are.

Another example of other-than-truthful talk might be the kind of communication taking place in art. Nietzsche often writes that art is a lie and artists are liars, but what he really means is that artists are particularly refined, skillful bullshitters. So Frankfurt writes: "[Bullshit] is more expansive and independent [than lying], with more spacious opportunities for improvisation, color, and imaginative play. This is less a matter of craft than of art. Hence the familiar notion of the 'bullshit artist'" (2005, p. 53).

When Francis Bacon describes fiction and poetry as "the lie which passeth through the mind," and which therefore does no harm, as opposed to "the lie that sinketh in and settleth in it" (1911, p. 12), he is illustrating the distinction I am trying to make. The lies, exaggerations, falsehoods, and misstatements of art, of politeness, and perhaps of bullshit do not play the same epistemological role for us as statements made in other communicative contexts. We do not attach the same weight to them, and so they do not interfere with our interaction with one another in the same way. This points toward a solution to the vexing problem of why true stories matter to us in a different way than fictional ones do: True stories become a part of our "getting it right" talk, fictional ones do not. We might say that bullshit is more like a performance than a conversation: A bullshitter is a bit like a stand-up comic, who can defensibly get away with jibes that, if they were presented in ordinary speech, would merit a punch in the nose.

On this account, then, and crucially, the bullshitter is never either sincere or insincere; he is never authentic or hypocritical. He is indeed the very type of the artist, who would say that laying claims of "true" or "untrue" upon the kind of speech he is engaged in not only misses the point, it is unreasonable and misleading. It is silly to insist that Tolstoy is lying when he tells the sad story of Anna and Vronsky, even though there never was a Madam Karenina who desperately hurled herself beneath the iron wheels on an oncoming train. It would be a rare piece of aesthetic ignorance to raise this complaint; but that is just the complaint, the bullshitter may say, being made against him. We can nevertheless admit that *Anna Karenina* has influenced, and will continue to influence, the thinking and even the behavior of thousands of people since its writing; and one suspects that Tolstoy would have been disappointed as a novelist, and the novel itself would not have become the classic that it is, were this untrue. The artist, the advertiser, and the bullshitter may all be the source or inspiration of the thinking and action of the audience, but, they will each insist, they cannot themselves be blamed for that fact, *so long as they have never claimed to be speaking the truth.* Here again the dogmatism and self-assuredness of the sincere person and the hypocrite look suspicious, while the playful irresponsibility of the artist looks as though it might be, at least in some instances, recommended to us.

The Moral of the Story: Williams on Sincerity and Authenticity

Returning briefly to *Truth and Truthfulness* for the moral of our little morality tale, Bernard Williams (2002) has an interesting discussion of the differences between Rousseau and Diderot on the questions of authenticity, self-knowledge, and what it takes to be a truthful person. Because, at the end of the day, we all agree that these are virtues we seek, and we do not want to live our own lives as chronic bullshitters, even if we might also be suspicious of insisting that we always and only tell the truth, or that we are always and only sincere. Williams argues that, for Rousseau, to be a truthful person one need only be completely sincere, and self-knowledge lay in the frank revelation of one's deep dark secrets (thus Rousseau's *Confessions*). This, Williams thinks, gives us a distorted view of the self, by assuming a transparency and stability of consciousness (and self-consciousness) that does not exist. We simply cannot grab hold of these stable truths about ourselves that we can know and therefore sincerely report (and thus the infamous unreliability of Rousseau's own report). Williams argues that the better account of self-hood is given by Rousseau's contemporary and sometime friend Diderot, who, like Nietzsche, and after Nietzsche, Freud, describes coming to know oneself as a difficult, lifelong project of self-creation and stabilization. The self as it is given to us "is awash with many images, many excitements, merging fears and fantasies that dissolve into one another" (2002, p. 195), and the attempt to sort through and manage that refractory collection is the struggle for authenticity.

Williams goes on to give his own account of authenticity, both before oneself and with one's community, in terms of "beliefs which [an agent] is committed to holding true in the context of his deliberation" (2002, p. 196). Here he provocatively argues, with Nietzsche, that the many different forms of wishful thinking and other kinds of modest self-deception are not impediments to the creation of an authentic self, but essential to the process of individual deliberation that alone allows such a self to develop. This reminds me again of Frankfurt's account of falling in love: We do not simply identify the features of our beloved and say: now, that is the reason I love her or him; rather, we engage in a creative process that involves our emotions, our reason, our will, and our ability to deceive both ourselves and the one we love. Maybe the process of self-knowledge and the project of authenticity is a bit more like this: A kind of creative engagement with oneself that helps one to, as Nietzsche puts it, "become who we are"(Nietzsche, 1985, p. 144), where the emphasis is on becoming. Once we allow that the self is a thing that grows and changes rather than a stable entity against which we can judge or measure our reports and actions any unironical attempt to be "wholly sincere" looks deceptive—and then we should hardly be surprised to find, as recent research on hypocrisy and a sense of moral superiority by Reynolds and Ceranic (2007) suggests, that the most sincere persons among us are also the most self-deceived, and perhaps the most hypocritical.

Acknowledgment

I would like to thank Andrew S. Bergerson, R. J. Hankinson, Kathleen M. Higgins, Steve Ostovich, Robert C. Solomon, and David Sosa, for comments on earlier drafts of this chapter. Thanks also to conference participants of the University of Texas at Austin Communication Studies Conference on "The Intersections of Truth and Deception," especially Matthew McGlone and Dan Ariely.

References

Arendt, H. (1971). *The life of the mind*. New York: Harcourt.

Aristotle. (1962). *Nicomachean ethics* (Martin Ostwald, Trans.). Englewood Cliffs, NJ: Prentice Hall.

Bacon, F. (1911). *Essays civil and moral*. London: G.G. Houewens and Sons.

Carson, T. (in press). Lying redefined: Truth, lies, and bullshit. In C. Martin (Ed.), *The philosophy of deception*. New York: Oxford University Press.

Collins, J. (1999). Should doctors tell the truth? In H. Kuhse & P. Singer (Eds.), *Bioethics: An anthology* (pp. 501–506). Oxford, UK: Blackwell.

Frankfurt, H. (2005). *On bullshit*. Princeton, NJ: Princeton University Press.

Frankfurt, H. (2006). *On truth*. New York: Knopf.

Grotius, H. (1925). *On the law of war and peace* (F. W. Kelsey, Trans.). New York: Bobbs-Merrill.

Machiavelli, N. (2005). *The prince* (P. Bondanella, trans). New York: Oxford University Press.

Martin, C. (in press). *The love of truth and lies*. New York: Farrar, Straus and Giroux.

Miller, W.I. (2003). *Faking it*. New York and London: Cambridge University Press.

Nietzsche, F. (1985). *Ecce homo* (W. Kaufmann, Trans.). New York: Vintage Books.

Nietzsche, F. (1996). *Human, All-too-Human* (R. J. Hollingdale, Trans.). New York: Cambridge University Press.

Nietzsche, F. (1997). *Daybreak: Thoughts on the prejudices of morality*. M. Clark & B. Leiter (Eds.), New York: Cambridge University Press.

Plato. (1961). *The collected dialogues* (E. Hamilton & H. Cairns, Eds). Princeton, NJ: Princeton University Press.

Reynolds, S., & Ceranic, T. L. (2007). The effects of moral judgment and moral identity on moral behavior: An empirical examination of the moral individual. *Journal of Applied Psychology, 92*, 1610–1624.

Rorty, R., & Engel, P. (2007). *What's the use of truth?* New York: Columbia University Press.

Sedgwick, E. (1991). *Epistemology of the closet*. Berkeley: University of California Press.

Sylvester, A. (1967, November 18). The government has the right to lie. *Saturday Evening Post*, 10–11.

Williams, B. (2002). *Truth and truthfulness*. Princeton, NJ: Princeton University Press.

Chapter 8

Accounts as Social Loopholes

Reconciling Contradictions Between Culture and Conduct

David Shulman

An applicant applies to binding early admission programs at two colleges and when accepted by both, reneges on one, "because that's what everyone is doing to increase their chances." A man physically attacks an immigrant on the street and states, "he had it coming." A customer steals from a clothing store's inventory, explaining, "that they won't miss it." A man apologizes for last night's offensive remarks against minorities by saying that he was "drunk."

In the aftermath of offensive acts, people often ask (with different levels of appropriate severity), "What kind of person could do such a thing?" The very question emphasizes segregating the bad actor from a more decent social collectivity. Yet, as these diverse opening examples demonstrate, and as numerous scholars have analyzed, many people work hard to justify discreditable or discrediting actions in order to avoid being labeled negatively. Individuals, to paraphrase Everett Hughes (1984), regularly perpetrate "dirty" actions while still maintaining a view of themselves as being "good" people. They attempt to present themselves in ways that restore an otherwise tarnished image and lessen their estrangement from a more ideal-type "decent" social body.

Scholars across academic disciplines have dissected the processes by which people carry out these exercises in deflecting judgment. A literature on verbal accounts has emerged to identify specific types of exculpatory claims that people offer when they attempt to reconcile their actions with countervailing social expectations. Erving Goffman (1959, 1963, 1969, 1974) conceptualized different remedial strategies that people use to fend off various forms of stigmatization. Other sociologists have identified "accounts" (Scott & Lyman, 1968), "aligning actions" (Stokes & Hewitt, 1976), "disclaimers" (Hewitt & Stokes, 1975), "discounts" (Pestello, 1991), "misunderstandings" (Young, 1995), "quasi-theories" (Hewitt & Hall, 1973), "techniques of neutralization" (Sykes & Matza, 1957), and "vocabularies of motive" (Mills, 1940) as additional types of accounts. So a variety of preemptive and post-hoc accounts that people use are now well established in the scholarly literature, with recent reviews of this literature (see Benoit, 1995; Fritsche, 2002; Orbuch, 1997) identifying literally dozens of different accounts. Empirical scholarship in this area continues to advance our understanding of how individuals and groups attempt to sustain their identities when these are threatened by discrediting past, present, or future conduct.

Scholars have emphasized studying accounts as a way that individuals attempt to protect identities; but in doing so, I argue that they have not focused enough on three important macrosociological aspects of using accounts. These are using accounts as a collective activity among social groups; appreciating accounts as a means to preserve the capacity to engage in untoward behaviors; and ultimately as a tool that allows violations of social norms to persist while not threatening the stability of those norms. A more macrosociological approach to accounts is needed to explore how they work and their larger significance.

We have all been witness to people behaving in ways that are wildly inconsistent with prevailing norms. People violate the Ten Commandments with gusto. They are supposed to be faithful in marriage, not cheat on tests or papers, not break laws, and not discriminate. Yet, statistics abound that demonstrate that conduct is often inconsistent with culture. The gap between what we say and what we do can be as deep as the ocean.

This inconsistency, if untreated, can lead to devastating social consequences. When behavior is too dissonant with cultural expectations, social life is poorly regulated. If conduct wholly conforms to expectations, social life may be too rigid and controlling. People are trapped between potential dysfunctions: either in overregulation or under-regulation.

The goal of collective social life is to have conduct accord with cultural ideals. Yet, innumerable examples exist where ideals and conduct contradict one another. People are encouraged to do anything in a dog eat dog world to get ahead but to be simultaneously ethical in their competitiveness. Ideal body images are venerated but are not to be attained through deleterious shortcuts (eating disorders/plastic surgery). When people do violate expectations, they use excuses to attempt to absolve themselves and their actions. However we also have to broaden our appreciation of a deeper aspect of accounts and excuses. We must explore how they allow contradictory actions to be available to people.

Accounts and excuses are specific verbal utterances that people use to repair an otherwise tainted identity. To work, however, they must invoke a deeper social context that can absolve discrediting behaviors and encourage observers to accept them. I analyze how some specific situational contexts constitute social loopholes that allow normal cultural ideals to be suspended. To that end, this chapter identifies "social loopholes" in norms that essentially license contradictory behaviors, along the way, laundering the perpetrators from negative labeling.

Attempts to restore individual images are important. Yet accounts are also used collectively. Social groups, occupations, organizations, and professional associations employ accounts in efforts to preserve the ability to engage in controversial activities. Private detectives follow people without their knowledge. Political consultants dig dirt on opposing candidates. A collective usage of accounts, not just to preserve identity, but also to preserve the capacity to keep engaging in controversial professional livelihoods has been overly neglected.

I begin this chapter with a brief review of verbal accounts. I then analyze how accounts reference deeper social contexts that constitute socially acceptable loopholes for bad behavior. Social loopholes are vital means of suspending normal standards for judging behavior. I then explore the deeper sociological significance of these loopholes. I argue that they help reduce the strains on social order that would otherwise result from having to address rampant and ubiquitous contradictions between culture and conduct.

One might even consider social loopholes examples of concerted self-deception at a macrosociological level. At an individual level, people use accounts and excuses to break norms without undermining their individual social standing. However, what allows rules to be broken without rules losing legitimacy? How can a society allow norms to be broken without undermining them and the stability of social order? How can good people do dirty work and not see themselves as bad people? How can so many people abide law in name but not in action? Our culture of idealizing truth confronts a deceptive reality of illicit conduct. I argue that our ability to overlook this contradiction is vital for social stability, and an important scholarly issue to explore. This chapter offers some theoretical foundations with which to begin that exploration. As Fritsche (2002) notes, the trick of accounting is to "break norms without fundamentally undermining them" (p. 374). The question I address here is how social loopholes perform this trick.

Background: The "Sociology of Accounts" Literature

The sociologist C. Wright Mills began the accounts/aligning actions literature when he developed the notion of vocabularies of motive. Mills (1940) emphasized that individual motives must be considered as more than inherent psychological states; motives are constituted in the vocabularies of social explanations and justifications that individuals present as explanations for their actions. He wrote that:

> A motive tends to be one which is to the actor and to the other members of a situation an unquestioned answer to questions concerning social and lingual conduct....Motives are accepted justifications for present, future and past programs or acts. (p. 907)

Following up on Mills's work, Scott and Lyman (1968) developed the concept of accounts. Scott and Lyman define an account as "a linguistic device employed whenever an action is subjected to valuative inquiry" (p. 46). Accounts consist of excuses and justifications that reconcile untoward actions and social expectations (Scott & Lyman, 1968). People who use excuses acknowledge committing a negatively viewed act but they disclaim personal responsibility for their actions. Everyday examples of excuses include: "It was an accident" or "I did it, but I was drunk." People who use justifications acknowledge committing a discreditable act but claim that extenuating circumstances legitimate that behavior. Everyday examples of justifications include: "I was following orders" or "Those people had it coming to them."

Scott and Lyman's (1968) paper inspired a prolific literature that has produced inventories of many accounts (for a description see Orbuch, 1997). Much of this scholarly literature has focused on members of highly stigmatized groups, including male hustlers (Reiss, 1964), juvenile delinquents (Sykes & Matza, 1957), disgraced professionals (Pogrebin, Poole, & Martinez, 1992), and convicted criminal offenders, such as white-collar criminals (Benson, 1985) and rapists (Scully & Marolla, 1984). Another strand of this literature has integrated accounts into research on the narratives that people tell in association with various life events, such as marriage and stressful situations (see Orbuch, 1997, for an extensive review). Meta-analyses of accounts have collapsed them into five categories: justifications, excuses, concessions, and refusals (Schonbach, 1990), with the recent addition of a set of accounts called referentializations (Fritsche, 2002).

Stokes and Hewitt (1976) contributed to advancing the theoretical aspects of the literature in their paper on "aligning actions." They conceived of aligning actions as mechanisms that attempt to "sustain a relationship between ongoing conduct and culture in the face of recognized failure of conduct to live up to cultural definitions and requirements" (p. 844). Of primary importance in that work is how aligning actions "call attention to and render sensible those numerous discrepancies between normative culture and ongoing conduct"—their use "implies an actual effort of some kind to bring conduct more into line with normative culture" (p. 847).

Moving Beyond the Literature

At their core, accounts represent an individual's attempts to assign responsibility for their discrediting actions to other actors or social forces, such as alcohol, scapegoats, or a superior's orders. All account giving reflects attempts to negotiate the level of stigma or punishment that is attached to an individual's action. Accounts are "stories and narratives" that represent ways that people organize images of them and others in the social world (Orbuch, 1997). These stories help to explain behaviors in a positive light. Harre (1983) argues that in producing accounts, actors show their knowledge of ideal ways of acting and idealized reasons for doing what they have done. Individuals offer accounts to offset responsibility and preserve a positive image (Orbuch, 1997).

The potential to invoke a positive self-image for discreditable actions means that individuals can overpower the grip of cultural ideals that reject taking those actions. Yet, individuals are not the only social group who seek that amnesty from judgment. A plethora of social groups, from professionals to government agencies, all seek exemptions from judgment when their actions might incur a negative assessment.

How do professionals use accounts to characterize occupational identity positively? How are accounts different when organizations, groups, or collectivities put them forth? Little research exists on how an organizational or group context for account-giving differs from private individual contexts, such as accounting for deviant acts in one's personal life. Nichols (1990) identifies failing to consider the collective or group use of accounts as an "elementary omission" (p.133) in scholarship on accounts. Potential differences exist between how groups construct and honor accounts according to their aims, power and stakeholders. A sharper analytic focus is needed to discern the distinctive qualities of offering accounts within a professional context.

While the literature has been advanced through scholars identifying new accounts, and by more empirically focused analyses of how people account for specific actions (see, for example, Benson, 1985; Hewitt & Stokes, 1975; Jacobs, 1992; Klockars, 1984, 1985; Mulcahy, 1995; Pestello, 1991; Reiss, 1964; Scully & Morolla, 1984; Stokes & Hewitt, 1976; Sykes & Matza, 1957; Young, 1995, 1997), this body of work has identified neither organizational contributions to accounts nor how accounts legitimate legal but controversial "dirty work."

Recent scholarly reviews of research on accounts (Hunter, 1984; Nichols, 1990; Orbuch, 1997; Young, 1997) stress paying more attention to how accounts are socially distributed and enacted. More emphasis is needed to consider who offers accounts and on the different contexts in which accounts are offered. How does one's professional affiliation also affect the ability to give a successful account? A key theoretical attribute of accounts to examine with professionals in mind is how accounts possess a cumulative power. This "cumulative" power refers to the capacity a particular account has to legitimate or excuse repeatedly engaging in a kind of behavior. For example, if someone knows that saying "boys will be boys" will always justify male aggression, that particular account can assume a cumulative power. Citing this account may allow someone to act more aggressively because the account perpetually excuses or justifies those actions.

Cumulativeness is important because knowing that an account will be cumulatively honored means that the power exists to exonerate repeated incidents of potentially discreditable behavior. The potential cumulative power of accounts is particularly relevant to occupations, because professionals involved in adversarial work have to engage in potentially discreditable behaviors for their livelihood. Accounts function to excuse and justify behaviors as social facts; they do more than rehabilitate individual reputations. A "cumulative" account preserves the capacity to engage in discrediting behaviors by successfully mitigating norms against those behaviors.

Shulman (2000) analyzed the accounts that private detectives use to justify their work-related deceptions. He identified individual practitioner excuses and justifications, but also emphasized as theoretical contributions, how their accounts reflected their professional context. He stressed that the importance of practitioner accounts reflected more than attempts by professionals to avoid losing face. What was crucial in the accounts was that controversial behaviors that are essential to professional livelihood could be sustained in the face of opposition.

So in the organizational and occupational context, accounts do more than negotiate a person's identity. Noting the importance of accounts to social collectivities is a shift from the persistent focus on individuals. It is more important to understand how accounts and social loopholes contribute to social order. The mechanics of social loopholes must be unpacked. What makes an observer more or less likely to honor an account? What context does an account invoke that can persuade observers? Accounts must be seen as potentially honorable in their content or to offer them would be fruitless.

Accounts must reference background expectancies. Background expectancies refer to sets of taken for granted contexts that permit people to interpret remarks as accounts in the first place. People need to anchor appropriate background expectancies to accounts. Consider how a student might explain cheating to a professor as compared to another student. In one case, the student might tell "a sad tale" to the professor, while telling another student that no harm was done.

In referring to background expectancies, accounts and excuses are referencing larger social norms that people could see as legitimating the questioned behavior in particular context. What is crucial is examining how accounts seem to offer such loopholes. What contextual claims seem to propel the acceptability and functionality of many accounts?

Accounts as Social Loopholes

In a legal and a folk sense, loopholes are often thought of as ambiguities in the wording of contracts or laws that people take advantage of

in order to avoid compliance or punishments for misdeeds. Social loopholes enable violations of social norms to persist while not threatening
the stability of norms that are violated. The concept of social loopholes
helps in reconsidering the larger theoretical relationship between culture
and conduct that originally motivated devising the concepts of accounts
and aligning actions (Mills, 1940; Stokes & Hewitt, 1976).

Social loopholes reference a deeper social context upon which an
account rests. Accounts are specific verbal utterances that people use
to repair an identity in crisis. Social loopholes, alternatively, refer to the
background expectancies and situational contexts that various accounts
emphasize in their attempts to become honored by others. Scott and
Lyman (1968) refer to background expectancies as "those sets of taken
for granted ideas that permit the interactants to interpret remarks as
accounts in the first place" (p. 54).

In creating a narrative that presents idealized reasons for controversial behavior, accounts must invoke specific social recipes that one thinks
can legitimate bad behavior. Social loopholes reference the base claim
for legitimating a specific account's effectiveness. They are the essential
thematic appeals of existing types of accounts and aligning actions. In
an exploratory manner, I here consolidate accounts into several categories of core social loopholes (see Table 8.1).

Some illustrations are helpful. People can invoke biological drives to
explain morbid obesity or a gambling problem. The social loophole in
accounts such as appeals to defeasibility and biological drives is loss of
personal control. The operating notion is that when people lack control
over their actions, or have that control impacted negatively, their resulting poor behavior is less blameworthy. Only when people fully "intend"

Table 8.1 Social Loopholes

Common Excuses & Justifications[1]	Social Loopholes
Aligning Actions	1. **Fading into Commonality**
Appeal to accidents	Anonymity, time zones, geography,
Appeals to defeasibility	mitigation by status.
Appeal to higher loyalty	
Condemnation of the condemners	
Biological drives	2. **Loss of Personal Control**
Discounts	Predisposition, genetic, social,
Scapegoating	biological
Denial of injury	
Denial of victim	3. **Protection**: Of self or others
Denial of responsibility	
Misunderstandings	4. **No Alternative**
Quasi-theories	

[1]*From:* Jacobs, 1992; Pestello, 1991; Scott & Lyman, 1968; Stokes & Hewitt, 1976; Sykes & Matza, 1957, Young, 1995)

or "choose" acts, and demonstrate deliberation and free will with no qualifications, should their conduct be judged with the most severity.

Consider a common rationalization for shoplifting: "The store won't miss it—they're rich anyway." This sentiment reflects the traditional accounts of denial of injury and denial of victim. A social loophole here is mitigation by status, with reasoning behind it that an affluent, impersonal, and gigantic entity is one that can withstand mild exploitations without harm.

This chapter's argument has been that accounts represent manifestations of larger social loopholes on which accounts base their appeal. As such, social loopholes represent larger social categories that exist as waivers for behavior. Particular manifestations of those loopholes may exist in different appeals, as represented in varied excuses and justifications. This chapter suggests shifting from studying a typology of how people attempt to mitigate their actions, to considering the bases through which people view behaviors as being potentially mitigated. The issue is to move more towards why accounts work and exploring the grounds people cite to have them work, at their most basic building blocks, rather than to identify new types.

The most crucial qualification here is that examining why accounts are honorable is a distinct enterprise from researching the process of honoring them. For example, an audience, in judging the specific mitigation of a behavior, may take the gender of an account-giver into consideration (Nichols, 1990). However, the goal here is to understand and examine the various thematic grounds for accounts as they have been offered in prior research, rather than to investigate the degree to which demographic and socio-economic characteristics make a particular group or individual's use of accounts more or less acceptable.

As a start, I identify four primary categories of social loopholes here and some subcategories within those loopholes (see Table 8.1). These social loopholes function behind the traditional accounts identified in the literature. I make no claim of exhausting the range of potential social loopholes; my goal instead is to articulate and illustrate the concept as a starting point.

Fading into Commonality

Fading into commonality is a social loophole encompassing several often-interrelated factors such as anonymity, geography, size, and time. Fading into commonality references a social loophole in which committing a deviant act within a particular social context where doing so is common, means that no cultural ideals are really being flouted. Anonymity, geography, time, and size are factors that exempt the deviance. Where people are commonly pursuing deviant activities, that very commonality allows for one's own misconduct (drinking, promiscuity, fighting, vandalism) to fade into some common shared identity as being in a place and time permitting such actions. For example, people often cite places and times where they can feel anonymous. The sense of not being recognized and simply fading into just being one of a mob of like others is sometimes cited as a waiver for misbehavior, such as in riotous mob actions.

Consider how particular zones of time and space privilege a common acceptance of untoward acts, hence the fading into commonality of deviant behaviors. Mardi Gras and Spring Break illustrate localized hedonic excess that is circumstantially accepted. Geographic location is a key factor in such deviance. In such cases, deviant action occurs in locations where identity is more transient and deviant actions are expected. In many cases, contradictory social actions are more tolerable as long as that deviance is confined to a specific area. At an individual level, a person often decides that a given zone offers a chance "to cut loose" or to "wild." Examples of such actions occur on Spring Breaks and "weekends with the gals/guys in Las Vegas," and bachelor and bachelorette parties.

Fading into commonality also exists temporally, when unusual behavior becomes particularly acceptable, such as on New Year's Eve. People are expected to party to the point of being out of control, and to not do so may, in fact, contradict the prevailing cultural ideal. People retain a sort of blanket anonymity in colluding in common deviance. Since all of those involved, i.e., friends on Spring Break or at a New Year's Eve party are acting similarly; an unstated rule of confidentiality is implied. Normal rules are suspended in these times and places. The "abnormal" rules become the norm, and social order is maintained ironically through a collective fading into deviance.

Fading into commonality occurs in much more particularistic ways, tied to the distinct place and time of the social circumstances of individuals using this loophole. For example, contradicting social ideals may be loopholed because "we graduate in a few weeks" or "we need to blow off steam after the semester/work project/sales pitch is finished." Excuses such as "the store won't miss it" or "everybody does it" also fit this category. The rationale is that since the contradicted act is common in itself, it should not be judged pejoratively. If everybody is speeding, how bad can that transgression be? If everyone is smoking marijuana or has a beer, is the contradiction really that pejorative? The very act of committing the same act that many, many others do is seen as reasonable grounds for mitigation.

Fading into commonality mitigates by size. In this sense, size references the large number of people committing the contradiction, a quantity that then forms grounds for exempting the behavior from a negative association. A further mitigation by size concerns the common justification that certain behaviors do not contradict social ideals if those behaviors are perpetrated on a powerful or large target. In interviews I have conducted for other research (addressing consumer deceptions), convenience and department chain store representatives consistently stated that thieves saw their acts as relatively harmless because—"the (generic large company) could not possibly suffer from this small loss." The large size of the target mitigates the taint of the act. A small size can also mitigate the behavior, such as when people steal pencils and pens from offices without considering such acts to be thefts. The fading into commonality in these circumstances is that given a particular large or small N associated with the event, the untoward behavior is qualified to no longer contradict ideals. Fading into commonality is a social loophole that numerous accounts use.

Loss of Control

A loss of control is often a generic social loophole behind many accounts. I consider a multitude of genetic/physiological/social/supernatural predisposition variables under the loophole that a loss of control exempts the act. For example, people's accounts regularly evidence this loophole with references to dysfunctional families, poverty and genes.

There are different types of loss of control social loopholes. By "genes," I refer to broad explanations that one's genetic or physiological components are primary causes of misconduct. A social predisposition argument references social factors that people see as having an almost involuntary causal pull in misconduct, such as the sense that poverty or social dysfunction "explains" misconduct, with a sense that this cause prohibits someone from having full control of their actions. Being in a specific subculture is also seen as a social predisposition. Supernatural causes, such as magic and more religiously oriented forces also can be identified as loss of control loopholes. In American society, we tend to use individual free will as a criterion for assigning blame. A loss of control social loophole nullifies poor behavior because free will is taken out of the equation.

Scientists study genetics to discover the influences of biology and genes on behavior. Not only does biology affect behavior, so does one's social environment. Cultural relativism can be used to loophole deviant behavior. The power of the loss of control social loophole lies in its ability to argue that the true cause of contradicting social ideals is not individual will, but an external force. In that sense, the individual is not to be fully blamed for their actions. In other words, the individual is not deciding to contravene dictates—exogenous independent variables are forcing the individual's hands. The social contradictions are out of the person's realm of control.

As an example, rhetorical use of biological bases for addiction is now pervasive in explaining obesity, gambling, and drug abuse. "Rage" defenses emerged in which a history of being the victim of racial discrimination is argued to loophole "retaliatory" violence. Poverty is invoked to explain an inability to choose behaviors that would avoid contradicting law—in its purer version, Anatole France's dictum that "It is equally against the law for the rich and the poor to sleep under bridges" comes to mind. Deviant behavior can be the result of being "bewitched." An individual from a country where bribery is more common may loophole similar behavior in the United States as simply being a product of the individual's "cultural programming."

Protection

A pervasive social loophole invokes contradicting social ideals because of the need to protect. For example, workplace deception interviews reveal a consistent theme of lying because of the need for collective and self-protection, i.e., "if I didn't take credit for the work, I would have been hurt or disadvantaged," or "I needed to lie to protect the company" (see Shulman, 2006). The literature on white-collar crime is replete with executives who argue that a competitive business climate requires cutting ethical corners. In environments with excessive competition, self-protection may lead to behaviors that contradict social ideals.

Akin to the protection loophole is a "the best defense is a good offense" sensibility. Interviews often reveal sentiments such as "they were gossiping about me, I had to get him or her back. You do not want to get a reputation for being pushed around; otherwise others will begin taking advantage of you and cause you further harm."

In a different vein, an account of appeals to higher loyalty references obligations to protect important social others. If a loved one is threatened, almost any action can be loopholed under the category of self-defense. A good example occurs when friends or coworkers cover up wrongdoings. There is a long tradition of pejorative terminology for those who are unwilling to lie to protect team secrets, such as tattletale, stool pigeon, and so forth. Certainly when an individual is threatened, protection is also often invoked, such as in the ceaseless rationalization for violence that starts with "he hit me first."

Social ideals often demand that people hide guilty knowledge as a signal of social solidarity. Ironically, one commits to and reaffirms trust through failing to reveal damaging social actions, such as in the plethora of cases where savvy workers help cover up misbehavior. A greater responsibility to social good is downgraded for being responsible instead to a smaller group affiliation.

No Alternative

An additional social loophole is that of "no alternative." The essential argument is that one engaged in the act "at gunpoint." This social loophole references the sense that organizational circumstances around someone can make contradicting social ideals inevitable, thus loopholing relevant discrediting behaviors.

This loophole reveals an individual and organizational disassociation. Organizational identity is seen as distinct from individual identity. A person may have no alternative but to act badly as part of a situated work identity. As individuals, they would not choose to do such things, but the work role gives them no alternative. That sense that work (or other factors) gives no alternative is often seen as a social loophole in scholarship studying business misconduct.

Social Loopholes: Resocializing Behavior, Degenerating Responsibility, and Overlooked Consequences of Wrongdoing

Social loopholes constitute social mores that allow people to avoid individual responsibility for misbehavior on a mass scale. One may or may not receive an exemption from judgment at an individual level, but social loopholes offer a sense of the grounds under which people attempt to successfully plea for breaching rules without punishment. Individuals misbehave and hope to reintegrate themselves when they have violated cultural ideals. Why have social loopholes that mitigate norm breaking? Why have exemptions that allow culture and conduct to contradict?

Three reasons, all pertaining to questions of social order come to mind. First, social loopholes enable rules to save face. Organizational theory is replete with examples of rules and ideals failing to be applicable in some circumstances, while being useful in other circumstances. Poverty and lack of opportunity may make flouting social ideals practically involuntary. Social loopholes allow ideals to retain some flexibility while also maintaining ideals as reasonable social bonds.

Second, some social loopholes aid social integration. To protect and acknowledge commonality are profoundly collective exercises in nature. A shared participation in less than exemplary behaviors still represents a social bond, one that social loopholes reaffirm. Third, there must be explanations to bridge the contradiction of having to live with people who consistently disobey social norms. How are people to save face, in and apart from having to assert faith in rules that people disobey?

While there may be functions of social loopholes that explain their presence, their negative consequences also must be emphasized. Accounts as social loopholes both aid individuals in doing wrong without seeing wrong and they degenerate an individual sense of responsibility to abide by social norms. Most importantly, they allow for the persistence of accounted for behaviors that represent contradictions between culture and conduct. These actions, whether criminal or not, may be perpetuated through the consistent successful association of the behavior with a loophole. If accounts enable social norms to be suspended, some of the functionality of social norms is lost, even if they appear stable.

To the extent that crimes occur, (i.e., murder, rape, predatory deceptions, theft, physical assault, degradation of others), cultural inhibitions are not thought to effectively sink into the moral calculus of social actors. Pundits may fault parents and schools for "not teaching children right from wrong;" clergy may invoke a failure to realize religiously informed ethical guidelines. Whatever the suggested cause, the prevailing idea is that there is a "socialization failure," and primary cultural ideals are lacking a binding force. Through examining how social loopholes allow people to violate cultural ideals for behavior, one can analyze the processes that aid a general degeneration of individual responsibility to abide by norms.

At a level below illegal acts, impression management itself requires a constant control of information so as to appear credible in presenting an image that may be cracked and fissured from hidden discrepancies. Cultural norms are not always easily followed and are sometimes laden with incentives to be broken. People are placed in contradictory binds that force them to violate norms while paying public homage to abiding by those same norms. As Fritsche (2002) writes, "societies with high levels of account giving activities should contain highly stable systems of normative beliefs and moral commandments" (p. 374). Social loopholes enable violations of social norms to persist while not threatening the stability of norms that are violated.

Deviating from socially approved goals and means also carries a personal price of knowing that one has failed to live in an idealized way. People seek to limit any personal damage from manifesting these contradictions and thus they seek to substitute an alternate social context for judging their actions. At the deepest level, social loopholes allow people to attempt to maintain membership in a social order while simultaneously breaching ideal normative codes of membership. Social loopholes smooth over instances of social hypocrisy, which preserves a social system in which the ideal grasp of collective social norms is in practice routinely discarded. Social loopholes also allow people the illusion of legitimately departing from social expectations when economic and social demands may make such departures inevitable. Further, American society is argued to be awash in increasing individualism, where bonds between individuals, groups, and organizations are loosening

(Bellah, 1985; Eliasoph, 1998; Patterson & Kim, 1992; Wolfe, 1998). In such circumstances, it is critical to understand what social loopholes allow people to avoid a sense of being responsible for obeying norms and cultural values that aid in maintaining collective life.

Research must pay greater attention to the collective macrosociological consequences of giving accounts. Both further empirical and theoretical work is needed to identify background expectancies that help give accounts their potential for mitigating social contradictions and to discern what type of account giver is demographically and socio-economically more legitimated than another. That a social loophole is claimed does not mean that it will be honored. Some researchers have identified variables that they think explain why some accounts are honored and while others are not. To complement that work, further analysis is needed of a wide variety of collective accounts and the loopholes on which they depend.

At the heart of the interplay between deception and truth is a belief that the borders between them should be clear. Social loopholes are a form of societal self-deception—a means by which social actors ignore that some cultural ideals are widely flouted. Like all self-deceptions, there are benefits to pretending that cheating is not cheating, and that our behavior is better looking than it really is. The downside is that when good people do dirty work and still think they look good, the dirty work still stays dirty. The person might look cleaner, but the act and its consequences remain.

References

Bellah, R. (1985). *Habits of the heart*. Berkeley: University of California Press.

Benoit, W. L. (1995). *Accounts, excuses, and apologies: A theory of image restoration strategies*. Albany: State University of New York Press.

Benson, M. (1985). Denying the guilty mind: Accounting for involvement in a white-collar crime. *Criminology, 23*, 583–607.

Eliasoph, N. (1998). *Avoiding politics*. Cambridge, England: Cambridge University Press.

Fritsche, I. (2002). Account strategies for the violation of social norms: Integration and extension of sociological and social typologies. *Journal for the Theory of Social Behavior, 32*, 371–395.

Goffman, E. (1959). *The presentation of self in everyday life*. Garden City, New York: Doubleday.

Goffman, E. (1963). *Stigma: Notes on the management of spoiled identity*. Englewood Cliffs, NJ: Prentice Hall.

Goffman, E. (1969). *Strategic interaction*. Philadelphia: University of Pennsylvania Press.

Goffman, E. (1974). *Frame analysis: An essay on the organization of experience*. Cambridge, MA: Harvard University Press.

Harre, R. (1983). Commentary from an ethogentic standpoint. *Journal for the Theory of Social Behaviour, 13,* 69–74.

Hewitt, J. P., & Hall, P. M. (1973). Social problems, problematic situations, and quasi-theories. *American Sociological Review, 38,* 367–374.

Hewitt, J. P., & Stokes, R. (1975). Disclaimers. American *Sociological Review, 40,* 1–11.

Hughes, E. (1984). *The sociological eye.* New Brunswick, NJ: Transaction Press.

Hunter, C. (1984). Aligning actions: Types and social distribution. *Symbolic Interaction, 7,* 155–174.

Jacobs, B. A. (1992). Undercover drug-use evasion tactics: Excuses and neutralization. *Symbolic Interaction, 15,* 435–453.

Klockars, C. (1984). Blue lies and police placebos: The moralities of police lying. *American Behavioral Scientist, 27,* 529–544.

Klockars, C. B. (1985). The Dirty Harry problem. In F. A. Elliston & M. Feldberg (Eds.), *Moral issues in police work* (pp. 55–71). Totowa, NJ: Rowman & Allanheld.

Mills, C. W. (1940). Situated actions and vocabularies of motive. *American Sociological Review, 5,* 904–913.

Mulcahy, A. (1995). Headhunter or real cop: Identity in the world of internal affairs officers. *Journal of Contemporary Ethnography, 24,* 99–130.

Nichols, L. (1990). Reconceptualizing social accounts: An agenda for theory-building and empirical research. *Current Perspectives in Social Theory, 10,* 113–144.

Orbuch, T. L. (1997). People's accounts count: The sociology of accounts. *Annual Review of Sociology, 23,* 455–478.

Patterson, J., & Kim, P. (1992). *The day America told the truth.* New York: Penguin.

Pestello, F. P. (1991). Discounting. *Journal of Contemporary Ethnography, 20,* 26–46.

Pogrebin, M., Poole., E., & Martinez, A. (1992). Accounts of professional misdeeds: The sexual exploitation of clients by psychotherapists. *Deviant Behavior, 13,* 229–252.

Reiss, A. J., Jr. (1964). The social integration of peers and queers. In Howard Becker (Ed.), *Outsiders* (pp. 181–210). New York: Free Press.

Schonbach, P. (1990). *Account episodes: The management or escalation of conflict.* Cambridge, England: Cambridge University Press.

Scott, M. B., & Lyman, S. M. (1968). Accounts. *American Sociological Review, 33,* 46–62.

Scully, D., & Marolla, J. (1984). Convicted rapists' vocabulary of motive: Excuses and justifications. *Social Problems, 31,* 530–544.

Shulman, D. (2000). Professionals' accounts for work-related deceptions. *Symbolic Interaction, 23,* 259–282.

Shulman, D. (2006). *From hire to liar: The role of deception in workplace culture.* Ithaca, NY: Cornell University Press.

Stokes, R., & Hewitt, J. P. (1976). Aligning actions. *American Sociological Review, 41,* 838–849.

Sykes, G. M., & Matza, D. (1957). Techniques of neutralization: A theory of delinquency. *American Sociological Review, 22,* 664–670.

Young, R. L. (1995). Misunderstandings as accounts. *Sociological Inquiry, 65,* 251–264.

Young, R. L. (1997). Account sequences. *Symbolic Interaction, 20,* 291–305.

Wolfe, A. (1998). *One nation after all.* New York: Viking Press.

Chapter 9

"I Read *Playboy* for the Articles"

Justifying and Rationalizing Questionable Preferences

Zoë Chance and Michael I. Norton

> So convenient a thing it is to be a reasonable creature, since it enables one to find or make a reason for everything one has a mind to do.
>
> Benjamin Franklin (1706–1790)

> He uses statistics as a drunken man uses lamp-posts—for support rather than illumination.
>
> Andrew Lang (1844–1912)

Humans are masters of lying and self-deception. We want others to believe us good, fair, responsible, and logical, and we place just as much importance on thinking of ourselves this way. Therefore, when people behave in ways that might appear selfish, prejudiced or perverted, they engage a host of strategies designed to justify questionable behavior with rational excuses: "I hired my son because he's more qualified." "I promoted Ashley because she does a better job than Aisha." Or, in the example from our title and the subject of an experimental investigation we report below, "I read *Playboy* for the articles."

Masking immoral behavior is not a new phenomenon, of course: A large body of research, dating back at least as far as Freud's (1894/1962) elaboration of defense mechanisms, suggests that people's perceptions of the world—and of themselves—are self-serving. Social scientists have long been interested in exploring cases where the human desire to appear moral fails to result in moral behavior, frequently focusing on situations in which people attempt to justify questionable or immoral behavior (Tsang, 2002). Indeed, the many ways in which questionable decisions, policies, or actions are justified and legitimized have been well-documented (Kelman, 2001; Scott & Lyman, 1968). Organizations gain the appearance of morality by conducting affairs in line with accepted standards and values even as they engage in unethical behavior (Elsbach & Sutton, 1992; Suchman, 1995). Individuals, too, are quite skilled at justifying their own immoral behavior while maintaining a view of themselves as moral. Examples abound: People viewed their own showers during a water shortage as justifiable but the showers of others as reflecting their lack of moral fiber (Monin & Norton, 2003), or, in an extreme example, doctors who participated in genocide in Nazi Germany failed to see how their behavior violated the Hippocratic oath (Lifton, 1986).

In this chapter, we first describe two means by which individuals rationalize and justify questionable behavior, one which focuses on *preemptive* actions people take before engaging in such behavior and one which focuses on *concurrent* strategies, examining how people restructure situations such that their behavior seems less questionable. We conclude by briefly reviewing two additional strategies for coping with such difficult situations: either *forgoing* making decisions, or *forgetting* one's decisions altogether.

Preemptive Justification of Questionable Behavior

One common means of rationalizing questionable behavior is using the moral "credentials" gained from good behavior in the past to justify behaving badly in the present; people thus engage in preemptive justification, using desirable behaviors to license questionable ones. In a series of clever experiments, Monin and Miller (2001) gave some people the opportunity to credential themselves in a preliminary exercise, and then examined the impact of such licensing on subsequent behavior. For example, participants who had the opportunity to disagree with blatantly sexist statements subsequently felt more licensed to express sexist opinions; similarly, participants who selected an obviously-qualified Black applicant for one position were then more likely to favor a White candidate in a second, more ambiguous situation.

Moral credentials can also apply to matters of personal willpower, with future virtue licensing present misbehavior. Khan and Dhar (2007) explored licensing in acts of self-control. They asked participants to choose between a virtue (fat-free yogurt) and a vice (a cookie), manipulating whether the decision was presented as a series of choices or in isolation. Because participants believed that they would choose the virtuous option in the future, when they viewed the current choice within the context of their future choices, they were more likely to select the vice in the present—and to feel less guilty about it. Most importantly, Khan and Dhar (2007) found that people were deceiving themselves about their likelihood of future virtuous behavior: Two thirds of participants predicted that they would make the virtuous choice in the second round of decisions, but when that time came, half of them chose the vice (see also Khan & Dhar, 2006). Thus licensing had a net negative effect on behavior, allowing people to engage in suboptimal behavior while feeling good about doing it.

Concurrent Justification of Questionable Behavior

In addition to this kind of preemptive justification, with preemptive good licensing subsequent bad, individuals are also skilled at justifying their behavior in the moment. In Batson, Kobrynowicz, Dinnerstein, Kampf, and Wilson (1997), people were asked to allocate two tasks between themselves and a partner. The person who performed the "positive consequences" task would have the opportunity to win money, while the other person would be forced to perform a "neutral consequences" task, described as dull and boring. Some people allocated the tasks by flipping a coin. If the process were truly random, coin flippers would have assigned the positive task to themselves roughly 50% of the time, of course; Batson et al., however, found that coin flippers allocated the positive consequences task to themselves 90% of the time, suggesting that many of those who called "heads" only to see the coin come up "tails" managed to concoct an exception that favored themselves.

Similarly, in Mazar and Ariely (2006), participants were allowed to grade themselves on a test with monetary incentives and take the appropriate payment from a jar of money, while others had their tests graded by the experimenter. Not surprisingly in light of Batson et al.'s (1997) results, those people who graded their own performance somehow managed to perform much better on the test—sometimes twice as well as those whose exams were graded by the experimenter—and therefore took home more money as a result. As a final example of concurrent justification, Hsee (1996) asked participants to take on the role of real estate appraiser and evaluate two condominiums; some were told to imagine that their fiancé was interested in buying (or selling) one of the condominiums, and others were not. Participants who appraised on behalf of their fiancé estimated a lower (or higher) buying price, presumably justifying their questionable behavior by rationalizing that their behavior was on behalf of a loved one.

"I Read *Playboy* for the Articles"

But what processes underlie this impressive ability to mask questionable behavior? How did those individuals who altered the outcome of their coin flip, for example, manage to convince themselves that this was a legitimate outcome? We conducted an experiment to examine one means by which people engage in concurrent justification, by explaining decisions made on the basis of questionable criteria—for example, choosing to buy a magazine because it contains pictures of scantily clad ladies—in terms of other, more acceptable criteria—for example, the quality of the articles in that publication.

We asked 23 male participants (M_{age} = 20.9) to complete this experiment as part of a class requirement. We told participants we were interested in the criteria they thought were important in choosing magazines, and introduced two sports magazines. Both had won the same number of Associated Press Journalism Awards, and had similar average issue lengths.

We manipulated two attributes of the magazines, such that each magazine dominated on one attribute. One magazine had a *higher* number of sports covered per issue than the other (9 vs. 6), while also having a *lower* average number of feature articles per issue (12 vs. 19). In addition, each magazine was advertised as having one special issue: either a Swimsuit Issue (a questionable preference) or a "Year's Top 10 Athletes" special issue. Most importantly, we varied which magazine came with the Swimsuit Issue; for half of our participants, it accompanied the magazine with more sports, while for the other half, it accompanied the magazine with more feature articles.

We expected our male participants to select the magazine subscription with the Swimsuit Issue regardless of whether it covered more sports or contained more articles, and then, in an effort to justify their questionable behavior, to inflate the value of the attribute favoring that magazine—either the number of sports covered or the number of articles per issue.

Participants examined the descriptions of the two magazines, circled the magazine they would choose, and then ranked criteria (average issue length, number of awards, annual special issues, number of sports covered, average number of articles, and "other") in terms of how important they were in their decision. Overall, and as expected, participants overwhelmingly picked the magazine with the Swimsuit Issue (74%), χ^2 (1) = 5.26, p < .03. While 92% of participants selected the magazine with more articles when that magazine was paired with the Swimsuit Issue, only 46% picked this magazine when it did not have the Swimsuit Issue paired with it, meaning that 54% of participants suddenly preferred the magazine with more sports covered, χ^2 (1) = 5.79, p < .02, which just *happened* to include the Swimsuit Issue (see Table 9.1).

Table 9.1 Preferences for Swimsuit Issues and Justifications for those Preferences

	% Selecting Magazine with More Articles	% Citing More Articles as More Important	% Selecting Magazine that Covers More Sports	% Citing More Sports as More Important
Swimsuit Issue has More Articles	92	83	8	17
Swimsuit Issue Covers More Sports	46	36	54	64

Most important for our argument is that participants also subsequently inflated the value of the attribute that favored the magazine with the Swimsuit Issue, justifying their questionable preference on the basis of less suspect criteria. We created a dichotomous variable by coding whether participants ranked number of sports or number of articles more highly. Mirroring the results above, while 83% of participants ranked number of articles higher when the magazine coupled with the Swimsuit Issue contained more articles, this number dropped to just 36% when this magazine covered more sports, meaning that 64% now reported that number of sports was more important, $\chi^2 (1) = 5.32$, $p < .03$ (see Table 9.1).

Similar effects of using acceptable criteria to mask preferences based on questionable criteria have been shown in many other domains. Norton, Vandello, and Darley (2004) asked men to choose between male and female candidates for a stereotypically male job, managing a construction company. Half the participants read that the man was better educated but had less experience; the other half, that the man had more experience but less education. In both conditions, the majority of participants selected the male applicant. When asked why they had made that choice, males claimed that gender had not influenced their decisions, instead citing education (when the male had more education) or experience (when the male had more experience) as the basis for their choice, in each case downgrading the criteria on which the female candidate was superior. This same strategy—citing acceptable criteria to justify questionable preferences—has been shown to be used to exclude Blacks and women from juries (Norton, Sommers, & Brauner, 2007; Sommers & Norton, 2007).

In addition, the strategy is remarkably flexible and can be used to justify decisions with completely different motivations. In Hodson, Dovidio, and Gaertner (2002), participants scoring high on a prejudice measure rated a Black candidate for college as worse than a similarly qualified White candidate, and then inflated the value of criteria that favored the White candidate (e.g., his grades). Individuals scoring low on the prejudice measure, however, demonstrated the opposite preference, rating the Black candidate as better, yet used the very same strategy to justify that decision, inflating the value of whichever criteria favored the Black candidate to support their judgment (see also Norton, Sommers, Vandello & Darley, 2006).

Are People Aware That They Are Justifying?

In the *Playboy* study reported above, participants might have been cognizant of the true reasons behind their choice ("I want to look at scantily-clothed women") and dissembled merely in an effort to deceive the experimenter ("I don't want to look like a pervert"); more troubling, however, is the possibility that people are blissfully unaware of the extent to which they rationalize their regrettable actions. The extent to which people are consciously deceiving versus unconsciously is obviously of great importance, yet asking our participants whether they are doing this might be futile, even if they were motivated to explain the true reasons underlying their decisions. In a series of classic studies, Nisbett and Wilson (1977) demonstrated that people frequently are unaware of the causes of their own behavior. For example, when asked to choose the highest-quality pantyhose between four identical pairs, participants were four times more likely to choose the pair on the right than the pair on the left. They were unaware of this "right bias," however, and "when asked directly about a possible effect of the position of the article, virtually all subjects denied it, usually with a worried glance at the interviewer suggesting that they felt either that they had misunderstood the question or were dealing with a madman" (p. 244).

Is it possible that when people restructure the world to appear moral in light of their questionable behavior, they may actually be similarly unaware they are doing so? Norton and Ariely (2008) found evidence that cheaters may believe their own lies. In a series of studies, college students completed intelligence tests with or without access to answer keys. Not surprisingly, those students with access to the answers outperformed those without such access. Interestingly, however, they also tricked themselves into believing they were as intelligent as their fraudulent scores indicated. Even when offered monetary incentives to accurately forecast their score on a second test without an answer key, they inflated predictions of their future performance, attributing their improved performance on the first test not to glancing at the answers, but to their own amazing abilities, which caused them to lose money when their test performance regressed to their true (no answer sheet provided) IQ level.

Can This Justification Be Stopped?

The fact that people seem—at least at times—unaware that they are masking their questionable behavior by justifying it complicates efforts to decrease such behavior: If people don't know when they are masking their questionable behavior, how could they know when to stop?

One possible means of reducing people's ability to engage in questionable behavior is to remove ambiguity from the situation. In our *Playboy* study, for example, we deliberately designed each magazine to be superior on one attribute: Offering a readily accessible alternative explanation for choosing the swimsuit issue increases the ambiguity of the true reason for that decision ("maybe he really *does* read it for the articles!").

Removing this kind of ambiguity has been shown to decrease people's tendency to engage in questionable behavior. In Snyder, Kleck, Strenta, and Mentzer (1979), participants were asked to sit in either of two rooms to watch a film. One room was empty; in the other, a person in a wheelchair was also waiting to watch the film. The experimenters varied whether the film was the same in both rooms (offering no excuse to avoid the disabled person) or different (offering a plausible justification for choosing to avoid the disabled person). Snyder et al. (1979) found that participants overwhelmingly chose to watch the movie alone when the two movies were different, but chose to sit with the disabled person when both movies were the same. Using the same paradigm, Bernstein, Stephenson, Snyder, and Wicklund (1983) replaced the disabled person with an attractive female, showing that nearly all men watched the film alone when the two films were the same (no excuse to sit next to the attractive woman), while nearly all men chose to watch the movie with the attractive woman when the two films were different, again ostensibly because they preferred that film over the other.

Unfortunately, however, real-life situations are usually more ambiguous than the situations we have described—and people are likely quite skilled in seeking such ambiguity when faced with difficult decisions—so while these studies demonstrate a moderator of people's ability to engage in questionable behavior, they do not necessarily offer a practicable real-world intervention. Another possibility for decreasing such behavior is to make people accountable for their decisions, requiring them to explain the reasons underlying their choices (Lerner & Tetlock, 1999). Given people's demonstrated desire to seek out acceptable justifications for questionable preferences, however, accountability pressures may simply motivate people to look even harder for justifications, rather than stop them from behaving poorly. In fact, in some situations accountability can enhance bias, as with its amplifying effect on commitment to decisions (Simonson & Staw, 1992). Indeed, when Norton et al. (2006) made participants accountable for their decisions in choosing between a Black and White high school student for admission to college, not only did requiring participants to explain themselves fail to decrease preferences based on racial bias, it made them look even more carefully through the resumes to find additional evidence in favor of their questionable decisions.

Forgoing and Forgetting Questionable Preferences

Having demonstrated a striking variety of strategies that people use to justify questionable behavior both preemptively and concurrently, we turn to outlining two additional routes to coping with difficult decisions: avoiding them altogether, and forgetting them after the fact. These additional strategies, in some sense, book-end the strategies outlined above;

taken together, they offer a full palette of opportunities for people to justify and rationalize their behavior.

Forgoing Questionable Behavior

One obvious means of dealing with situations that might require one to engage in questionable behavior would be simply to avoid the situation altogether, obviating the need to justify that behavior. Of course, in many cases people engage in such behavior to benefit themselves, meaning that forgoing behavior—while an efficient means of avoiding guilt— also means forgoing benefits. Still, research suggests that in some cases individuals are willing to pursue this route.

Dana, Cain, and Dawes (2006) demonstrated one such instance of this strategy by modifying a classic paradigm, the Dictator Game. Behavioral economists have asked thousands of people to engage in this simple two-person game, in which the Dictator is given a sum of money (say, $10) and is then asked to decide how much, if any, to keep, and how much, if any, to give to an anonymous other player who will never know with whom they were paired. Basic economic theory predicts, of course, that the Dictator will keep all the money because this is the choice that will leave him the most well-off; in reality, most Dictators give some of the money away, seeming to demonstrate unselfish altruism (Fehr & Schmidt, 1999; Loewenstein, Thompson, & Bazerman, 1989).

Dana et al. (2006), however, added a creative twist to this standard game which calls the nature of this altruism into question. In this experiment, after stating the fraction of $10 they wished to allocate to their partner, Dictators had the option of buying a "quiet exit" for $1—in essence, forgoing the decision of how much to give to their partner. Thus, they could keep $9 and ensure that their partner would never know the game had taken place. Nearly 30% of players chose this option, even though it left them worse off than a $10/$0 allocation and—most importantly—it left the other player worse off than a $9/$1 allocation. Opting out of this choice allowed Dictators to avoid the responsibility for choosing an inequitable split, even as they behaved selfishly. In a related line of research, Ehrich and Irwin (2005) showed that consumers forgo obtaining information on the ethicality of manufacturers—demonstrating "willful ignorance"—in order to enjoy their possibly unethical products. Disturbingly, they found that willful ignorance manifested most strongly among those people who had claimed to care most about the ethical issue at hand.

One final example of forgoing potentially questionable behavior comes from an investigation of political correctness. Whites are generally reluctant to use race—or even mention race—when deciding between or describing Blacks (Norton, Sommers, Apfelbaum, Pura, & Ariely, 2006);

a paradigm developed by Norton, Vandello, and Biga (2008) leveraged this hesitancy to demonstrate another instance of avoiding choice. When they asked White participants to express preferences between members of different races based solely on their pictures—for example, which person was more likely to be class valedictorian or to have committed a violent crime—Whites were quite willing to choose between two White individuals, but less likely to express a preference between a White and Black person. Whites were even willing to forgo money to appear politically correct, refusing to choose between members of different races even when a correct answer was worth $1.00. Though Whites were willing to assume some costs to appear colorblind, they overcame their reluctance to choose when given sufficient monetary incentive—$5.00 was enough to convince them that the benefits of forgoing choice were no longer worth more than the cost of forgoing money.

Forgetting Questionable Behavior

Finally, we turn to one last method for reducing guilt or regret over our decisions—simply forgetting we ever made those decisions in the first place. Some research shows that this may be a relatively common method for coping with decisions, particularly difficult ones. Chance and Norton (2008) tested people's memory for difficult decisions in a variety of familiar and exotic choice domains (including vacation destinations, consumer products, colored geometric shapes, and ways to die). Participants first chose between pairs of options and rated the difficulty of each choice; later, they completed a surprise memory quiz. People were less likely to remember their difficult decisions than their easy ones, although they had spent more time deliberating on them. In fact, they were less likely to remember having seen those options at all—despite having looked at the difficult pairs longer when making their decision. These results contradict the general finding that duration of exposure to a stimulus improves recall (Hamid, 1973; Janiszewski, 1993; Seamon, Marsh, & Brody, 1984).

In addition, forgetting our questionable decisions may not only alleviate guilt or minimize regret, but also help us trick ourselves into believing we got just what we wanted. In a clever sleight-of-hand experiment, Johansson, Hall, Sikstrom, and Olsson (2005) demonstrated that people can give perfectly lucid reasons for having *chosen* options that they actually rejected mere seconds ago. Participants first chose which of two female faces they found more attractive. The experimenter would then show one of the faces again and ask, "Why did you pick this one?" In most cases, the presented face would be the one that respondents had, in fact, selected, but sometimes it would be the rejected face. Respondents not only failed to notice the switch, but provided logical reasons why they had "chosen" the face they had in fact rejected.

Taken together, these results suggest that when people do not get what they want, they may fool themselves into believing they wanted what they got. People appear to forget their original decisions when those decisions were difficult, allowing them to later be happy with options they may have rejected earlier. This sequence of events may also explain, for example, why voters over-report having voted for election winners (Atkeson, 1999).

Conclusion

We have discussed a number of ways in which people cope with questionable behavior, from forgoing to rationalizing to justifying to forgetting it altogether, a remarkable—and yet far from exhaustive—range of strategies. Because people do not want to be perceived as—or feel like—unethical or immoral individuals, they devise logical justifications and rationalizations, as the Benjamin Franklin quote with which we opened aptly reflects: "I read *Playboy* for the articles." "I'm not selfish, I just prefer not to play the Dictator game." "I'll pick the fat-free yogurt tomorrow."

We should note that, although we have focused on the negative aspects of rationalization and justification, these strategies are not without their benefits. First, from a strictly utilitarian point of view, it enables an individual to engage in self-serving behavior without incurring psychological costs. Second, preserving a sense of one's morality despite evidence to the contrary allows individuals not just to see themselves as good, but as better and more moral than others (Chambers & Windschitl, 2004; Codol, 1975; Epley & Dunning, 2000). Individuals who deceive themselves in these ways may be happier than others—normal psychology is characterized by people seeing themselves as "above-average," while depression is linked to realism (Dunning & Storey, 1991). Thus rationalization and justification can involve a tradeoff between the truth—people admitting the real reasons for their questionable behavior—and their well-being—denying those reasons leads them to be happier. We would suggest that while the benefits may outweigh the costs for an individual, those costs are likely assumed by that person's peers: We would likely not want to be the partner, roommate, or subordinate of a person comfortable sacrificing truth for personal happiness.

References

Atkeson, L. R. (1999). 'Sure, I voted for the winner!' Overreport of the primary vote for the party nominee in the national election studies. *Political Behavior*, 21, 197–215.

Batson, C. D., Kobrynowicz, D., Dinnerstein, J. L., Kampf, H. C., & Wilson, A. D. (1997). In a very different voice: Unmasking moral hypocrisy. *Journal of Personality and Social Psychology*, 72, 1335–1348.

Bernstein, W., Stephenson, B., Snyder, M., & Wicklund, R. (1983). Causal ambiguity and heterosexual affiliation. *Journal of Personality and Social Psychology, 19,* 78–92.

Chambers, J. R., & Windschitl, P. D. (2004). Biases in social comparative judgments: The role of nonmotivated factors in above-average and comparative-optimism effects, *Psychological Bulletin, 130,* 813–838.

Chance, Z., & Norton, M. I. (2008). *Decision amnesia: Motivated forgetting of difficult choices* (Working paper). Cambridge, MA: Harvard Business School.

Codol, J. P. (1975). On the so-called 'superior conformity of the self' behavior: Twenty experimental investigations. *European Journal of Social Psychology, 5,* 457–501.

Dana, J., Cain, D. M., & Dawes, R. M. (2006). What you don't know won't hurt me: Costly (but quiet) exit in dictator games. *Organizational Behavior and Human Decision Processes, 100,* 193–201.

Dunning, D., & Storey, A. L. (1991). Depression, realism, and the overconfidence effect: are the sadder wiser when predicting future actions and events? *Journal of Personality and Social Psychology, 61,* 521–532.

Ehrich, K. R., & Irwin, J. R. (2005). Willful ignorance in the request for product attribute information. *Journal of Marketing Research, 42,* 266–277.

Elsbach, K. D., & Sutton, R. I. (1992). Acquiring organizational legitimacy through illegitimate actions: A marriage of institutional and impression management theories. *Academy of Management Journal, 35,* 699–738.

Epley, N., & Dunning, D. (2000). Feeling holier than thou: Are self-serving assessments produced by errors in self or social prediction? *Journal of Personality and Social Psychology, 79,* 861–875.

Fehr, E., & Schmidt, K. M. (1999). A theory of fairness, competition and cooperation. *Quarterly Journal of Economics, 114,* 817–868.

Freud, S. (1962). The neuro-psychoses of defense. In J. Strachey (Ed. and Trans.) *The standard edition of the complete works of Sigmund Freud* (Vol. 3, pp. 45–61). London: Hogarth Press. (Original work published 1894)

Hamid, P. N. (1973). Exposure frequency and stimulus preference. *British Journal of Psychology, 64,* 569–577.

Hodson, G., Dovidio, J. F., & Gaertner, S. L. (2002). Processes in racial discrimination: Differential weighting of conflicting information. *Personality and Social Psychology Bulletin, 28,* 460–471.

Hsee, C. K. (1996). Elastic justification: How unjustifiable factors influence judgments. *Organizational Behavior and Human Decision Processes, 66,* 122–129.

Janiszewski, C. (1993). Preattentive mere exposure effects. *The Journal of Consumer Research, 20,* 376–392.

Johansson, P., Hall, L., Sikstrom, S., & Olsson, A. (2005). Failure to detect mismatches between intention and outcome in a simple decision task. *Science, 310,* 116–119.

Kelman, H. C. (2001). Reflections on social and psychological processes of legitimization and delegitimization. In J. T. Jost & B. Major (Eds.), *The psy-*

chology of legitimacy: Emerging perspectives on ideology, justice, and inter-group relations (54–73). New York: Cambridge University Press.

Khan, U., & Dhar, R. (2006). Licensing effect in consumer choice. *Journal of Marketing Research, 43*, 259–266.

Khan U., & Dhar, R. (2007). Where there is a way, is there a will? The effect of future choices on self-control. *Journal of Experimental Psychology-General, 136*, 277–288.

Lerner, J. S., & Tetlock, P. E. (1999). Accounting for the effects of accountability. *Psychological Bulletin, 125*, 255–275.

Lifton, R. J. (1986). *The Nazi doctors: Medical killing and the psychology of genocide*. New York: Basic Books.

Loewenstein, G., Thompson, L., & Bazerman, M. (1989). Social utility and decision making in interpersonal contexts. *Journal of Personality and Social Psychology, 57*, 426–441.

Mazar, N., & Ariely, D. (2006). Dishonesty in everyday life and its policy implications. *Journal of Public Policy and Marketing, 25*, 1–21.

Monin, B., & Miller, D. T. (2001). Moral credentials and the expression of prejudice. *Journal of Personality and Social Psychology, 81*, 5–16.

Monin, B., & Norton, M. I. (2003). Perceptions of a fluid consensus: Uniqueness bias, false consensus, false polarization, and pluralistic ignorance in a water conservation crisis. *Personality and Social Psychology Bulletin, 29*, 559–567.

Nisbett, R. E., & Wilson, T. D. (1977). Telling more than we can know: Verbal reports on mental processes. *Psychological Review, 84*, 231–259.

Norton, M. I., & Ariely, D. (2008). *Self-deception: How we come to believe we are better than we truly are* (Working paper). Cambridge, MA: Harvard Business School.

Norton, M. I., Sommers, S. R., Apfelbaum, E. P., Pura N., & Ariely, D. (2006). Color blindness and interracial interaction: Playing the Political Correctness Game. *Psychological Science, 17*, 949–953.

Norton, M. I., Sommers, S. R., & Brauner, S. (2007). Bias in jury selection: Justifying prohibited peremptory challenges. *Journal of Behavioral Decision Making, 20*, 467–479.

Norton, M. I., Sommers, S. R., Vandello J. A., & Darley, J. M. (2006). Mixed motives and racial bias: The impact of legitimate and illegitimate criteria on decision making. *Psychology, Public Policy, and Law, 12*, 36–55.

Norton, M. I., Vandello, J. A., & Biga, A. (2008). *Colorblindness inhibits the expression but not the formation – of racial preferences* (Working paper). Cambridge, MA: Harvard Business School.

Norton, M. I., Vandello J. A., & Darley, J. M. (2004). Casuistry and social category bias. *Journal of Personality and Social Psychology, 87*, 817–831.

Scott, M. B., & Lyman, S. M. (1968). Accounts. *American Sociological Review, 33*, 46–62.

Seamon, J. G., Marsh, R. L., & Brody, N. (1984). Critical importance of exposure duration for affective discrimination of stimuli that are not recognized. *Journal of Experimental Psychology: Learning, Memory, and Cognition, 10*, 544–555.

Simonson, I. & Staw, B. M. (1992). Deescalation strategies: A comparison of techniques for reducing commitment to losing courses of action. *Journal of Applied Psychology, 77,* 419–426.

Snyder, M. L., Kleck, R. E., Strenta, A., & Mentzer, S. J. (1979). Avoidance of the handicapped: An attributional ambiguity analysis. *Journal of Personality and Social Psychology, 37,* 2297–2306.

Sommers, S. R., & Norton, M. I. (2007). Race-based judgments, race-neutral justifications: Experimental examination of peremptory use and the Batson challenge procedure. *Law and Human Behavior, 31,* 261–273.

Suchman, M. C. (1995). Managing legitimacy: Strategic and institutional approaches. *Academy of Management Review, 20,* 571–610.

Tsang, J. (2002). Moral rationalization and the integration of situational factors and psychological processes in immoral behavior. *Review of General Psychology, 6,* 25–50.

Chapter 10

Lying for Love in the Modern Age

Deception in Online Dating

Catalina L. Toma and Jeff T. Hancock

Within the span of a few short years, computer technologies have not only become a part of most households, but they have also revolutionized each of the fundamental aspects of the human condition: work, play, and relationships. We now have the ability to work from home on our remote desktops, entertain ourselves with video games and home-authored videos, and reconnect with long-lost friends—all from our own living rooms. One of the latest success stories in computer innovation affects what many people consider to have the greatest impact on their personal happiness: romantic relationships. Indeed, online dating is contributing new and powerful tools to people's quest for a romantic partner, such as access to extensive databases of singles and the ability to pre-screen potential dates based on relevant information (e.g., age, occupation, family situation).

However, with this newfound power, online dating has also brought about new challenges. Perhaps chief among them are concerns about deception (Brym & Lenton, 2001), which likely stem from the separation between the online persona and daters' embodied selves. The absence of a corporeal presence appears to elicit strong suspicions regarding the veracity of online dating profiles and has fueled numerous stories of outrageous online dating deceptions in the popular media. Paradoxically, the popularity of online dating has soared in recent years, with online dating companies securing large revenues, and numerous serious relationships and marriages stemming from online dating encounters. How then can we reconcile the widespread concerns regarding the prevalence of online deception with the success of online dating? Is online dating really as rife with deception as generally thought?

In the present chapter, we address this question by (a) examining the theoretical reasons surrounding when, why, and by how much online daters can be expected to lie in their profiles; (b) providing a framework for operationalizing deception in the context of online self-presentation; and (c) presenting the results of a large empirical study on the actual deceptive practices of online daters. We conceptualize deception along the lines of the standard psychological definition of deception, namely that it involves an intentional attempt to create a false belief in the target of the message (see Ekman, 1985; Vrij, 2000). We approach deception as a resource for self-presentation that can be used to enhance attractiveness to potential mates, and we argue that the decisions online daters make about whether or not to access this resource are shaped by several social and technological factors that we describe below.

We first examine the social demands of establishing romantic relationships, whether online or offline, and how they may affect the use of deception. We then discuss the technological affordances of the online dating environment that may either constrain or facilitate deceptive behavior. Next, we review gender differences that may influence what online daters decide to lie about. Lastly, we consider how these socio-technological factors work in conjunction with each other to determine the frequency, magnitude, and content of online dating deceptions. In the process, we hope to advance our understanding of how deception plays a role in this new and modern twist on how we describe ourselves in the pursuit of love and happiness.

Deception in Romantic Relationships

Compared to other kinds of relationships, romantic relationships seem to be a particularly fertile ground for deception. Indeed, DePaulo, Kashy, Kirkendol, and Epstein (1996) observed that people tell at least one lie in every three interactions with their romantic partners. Similarly, Feldman and his colleagues (Feldman, Forrest, & Happ, 2002) showed that, when given the goal of coming across as likeable, people lied significantly more during conversation than when they were not trying to be likeable.

In fact, research suggests that deception may be more prevalent in the early stages of relationships (i.e., dating) than in more established relationships, for a variety of reasons. First, as potential partners are trying to get to know each other and decide whether or not to pursue the relationship, *interpersonal scrutiny* is particularly high (Derlega, Winstead, Wong, & Greenspan, 1987). These high levels of information seeking have been shown to increase the occurrence of falsification and distortion relative to more established relationships (Berger, 1987; Ekman, 1985)—daters are willing to go to great lengths to come across as likeable. Second, DePaulo and Kashy (1998) note that the dating environment can highlight people's insecurities about attractiveness and stimulate their fear of being rejected. Daters' *need for approval* coupled with their *vulnerability to rejection* may lead them to resort to deception more often than in the context of established relationships, where acceptance has already been secured and there is no longer a pressing need to impress. Third, the use of deception in the early stages of relationships may be a response to a *sense of competitiveness* with other daters. For instance, Buss (1988) notes that the most frequently used strategy in attracting a date is making oneself appear more attractive or competent than competitors.

Clearly, there are important theoretical reasons why deception should play an important part in the early stages of romantic relationships, whether these relationships commence in face-to-face or online settings. However, the previously described concerns of interpersonal scrutiny, need for approval, vulnerability to rejection, and sense of competitiveness may be more pronounced for online daters relative to traditional daters. First, interpersonal scrutiny is unavoidable in the online dating arena, simply because posting a detailed profile describing oneself is an inherent part of the online dating process. While online daters have some control over the content of their profiles, they cannot circumvent self-disclosure altogether. In fact, online daters are often expected to reveal private information that usually does not come up in initial face-to-face interactions, such as their age, approximate income, or education. Given the demands for providing detailed personal information to a group of strangers, deception may emerge as a particularly appealing strategy. Second, the public nature of the online profile, which can be accessed by an unknown but presumably large audience, should also intensify daters' need for approval and fear of rejection. As they "perform" (Goffman, 1959) in front of a potentially large audience, online daters should feel increased pressure to present themselves as attractive and desirable, which, in turn, should lead to increased use of deception relative to face-to-face environments. Third, since the online dating arena counts millions of subscribers, the sense of competitiveness with other daters should be high, and the use of deception as a means of making oneself look better than competitors should also be increased.

To summarize, previous research suggests that deception is relatively common in the initial stages of relationships, as potential partners try to impress each other and assuage their insecurities. These levels of deception may be magnified by the public nature of online dating, which features a large audience that may scrutinize daters' personal information, and potentially millions of competitors. But does the mediated nature of online dating simply amplify the presence of deception, or does technology have more complex effects? For instance, do people lie more in general when communicating via technology compared to face-to-face, or are there technological factors that may constrain the use of deception? Below we address these questions by reviewing the literature on digital forms of deception.

Deception in Computer-Mediated Communication

As noted earlier, it is important to acknowledge the role played by communication technology in shaping deception. Contrary to popular belief, technology doesn't act in a unilateral way by simply exacerbating deception, but rather presents a multitude of affordances that have a differential effect on deception production. Specifically, communication technologies present characteristics that facilitate deception by making it easier to lie, but they also have characteristics that appear to promote honesty (Hancock, 2007). For instance, anonymous chat rooms, where interactions are purely textual, make it possible for users to engage in egregious deceptions, such as gender switching (i.e., pretending to be the opposite gender), with virtually no possibility of being caught lying (Herring & Martinson, 2004). However, other technological spaces, such as online support groups or diet blogs, have been shown to contain extremely candid and deeply personal self-disclosures—the kind of intimacies that are rarely discussed outside of counseling sessions. Some have referred to this form of online self-disclosure as the modern version of the stranger on a train phenomenon (Joinson, 2003), where the fleeting and partially anonymous nature of the interaction encourages people to reveal burdensome secrets that they are unable to share with their social circle. With technological features having the ability to foster a range of communicative behaviors, from the profoundly honest to the profoundly deceptive, the question arises as to how the specific features of online dating impact the use of deception. Below we outline the technological features of online dating that enable deception, as well as also the ones that promote honesty.

As mentioned earlier, probably the most striking difference between face-to-face and computer-mediated communication is that the latter allows users to interact with others without being physically co-present. The disembodied nature of mediated communication generates ample opportunity for deception, including, in extreme cases, creating a fictitious online persona that bears little or no resemblance to reality. However, such complete fabrications can only be maintained to the extent that the interaction never progresses to face-to-face environments—an unlikely scenario for online daters, who typically seek to establish face-to-face relationships.

In addition to the disembodied nature of online communication, there are other features of communication technologies that may enable deceptive behavior. Notably, online communication provides fewer communication cues (e.g., gestures, facial expressions, intonation, etc.) than parallel face-to-face interactions (Walther, 1996). While current technology is seemingly closing this gap by supporting audio and video channels, mainstream online dating portals still rely chiefly on text (the profile) and static visual information (profile photographs). This *reduction in communication cues* may enable deception for several reasons. First, it allows daters to distort information in ways that would not be possible face-to-face (e.g., claim to be taller, younger, or more extroverted than they actually are), or simply to omit disclosing undesirable characteristics (e.g., disguise weight by posting a photograph of a face close-up, rather than a full-body shot). Second, the reduction of nonverbal cues may cloak some telltale signs of lying, such as changes in nonverbal behavior (e.g., sweaty palms, avoidance of eye contact) or in the pitch of the voice (DePaulo et al., 2003). Although very few nonverbal cues are reliable in the human detection of deception, people hold strong beliefs about their ability to catch a liar nonverbally (Vrij, 2000). The fact that these supposed cues to deception are removed from online dating profiles may lead daters to conclude that they are less likely to be caught lying.

Another characteristic of computer-mediated communication that may affect deception practices is *synchronicity* (Walther, 1996), or the time lag that occurs between conceiving and transmitting a message, and receiving a response from one's interaction partner. Communication environments differ in the degree of synchronicity they provide; for instance, email is asynchronous (messages can be composed in an unhurried fashion and a response is only expected hours or days later), instant messaging is near-synchronous (conversation partners can take some time between formulating their responses, but the communication takes place with both partners interacting in real time), while face-to-face communication is synchronous (message production is extemporaneous and a response is expected immediately). Online dating profiles are asynchronous, in that users can take as much time as they need to compose their profiles, and they do not receive immediate feedback from potential mates.

The asynchronicity offered by online dating portals presents several possible benefits for deception. First, online daters are allowed an unlimited amount of time to formulate their self-presentation in composed and thoughtful ways—a luxury that traditional daters lack. Stories abound on how face-to-face daters, anxious to make a good first impression, inadvertently say the wrong thing, wear the wrong apparel, or behave inappropriately. By contrast, the *relaxation of time constraints* afforded by online interaction makes it possible for online daters to take as much time as they need to construct a self-presentation with which they are happy.

Relatedly, asynchronicity allows online daters to *edit* their self-presentation in both small and drastic ways. Unlike traditional daters, who cannot take back a faux pas, online daters can modify their profiles, possibly incorporating feedback from others, until they are pleased with their self-presentation. For example, the words describing oneself can be easily and repeatedly changed. Similarly, profile photographs can be altered in numerous ways in order to boost daters' physical attractiveness. During the photo shoot, daters can select flattering poses and lighting, or advantageous technological parameters (e.g., a camera with low resolution may hide skin imperfections). After the photo has been taken, it can be improved through retouching or through software packages that can remove wrinkles, sun damage and other skin imperfections, make hair shinier and fuller, or whiten teeth (Messaris, 1997). Daters are at liberty to select and post their most flattering photographs, and can even select older photographs that make them look younger.

Third, asynchronicity offers online daters the advantage of not needing to juggle the many mental tasks required by face-to-face interaction while composing their self-presentation (e.g., saying the right thing at the right time, managing body language, all the while trying to appear attractive). Instead, online daters can focus solely on the construction of an appealing profile. This property of asynchronous online communication has been referred to as the *reallocation of cognitive resources* (Walther, 1996), and it may promote the use of deception by freeing mental space that can be used for composing skillful deceptive messages.

The combined forces of reduced communication cues, the relaxation of time constraints, editability, and the reallocation of cognitive resources allow online daters to engage in *selective self-presentation*—a more controlled and optimized version of face-to-face self-presentation (Walther, 1996; Walther & Parks, 2002). Because of selective self-presentation, online daters are able to create mindful and deliberate messages, and to present themselves in more flattering ways, some of which may be considered deceptive. In fact, if daters do decide to use deception as a self-presentational resource, this set of affordances certainly facilitates the planning and posting of skillful deceptive messages.

So far we have reviewed the technological affordances of online dating profiles that may facilitate deception. However, online dating also includes a set of affordances that may promote honesty, or at least constrain the use of deception as a self-presentational resource. First, online dating profiles are recordable. Once accessed, they may be saved and archived, thus preserving a record of any deception (Hancock, Thom-Santelli, & Ritchie, 2004). Users may not feel comfortable knowing that their lies can be captured and stored, leaving no possibility of denying them. Second, and most importantly, the default assumption behind online dating services is that they are merely a tool for facilitating *face-to-face* dating. While there may be exceptions to this expectation, it is reasonable to assume that the majority of those willing to pay a fee for the opportunity to establish romantic relationships plan on leaving virtuality and meeting potential mates in person. The *anticipation of face-*

to-face interaction (Walther, 1996) represents a significant constraint on deception because the face-to-face environment provides a venue for detecting deception, either instantly (e.g., deception related to physical appearance) or over time (e.g., deception related to relationship status, children, occupation, income, etc.). Since being perceived as dishonest negatively affects dating, the anticipation of future interaction should constrain the degree to which online daters use deception to enhance their attractiveness.

Gender Differences in Deception

So far we have discussed the technical and social factors that may affect online daters' decisions of whether or not to engage in profile deception. The next question of interest is what exactly daters can be expected to lie *about*. Since the purpose of online dating is to attract suitable mates, it is reasonable that daters will enhance those attributes that potential mates value. In other words, in the context of heterosexual dating, the content of profile lies should be driven by daters' perceptions of what the opposite sex finds desirable.

A large body of research suggests that, indeed, there are significant differences between what men and women consider attractive in a potential partner. Specifically, men look for youth and physical attractiveness (as indicated by luscious hair, large eyes, full lips, small noses, and clear and smooth skin), whereas women look for ability to provide and indicators of social status, such as education and career (Lance, 1998; Woll & Cozby, 1987; Scheib, Gangestad & Thornhill, 1999). Research in the dating arena has shown that richer men tend to pursue more physically attractive women and that men with better occupations are more successful in attracting women, although the same is not true for women (Hitsch, Hortacsu, & Ariely, 2004). When reviewing personal advertisements, women have been shown to prefer older and financially secure partners, whereas men seek physical attractiveness and youth (Lynn & Bolig, 1985). Similarly, when marketing themselves in newspaper personals, men emphasize their financial resources, status and occupation, whereas women draw attention to their physical attractiveness and body shape (Ahuvia & Adelman, 1992; Hirschman, 1987; Jagger, 2001). Additionally, Gibbs, Ellison, and Heino (2006) found that men reported deceptively enhancing their height, an indicator of physical strength and ability to protect, while women reported under-representing their weight, an indicator of physical attractiveness.

The same pattern of lying designed to meet the expectations of the opposite sex should be observed in online dating as well. Specifically, we expect men to strategically enhance their height and social standing, and women to enhance their youth and physical attractiveness.

Operationalizing Deception in Online Dating Profiles

We have just reviewed an assortment of social and technological factors that may impact the frequency, magnitude and content of deceptions in online dating profiles. Considered together, these factors paint a detailed picture of what we can expect online dating deception to look like. Specifically, online dating deceptions should be (a) frequent, because dating partners tend to boost their appeal by resorting to deception, and because online technologies offer many affordances that facilitate deception; (b) small in magnitude, because online daters do not want to be caught lying in subsequent face-to-face interactions, nor do they want records of deceptions preserved; and (c) gender-specific, with women lying to meet the demands of men and vice-versa.

Before these hypotheses can be empirically examined, however, it is necessary to determine what exactly counts as deception in online dating profiles, and how it can be measured. Given the kinds of questions featured in online dating profiles (age, height, favorite hotspots, photographs), what should reasonably be labeled as deceptive, and what standards should we apply in doing so?

A good starting point in operationalizing deception in online dating profiles is to analyze the actual makeup of these profiles. Let us begin by pointing out that there are currently two kinds of online dating services. The first relies on a matching system that pairs users based on personality characteristics (e.g., EHarmony). The second, which is the focus of our research, allows users to create their own profiles and then contact other users directly (e.g., Match.com). These profiles are not blank slates but instead offer daters an array of predetermined multiple choice questions, short answer questions, and a photograph upload tool. These questions guide users' self-presentation and therefore constrain what deception in online dating profiles means, and how it can be measured.

Although there is some variation in the kinds of profile questions that different services put forth, the majority of them tend to showcase users' height, weight, age, relationship status, interests/hobbies/activities, political views, religious views, and photographs. Some of these categories are quantifiable and easily verifiable (height, weight, age), whereas others are not (interests, politics, religion, photographs).

When it comes to the quantifiable categories of height and weight, the identification of deception should be as simple as measuring participants and comparing their profile claims with their actual measurements. However, this approach presents some practical problems. For instance, weight fluctuates on a daily basis and clothes can add some pounds to lab measurements. Similarly, height fluctuates during the lifespan, and can also vary subtly on a daily basis. Another problem associated with height measurements is that it is common to round them up to the nearest inch (for instance, someone who is 5'4½" would probably consider herself to be 5'4"). To account for this variability, we believe the best method is determining a range of weight and height measurements that can be considered accurate for each person. For weight, allowing a 10 pound range around a person's actual weight should account for daily variations in weight, as well as for the weight of clothes at the time of measurement. We believe that discrepancies of more than 5 pounds above or below actual weight can reasonably be considered deceptive. For height, allowing for a half inch above and below the actual height should account for rounding error and daily fluctuations. Discrepancies of more than half an inch are probably deceptive.

Accuracy on the more subjective categories of interests, politics, and religion is difficult to measure and to verify objectively. For these aspects of the profile, the daters' self-reported veracity is the most efficient method of assessing deception. Of course, asking people to be honest about their deceptive behavior is problematic (see DePaulo et al., 1996), but short of actually investigating daters' past activities for evidence of their interests and opinions, self-report is the best option.

In operationalizing deception, perhaps the most problematic aspect of the online dating profile is the profile photograph. What makes a personal photograph deceptive? The literature on photographic deception does not offer a straightforward answer to these questions, oscillating between divergent positions in regards to the issue of photographic accuracy. At one end of the debate lies the position that photography is inherently deceptive because the technology involved in its creation differs so fundamentally from the way the human eye works that a photograph can never show us what we would have seen had we been there ourselves (James, 2005; Mercedes, 1996; Snyder & Allen, 1975). At the other end, photographs are considered intrinsically accurate as documentary objects, attesting to the fact that the person or object portrayed did in fact exist (Walton, 1984).

We take a more moderate position, specifically that photographs can indeed be accurate if they provide a *realistic likeness* of the person portrayed, and that they can be deceptive if this likeness is missing. We agree that a photograph cannot be a perfect representation of the person it purports to stand for, but we argue that it is capable of providing viewers with a reasonable approximation of what that person looks like in the flesh. Below we propose a methodology for (a) assessing the accuracy of online dating profile photographs, (b) identifying specific discrepancies between photographs and reality, and (c) establishing which of these incongruities lead viewers to judge the photograph as deceptive.

We begin by determining if online dating photographs tend to provide a realistic likeness of the daters, or if they stray from this likeness. Because the daters themselves are likely to have self-serving biases about the accuracy of their photographs (i.e., rate flattering photographs as accurate and unflattering ones as inaccurate), one method for assessing deceptiveness is to ask independent judges to determine the extent to which online daters' photographic depictions resemble their current appearance. In our experience, independent judges tend to be reliable in making judgments about how accurate a photograph is for a given person.

While untrained judges' evaluations are reliable in assessing how deceptive online dating photographs are in general, they are not useful in identifying what exactly makes a photograph deceptive. In fact, it is often difficult to pinpoint the exact reasons for which people look differently in reality than in their photographs, and judgments of deception can be made without conscious access to those reasons. In order to uncover the specific elements that take away from the accuracy of photographs, we propose a two-part methodology. First, we train raters to identify specific discrepancies between profile photographs and online daters' current appearance. These discrepancies can refer to both online daters' physical appearance (hair length, hair color, eye color, nose, lips, skin, weight, etc.), as well as to photographic alterations (cropping, retouching, or professional photographs). These judgments provide a tally of the number and types of discrepancies in a profile photograph relative to the person's current appearance. Next, to determine whether these discrepancies are related to perceptions of deception, we correlate the presence of these discrepancies with the accuracy judgments made by the first group of independent judges. For instance, cropping might not be considered deceptive, but posting a photograph that shows a substantially thinner version of the person may be.

With these operationalizations of what counts as deception in online profiles, we now turn to a large empirical study that we conducted to examine the frequency, magnitude, and content of online dating profile deceptions.

An Empirical Study Examining Deception Practices in Online Dating

How much do online daters *actually* lie on the various profile items, and what precisely do they lie about? To answer these concrete questions, we selected a sample of 80 heterosexual daters in the New York City metropolitan area who had been using mainstream online dating services (Match.com, Yahoo Personals, American Singles, Webdate.com) for at least 1 month (see Hancock, Toma, & Ellison, 2007; Toma & Hancock, 2008; Toma, Hancock, & Ellison, 2008). We then downloaded their profiles, invited them to our lab, and interviewed them individually regarding their profile deceptions.

To obtain a comprehensive account of online dating deception, we employed four distinct deception detection methods—the first two aimed at uncovering deception on profile questions, and the latter two directed towards deception in profile photographs. For detecting deception in profile questions (e.g., height, weight, age), we attempted to verify the accuracy of quantifiable claims. Specifically, we measured daters' height and weight (using a standard measuring tape and scale, respectively), and we recorded their date of birth from their drivers' licenses. This objective measure of deception circumvents a major problem with deception research—namely, trusting people to report the truth about their own lies—and hence provided us with a reliable estimate of online dating profile deception.

However, since it is difficult to verify all of participants' quantifiable claims (e.g., education, job, income), and virtually impossible to verify the more subjective ones (e.g., sense of humor, favorite books), we relied on the participants themselves to identify inaccuracies in the rest of the profile items. We attempted to eliminate social desirability bias in this self-report measure (i.e., participants' unwillingness to admit to lying) by forewarning them that we were going to objectively verify some of their claims, without telling them exactly which. We reasoned that participants would be more likely to report the truth about their lies if they knew the truth was going to surface anyway.

To determine the accuracy of profile photographs, we had independent judges compare profile photographs with photographs we had taken of the daters in the lab. As discussed earlier, the lab photographs provided a representation of what daters look like on a daily basis. A group of independent judges were shown side-by-side photographs of participants (the lab photo vs. the profile photo) and were asked to score how similar the two were. This measure indicated the *extent* of photographic deception. Second, we sought to determine the *content* of photographic deception by examining the ways in which the profile photographs differed from the lab photographs. A group of independent raters identified these discrepancies based on a coding scheme that included incongruities related to physical appearance, as well as incongruities generated by the photographic process (see earlier discussion).

Results for the questionnaire-based part of the profile showed that, indeed, deception was frequently observed, but that the deceptions tended to be small in magnitude. Our measurements revealed that approximately 8 out of 10 online daters (81%) lied about their height, weight, or age. On average, daters misrepresented their height by less than an inch, their weight by about 6 pounds, and their age by about half a year. For both men and women, the more participants departed from physical norms (e.g., by being very short or very heavy), the more

they tended to lie. As we predicted, these subtle deceptions may be difficult to detect in person, thus allowing daters to portray themselves as
slightly more appealing tha, they are without the risk of being caught
lying by potential mates when meeting face-to-face.

Also noteworthy is that participants who lied on one characteristic
were not more likely to lie on the others as well (e.g., someone who portrayed herself as thinner did not necessarily portray herself as younger),
suggesting that online daters do not lie indiscriminately simply because
they can, but rather that they strategically select those deceptions that
would enhance their appeal.

The pattern of frequent but subtle deceptions we observed through
measurements also emerged when participants self-reported the accuracy
of their profile answers. On a scale from 1 to 5, with 1 being completely
inaccurate and 5 being completely accurate, participants reported an
average accuracy of above 4.5 across the profile items. These self-report
measures lead us to conclude that, contrary to popular belief, online dating profiles tend to be accurate, with only slight tweaks.

Now that we have determined how much online daters lie in the questionnaire part of their profiles, let us consider what they lie *about*. As
described above, online daters tended to misrepresent their weight and
height, although they were fairly accurate about their age. This appears
to be a strategic choice, as weight and height are characteristics that can
fluctuate and may be altered such that online daters are not caught lying
in face-to-face meetings with potential dates (e.g., by wearing flattering
clothes or heels, or by simply losing weight over time). Online daters can
also explain away their weight and height-related deceptions by claiming
ignorance on their *precise* measurements, thus eschewing being labeled
as liars. By contrast, age is a stable characteristic, that does not fluctuate
on a daily basis, and about which it is impossible to claim ignorance.
Under these circumstances, any age-related deception, if uncovered, may
earn daters the social stigma of being a liar.

Of particular interest is the fact that men lied significantly more than
women about their height, while women lied significantly more than men
about their weight. This was consistent with our expectations that men
and women would lie strategically about those characteristics that the
opposite sex finds attractive. For instance, when asked, men considered
it acceptable to lie about their social status (education and occupation).
Men's approval of deception about their social status indicates that they
may be giving themselves permission to lie about these characteristics,
if necessary, in order to attract women, and underscores their strategic
approach to online dating deception.

Overall, online daters were the most accurate about their relationship
status (i.e., single, divorced, separated) and about whether or not they
have children. This information is of vital importance in developing rela-

tionships, and being caught lying about it tends to be a deal-breaker for most relationships. The high level of accuracy reported on this topic may explain why online dating is so popular despite media concerns over its inherent untrustworthiness.

The same pattern of relative accuracy cannot be claimed for profile photographs. Although the online daters in our sample reported a moderate degree of accuracy for their photographs (an average of 4 on the 1–5 accuracy scale used), they still rated their photos as the least accurate element of their profiles. More importantly, independent judges found the photographs to be substantially less accurate than the participants themselves did. As a matter of fact, judges considered about one third of the photographs to be deceptive representations of online daters' current appearance. This pattern of inaccuracy was especially pronounced for women, whose photographs were rated as significantly more deceptive than men's. Almost half of the female photographs were rated below the midpoint of the accuracy scale, while only 15% of the male photographs were.

In what ways did men and women's photographs differ from the reality of their day-to-day appearance? Recall that we identified several possible physical discrepancies between how daters look in real life and how they look in their profile photos (e.g., age, weight, hair color, skin clearness, etc.). These discrepancies may arise from posting older photographs (in which participants look younger), selecting particularly flattering yet technically unaltered photographs, or altering photographs through retouching, cropping, or hiring a professional photographer. In our sample, women's photographs contained three times more discrepancies than men's photographs. Furthermore, female photographs included discrepancies related to age, hair style, and skin, and women were more significantly more likely than men to retouch their photographs, hire a professional photographer, and post older photographs.

These data suggest that women sought to portray themselves as younger and more physically attractive, an observation that falls in line with expectations that women will inflate characteristics that men find attractive. For instance, women's enhancement of their skin and hair in their photographs indicates their strategic awareness of the importance of these physical descriptors for attracting men. Indeed, evolutionary psychologists (Scheib, Gangestad, & Thornhill, 1999) have found that clear skin and lustrous hair in women are strong indicators of youthfulness and fertility.

It is important to note that, while men rated their photographs as less accurate the more discrepancies they contained, women did not do the same. In other words, women considered their photographs to be accurate even though they contained a number of incongruities with their everyday appearance. It is possible, yet unlikely, that women unconsciously chose more flattering photographs without being aware of how much they diverged from reality. Rather, we postulate that women's physical appearance, more so than men's, is considerably different on dates than it is on a daily basis. Women spend a lot of time and effort beautifying themselves, and hence it is reasonable to expect them to look better on a date than when they show up for an experiment. Women may not have rated their photographs as less accurate simply because they expected those discrepancies to be attenuated or disappear when they prepared for their date.

Conclusion

To summarize, our research on the actual deceptive practices of online daters shows that lies tend to be frequent, subtle and strategic (Hancock et al.,, 2007; Toma & Hancock, 2008; Toma et al., 2008). Online daters tend to lie the least about relationship deal-breakers, such as their marital status and whether or not they have children, and the most about their profile photographs. Men and women lie strategically in order to meet the expectations of the opposite sex. Men lie more about their height, and also report being willing to lie about their education and occupation. Women lie more about their weight, and also tend to enhance their physical appearance and youthfulness by posting enhanced photographs (through retouching or hiring a professional photographer).

This pattern of results supports the concept of selective self-presentation online, which assumes that online communicators are savvy about the self-presentational opportunities (editability, reduced communication cues) and limitations (recordability, anticipated future interaction) of computer-mediated communication, and use them in strategic ways so as to maximize their relational goals (in our case, finding relationship partners). Online daters do not seem to engage in deception simply because they can, but rather construct strategies about how to best enhance themselves without coming across as liars in face-to-face meetings.

As indicated by the literature on deception in the beginning stages of romantic relationships, online daters do tend to lie frequently—probably more so than those in established relationships. This frequent pattern of deception is consistent with the pressures of increased interpersonal scrutiny, increased competitiveness with millions of other online daters, and increased anxiety about putting themselves out there in front of a large, undifferentiated audience.

Future research is still needed to empirically determine whether the lying patterns of online daters differ from those of traditional daters. Our research seems to suggest that, despite the lack of a corporeal presence that may gave participants more freedom to embellish descriptions of their physical characteristics, online daters tended to use deception in their profiles in ways predicted by previous research concerned with face-to-face self-presentation, sparingly and tailored to their audience.

References

Ahuvia, A. C., & Adelman, M. B. (1992). Formal intermediaries in the marriage market: A typology and review. *Journal of Marriage and the Family, 54,* 452–463.

Berger, C. R. (1987). Communication under uncertainty. In M. E. Roloff & G. R. Miller (Eds.), *Interpersonal processes: New directions in communication research* (pp. 39–62). Beverly Hills, CA: Sage.

Brym, R. J., & Lenton, R. L. (2001). Love online: A report on digital dating in Canada. Retrieved January 13, 2006, from http://www.nelson.com/nelson/harcourt/sociology/newsociety3e/loveonline.pdf

Buss, D. M. (1988). The evolution of human intrasexual competition: Tactics of mate attraction. *Journal of Personality and Social Psychology, 54,* 616–628.

DePaulo, B. M., & Kashy, D. A. (1998). Everyday lies in close and casual relationships. *Journal of Personality & Social Psychology, 74,* 63–79.

DePaulo, B. M., Kashy, D. A., Kirkendol, S. E., & Epstein, J. A. (1996). Lying in everyday life. *Journal of Personality and Social Psychology, 70,* 979–995.

DePaulo, B. M., Lindsay, J. J., Malone, B. E., Muhlenbruck, L., Charlton, K., & Cooper, H. (2003). Cues to deception. *Psychological Bulletin, 129,* 74–118.

Derlega, V., Winstead, B., Wong, P., & Greenspan, M. (1987). Self-disclosure and relationship development: An attributional analysis. In M. E. Roloff & G. R. Miller (Eds.), *Interpersonal processes: New directions in communication research* (pp. 172–187). Thousand Oaks, CA: Sage.

Ekman, P. (1985). *Telling lies: Clues to deceit in the marketplace, politics and marriage.* New York: W.W. Norton.

Feldman, R. S., Forrest, J. A., & Happ, B. R. (2002) Self-presentation and verbal deception: Do self-presenters lie more? *Basic and Applied Social Psychology, 24,* 163–170.

Gibbs, J. L., Ellison, N. B., & Heino, R. D. (2006). Self-presentation in online personals: The role of anticipated future interaction, self-disclosure, and perceived success in Internet dating. *Communication Research, 33,* 1–26.

Goffman, E. (1959). *The presentation of self in everyday life.* New York: Anchor.

Hancock, J.T. (2007). Digital deception: When, where and how people lie online. In K. McKenna, T. Postmes, U. Reips, & A.N. Joinson (Eds.), *Oxford handbook of internet psychology* (pp. 287–301). Oxford: Oxford University Press.

Hancock, J., Thom-Santelli, J., & Ritchie, T. (2004). Deception and design: The impact of communication technology on lying behavior. In E. Dykstra-Erickson & M. Tscheligi (Eds.), *Proceedings of the 2004 Conference on Human Factors in Computing Systems* (pp. 129–134). New York: ACM.

Hancock, J. T., Toma, C., & Ellison, N. (2007). The truth about lying in online dating profiles. *Proceedings of the ACM Conference on Human Factors in Computing Systems*, 449–452.

Herring, S. C., & Martinson, A. (2004). Assessing gender authenticity in computer-mediated language use: Evidence from an identity game. *Journal of Language and Social Psychology, 23*, 424–446.

Hirschman, E. C. (1987). People as products: Analysis of a complex marketing exchange. *Journal of Marketing, 51*, 98–108.

Hitsch, G. J., Hortacsu, A., & Ariely, D. (2004). What makes you click: An empirical analysis of online dating (Working Paper). Retrieved July 18, 2005, from http://rover.cs.northwestern.edu/~surana/blog/extras/online_dating.pdf

Jagger, E. (2001). Marketing Molly and Melville: Dating in a postmodern, consumer society. *Sociology, 35*, 39–57.

James, S. (2005–2006, Dec.–Jan.). The truth about photography. *Art Monthly, 292*, 7–10.

Joinson, A. N. (2003). *Understanding the psychology of internet behaviour: Virtual worlds, real lives*. Basingstoke, England: Palgrave.

Lance, L.M. (1998). Gender differences in heterosexual dating: A content analysis of personal ads. *The Journal of Men's Studies, 6*, 297–305.

Lynn, M., & Bolig, R. (1985). Personal advertisements: Sources of data about relationships. *Journal of Social and Personal Relationships, 2*, 377–383.

Mercedes, D. (1996). Digital Ethics: Computers, photographs, and the manipulation of pixels. *Art Education, 49*, 44–50.

Messaris, P. (1997). *Visual persuasion: the role of images in advertising*. Thousands Oaks, CA: Sage.

Scheib, J. E., Gangestad, S. W., & Thornhill, R. (1999). Facial attractiveness, symmetry and cues of good genes. *Proceedings of the Royal Society, London B., 266*, 1913–1917.

Snyder, J., & Allen, N. W. (1975). Photography, vision, and representation. *Critical Inquiry, 2*, 143–169.

Toma, C., & Hancock, J. (2008). Putting your best face forward: The accuracy of online dating photographs. Paper presented at the *International Communication Association Convention*, Montreal, May 22–26.

Toma, C., Hancock, J., & Ellison, N. (2008). Separating fact from fiction: An examination of deceptive self-presentation in online dating profiles. *Personality and Social Psychology Bulletin, 34*, 1023–1036.

Vrij, A. (2000). *Detecting lies and deceit: The psychology of lying and the implications for professional practice*. Chichester, England: Wiley.

Walther, J. B. (1996). Computer-mediated communication: Impersonal, interpersonal, and hyperpersonal interaction. *Communication Research, 23*, 3–44.

Walther, J. B., & Parks, M. R. (2002). Cues filtered out, cues filtered in: Computer-mediated communication and relationships. In M. L. Knapp & J. A. Daly (Eds.), *Handbook of Interpersonal Communication* (3rd ed., pp. 529–563). Thousand Oaks, CA: Sage.

Walton, K. L. (1984). Transparent pictures: On the nature of photographic realism. *Critical Inquiry, 11*, 246–277.

Woll, S., & Cozby, P. C. (1987). Videodating and other alternatives to traditional methods of relationship initiation. *Advances in Personal Relationships, 1*, 69–108.

Chapter 11

Exoneration of Serious Wrongdoing via Confession to a Lesser Offense

R. Weylin Sternglanz

Several years ago, Senator Bob Kerrey was accused by fellow veteran Gerhard Klann of being involved in atrocities during the Vietnam War. Klann claimed that Kerrey personally assisted with the throat-cutting of an elderly peasant, and that some babies were executed along with the other members of the village.

Regardless of whether these allegations were true or not, Kerrey was put in a difficult political position. The possibility had been planted in the public's mind that Kerrey could be guilty not only of committing this atrocity, but of keeping it secret all these years. How, in this high-stakes situation, could Kerrey most convincingly establish his innocence?

One point of view is that serious charges which are ignored will fade away. This is the apparent position of press secretaries who dismiss questions about charges by saying that they are not going to dignify the charge with a response. Such a tactic has a certain appeal for the person who is accused, as it gives the press and public no opportunity to dissect the response of the accused for evidence of deceptiveness or of trying to weasel out of the charge. But it also raises very serious risks. Disparaging characterizations can stick even when they are made subtly by way of innuendo (Wegner, Wenzlaff, Kerker, & Beattie, 1981); ignoring a direct accusation may be especially risky.

Another response is to claim complete innocence. For the person who truly is innocent, this may well be the most likely response. But it is probably also a tempting response even for guilty people. However, a simple claim of innocence may not answer the question that people who have heard the accusation may harbor: If the accused really is innocent, then why did the accuser make the accusation?

The accused may respond by claiming that the accuser has ulterior motives. This strategy is often seen in the political arena, and it often devolves into a flurry of back-and-forth accusations. This may also happen in everyday interpersonal arguments. There is one serious risk to a counter-accusation strategy: The accuser may come off as a vindictive mudslinger. People who become known for giving negative evaluations of others are seen as less likable than those known for giving positive evaluations (Folkes & Sears, 1977).

Senator Kerrey's situation was unusual because of the extraordinarily serious charges it involved, and because of Kerrey's high position. But the experience of being accused of lying about some serious wrongdoing is not so unusual. Almost all people have suspected that someone else has lied to them about something serious, and almost all people admit to having told occasional serious lies themselves (DePaulo, Ansfield, Kirkendol, & Boden, 2004). It may behoove people who are accused of a serious lie to develop a strategy—particularly if they are guilty of lying.

Strategies for Deception

Despite the abundance of literature on nonverbal self-presentation (see DePaulo, 1992), relatively little attention has been given to the deliberate verbal and nonverbal strategies that people use when accused of deception. It has long been known that people use nonverbal cues, not only unconsciously but consciously, in order to convey a desired impression (Goffman, 1959; Ekman & Friesen, 1964). People who do not want to be labeled as liars may develop strategies to establish their innocence, particularly if they actually are guilty of lying. Theoretically, developing a strategy ahead of time could help one to deliver a lie more smoothly and prevent nonverbal leakage. In a study by DePaulo, Lanier, and Davis (1983), participants were given the opportunity to plan some of their lies in advance, whereas other lies they had to make up on the spot. It turned out that lies planned in advance were no more or less detectable than those not planned. However, deceptive as well as truthful planned responses were perceived as more deceptive than unplanned responses. It would seem that people are better off not planning a strategy ahead of time, regardless of whether they are telling the truth or lying. There was one important limitation to the DePaulo et al. (1983) study, as well as other similar studies in the literature: The nature of the strategies that people devised when given the opportunity to plan their lies were never examined. Perhaps the skills of those people who did come up with effective strategies were masked by the limitations of those people whose strategies were ineffective.

One might predict that deceptive strategies would be successful when people are especially motivated to get away with their lies. However, results have consistently shown that such motivation tends to backfire; participants who try harder to hide their deception actually give off more nonverbal cues to deception (DePaulo et al., 1983; DePaulo, LeMay, & Epstein, 1991). Possibly the people who are highly motivated to get away with their lies try deliberately to regulate and suppress their nonverbal cues, ironically giving the impression that they have something to hide (DePaulo, 1992; Wegner, 1994).

Based on research thus far, it would seem that ordinary self-presentational strategies are unlikely to be useful in managing an appearance of honesty. However, the research on this topic has been done almost exclusively with the "little" lies told in everyday life, rather than the more serious lies that may have serious consequences for both the would-be liars and the targets of such lies.

Suspicion of Serious Lies

> ... if you are ever suspected of something, try to make the evidence point to a lesser offense. Never try to prove lily-white innocence. Human nature being what it is, your chances are better. (Heinlein, 1953, p. 24)

Most lies told in everyday life are not particularly disruptive to social interaction (DePaulo, Kashy, Kirkendol, Wyer, & Epstein, 1996), perhaps, in part, because people rarely detect them (DePaulo & Pfeifer, 1986; DePaulo, 1994). This may be the case because, while everyday lies can be told relatively effortlessly (Vrij, 1994), disbelieving requires cognitive exertion. Gilbert and his colleagues (Gilbert, 1991; Gilbert, Krull, & Malone, 1990) suggest that comprehending a message entails accepting that message; in other words, believing is our "default." However, in unusual circumstances—for instance, when people are suspicious that a serious lie has been told—people may be more likely to make the extra cognitive effort to disbelieve.

In fact, when people are primed to expect deception, they do become less trusting; however, usually they do not become more accurate at distinguishing liars from truth-tellers (Toris & DePaulo, 1985; however, see also McCornack & Levine, 1990). In most studies of deception, suspicions are created and tested solely on the basis of the verbal and nonverbal cues available in the immediate interaction. In a study in which participants were asked directly how they figure out when someone is lying, however, Park, Levine, McCornack, Morrison, and Ferrerra (2001) found that people frequently use information from third parties and physical evidence to detect deception. Perhaps suspiciousness is more commonplace than many researchers believe.

Calling someone a liar or a guilty person can be a serious allegation, and people may be reluctant to make such a charge. Still, there may be ways in which people react differently to someone who someone who is lying than to someone who is telling the truth, if they do not make outright accusations of deceit. There is growing evidence that perceivers (or "judges") do feel differently when they just heard a lie than when they just heard a truth. For example, meta-analytic results have shown that judges feel more confident about their attributions of credibility when the story they heard was the truth rather than a lie, regardless of whether they accurately identified it as truthful (DePaulo, Charlton, Cooper, Lindsay, & Muhlenbruck, 1997). In addition, people sometimes view liars as less comfortable and more wary than truth-tellers (Anderson, DePaulo, & Ansfield, 2002; DePaulo & Morris, 2004). DePaulo (1994) has described these findings as indicative of implicit or indirect deception detection. From judges' responses, it seems that they are, on some level, bothered by deception. Nevertheless, because judges can sometimes distinguish truths from lies in these indirect ways even when they cannot distinguish them directly (i.e., by rating the lies as more deceptive than the truths), it appears that judges do not necessarily know how to interpret their own misgivings.

Because judges have more of these misgivings about people who really are lying than about those who are telling the truth, it is the liars who need to deal in some way with the potential misgivings or suspicions they may have created in the targets of their lies. Liars, then, may be most at risk for being disbelieved, or perceived more negatively in other ways, if they simply claim innocence without also trying to deal with other people's misgivings.

One possible strategy for people accused of lying is to try to explain why the accuser may have come to a false conclusion. For example, the accused can suggest that the accuser misinterpreted the evidence in a plausible way. The advantage to this approach is the appearance of taking the high road. The accused person avoids the perils of mudslinging, and even offers a face-saving way of explaining why the accuser made such a serious accusation that was actually untrue.

Will this approach work? Possibly, but it has a distinct disadvantage. Suspicion may be much more than a "cold," or unmotivated, reasoning process. There may be a feeling of discomfort, of "fishiness," that accompanies the suspicion that someone has told a serious lie, even in those cases when the judge is not directly affected by the lie. The judge may perceive that something feels wrong about the accused person's story. If the judge is suspicious that a serious lie has taken place, merely being able to explain the evidence away may not be enough. To remove the discomfort or "fishy feeling" associated with suspicion, the accused person may have to admit to at least some wrongdoing. Might someone accused of a very serious lie be better off confessing to a lesser offense, thus redirecting the judge toward a less serious transgression?

Suspicion as an Example of the Fundamental Attribution Error

Senders who redirect a judge toward a less serious transgression may have the advantage of making themselves appear forthright about their wrongdoing. Appearing forthright may play a substantial role in getting away with deception. O'Sullivan (2003) recently proposed that human lie detectors commit the fundamental attribution error—that is, they look for characteristics about the accused person, rather than the situation, and thus often make inaccurate judgments about the veracity of a particular statement. A judge may think that someone who freely admits wrongdoing when there was no obvious external pressure to do so is inherently honest; consider George Washington's alleged admission that he cut down the cherry tree.

The Theory

It was theorized that people who have been accused of a serious offense will be seen as more honest if they confess to a lesser offense than if they claim to be entirely innocent or use other defenses, such as explaining away the evidence or making a counter-accusation. There are two possible reasons why this process may take place. First, senders who confess to a lesser offense may be offering an alternative attribution for judges' discomfort and "fishy" feelings. Second, senders who confess to a lesser offense may be characterized as having a particularly honest disposition, and thus unlikely to deny something of which they are actually guilty. If this second explanation is accurate, perhaps senders who confess to any offense, even one not directly relevant to the one of which they were accused, would be perceived as particularly trustworthy people, and therefore truthful in a given situation.

In Study 1, I tested the hypothesis that people who were accused of a serious lie would be more likely to be perceived as honest and innocent when they confessed to a lesser offense than when they claimed to be completely innocent. In Studies 2 and 3, I compared the strategy of confessing to a lesser offense to various other strategies, such as offering a plausible explanation, making a counter-accusation, or admitting to an irrelevant offense.

Study I

Overview

Participants were randomly assigned to read one of two types of vignettes. In both vignettes, participants were asked to consider how they would react when told that a fellow student has been accused of a serious transgression: cheating off another student's exam. However, in one version of the vignette, participants were told that this fellow student denied the accusation completely (see Appendix A), whereas in the other version of the vignette, participants were told that the fellow student denied cheating off another student's exam, but admitted to noticing his or her friend cheating and failing to report it (see Appendix B). The student was described as either a male or female friend, or a male or female stranger.

Participants

A total of 322 undergraduates at the University of Virginia took part in the study. Participants received credit toward the experiment participation requirement for an introductory psychology course. All participants were run in groups of 4 to 12.

Design

The study employed a 2 (hypothetical accused student is a friend vs. a stranger) × 2 (student's defense against the accusation) between-participants design. Approximately equal proportions of male and female participants participated in each cell of the design. The dependent measures consisted of two items which are of relevance to this study. The first item was, "How likely is it that this person is guilty of actually exchanging and receiving answers on the exam?" Participants answered this question on a 7-point scale ranging from "very unlikely" to "very likely." The second item was, "If you had to make an educated guess, do you believe the accused person was lying?" This was a dichotomous measure; participants responded with either a "yes" (coded as 1) or "no" (coded as 0).

Procedure

Four experimental conditions were run, with approximately equal numbers of participants (between 77 and 82) in each. In the first stimulus condition, participants were told to imagine the accused student was a platonic male friend at the University of Virginia. In the second, participants were told to imagine the accused student was a platonic female friend at the University of Virginia. In the third, the accused was a male stranger, and in the fourth, she was a female stranger.

Upon beginning an experimental session, participants were asked to sign consent forms. Then, the experimenter gave approximately half of the participants (randomly assigned) the vignette in which the accused student denies the accusation completely, and gave the other participants the vignette in which the accused student admits to noticing his or her friend cheat. The experimenter asked participants to fill in the blank spaces in the vignette with the appropriate name. Depending on the condition, the name was either that of a platonic male friend at the University of Virginia, a platonic female friend at the University of Virginia, the name "Bob Stevenson" (a male stranger), or the name "Lisa Stevenson" (a female stranger). Participants were then asked to read the vignette and write a description filling out the details of the hypothetical scenario they had just read. Participants were given 3 minutes for this task. They then completed the dependent measures, after which they were thanked for their time, given course credit, and debriefed.

Results and Preliminary Conclusions

A 2 (accused student is a friend vs. a stranger) × 2 (student's defense against the accusation) between-participants ANOVA was conducted. The question, "How likely is it that this person is guilty of actually exchanging and receiving answers on the exam?" served as the dependent measure. Unsurprisingly, strangers ($M = 4.47$) were rated as significantly more likely to be guilty than were friends ($M = 2.58$), $F (1, 319) = 130.8, p < .001$.

There was no significant difference overall between participants' ratings of the accused students described as denying the accusation completely and the accused students described as admitting to a lesser offense, $F (1, 319) = 1.07, p = .32$. However, there was an interaction between the relationship of the accused to the participant (friend vs. stranger) and the accused student's defense against the accusation (complete denial vs. admitting to a lesser offense), $F (1, 319) = 3.78, p = .05$. Friends were rated as significantly more likely to be guilty if they admitted to a lesser offense ($M = 2.82$) than if they denied the accusation completely ($M = 2.33$), whereas strangers were rated as slightly (though nonsignificantly) less likely to be guilty if they admitted to a lesser offense ($M = 4.39$) than if they denied the accusation completely ($M = 4.55$).

Another ANOVA, with the same independent variables, was conducted using participants' dichotomous judgments (accused person was lying vs. not lying) as the dependent measure. (See Rosenthal & Rosnow, 1991; Snedecor & Cochran, 1967; and Winer, 1971, for use of an ANOVA with dichotomous dependent variables.) Once again, friends were seen as substantially less dishonest than strangers, $F (1, 319) = 58.92, p < .001$. In addition, the accused students were judged as less dishonest if they admitted to a lesser offense than if they denied the accusation completely, $F (1, 319) = 4.13, p = .04$. However, this latter effect was qualified by an interaction between the relationship of the accused to the participant (friend vs. stranger) and the accused student's defense against the accusation (complete denial vs. admitting to a lesser offense), $F (1, 319) = 5.42, p = .02$. Friends were rated as dishonest at almost identical low rates regardless of whether they denied the accusation completely (16%) or confessed to the lesser offense (18%), whereas strangers were rated as dishonest more often when they denied the accusation completely (65%) than when they admitted to a lesser offense (44%).

Taken together, these results indicate that the predicted advantage of confessing to a lesser offense over claiming total innocence is likely to be enjoyed by strangers but not by friends. Strangers were seen as non-significantly less guilty and significantly less likely to be lying when they admitted to a lesser offense than when they claimed to be completely innocent of all wrongdoing. In contrast, the friends were not seen as any more or less likely to be lying in one condition than in the other. The friends were, however, seen as significantly more likely to be guilty if they confessed to the lesser offense than if they denied the accusation completely. Perhaps, unless the evidence is truly overwhelming, people do not become at all suspicious that any deception has taken place when a friend denies an accusation. However, when a friend confesses to a lesser offense, people may awaken to the idea that there is at least some chance a friend could be guilty of serious wrongdoing. On the other hand, because people do not have preconceived notions about strangers' integrity and honesty, even a small amount of damning evidence may be enough to engage people's suspicions, regardless of what defense the stranger uses. Once participants' suspicions have been engaged, these suspicions may be assuaged more easily when the stranger admits to a lesser offense than when he or she denies the accusation completely.

The results for friends were unexpected, and future research will be necessary to advance our understanding beyond the speculations I have offered here. In the present research, I wish to focus primarily on strangers; thus, in Studies 2 and 3, I have included only participants who are strangers to the people they are judging.

Study 2

Participants

A total of 51 undergraduates (33 females and 18 males) at the University of Virginia took part in the second study. Participants received credit toward the experiment participation requirement for an introductory psychology course. Twelve of the participants (6 men and 6 women) were designated as "confederates." Confederates were run through the study individually. The remaining 39 participants were designated as "judges." Judges were run in groups of 4 to 12.

Design

Judges were the units of analysis in a 2 (confederate's gender) × 6 (confederate's defense against the accusation) repeated-measures analysis. The dependent measures consisted of a questionnaire with direct and indirect measures of judges' perceptions of guilt (see Appendix C).

Procedure

All 12 confederates were videotaped discussing an event in which they were supposedly accused of a serious offense (see Appendix D). The serious accusations in question were based on a questionnaire given to undergraduate students not involved in this study; these students described real events in their own lives in which they had been accused of serious offenses.

Each confederate was videotaped discussing the events immediately preceding and during this hypothetical accusation. The confederate's description of these events was exactly the same across conditions. However, after describing the hypothetical accusation, the confederate was videotaped offering six distinct defenses for the accusation, which differed as follows:

1. The confederate described the accusation, but did not present any additional information.
2. The confederate described the accusation, and then denied that it was true.
3. The confederate described the accusation, denied that it was true, and offered a brief explanation for the accuser's suspicions.
4. The confederate described the accusation, denied that it was true, and made a counter-accusation against the accuser.
5. The confederate described the accusation, denied that it was true, and admitted to a relevant lesser offense than the one of which he or she was accused.
6. The confederate described the accusation, denied that it was true, and admitted to an irrelevant lesser offense (of which he or she was not accused).

In the second phase of the study, the judges viewed these videotapes. Four different stimulus tapes had been created for generalizability, each of which had a total of 12 video clips (1 male and 1 female confederate for each of the six conditions, in randomized order). Although all 12 confederates were videotaped using all six defenses against their hypothetical accusation, the judges viewed a stimulus videotape on which each confederate used only one defense. Thus, a judge in one session would see a given confederate use one defense, while a judge in another session would see that same confederate use a different defense. Any effects due to the confederate's physical appearance or visible personality quirks should therefore be approximately equal across conditions.

Groups of 4 to 12 judges viewed the stimulus tapes. After filling out consent forms, judges were told that they would watch videotapes of some people who would describe a time when they had been accused of committing a serious offense. Judges were told that some of the people were guilty of these serious offenses, but others were not. Finally, judges were told that after they watched each videotape, they would be asked to try to determine who is guilty, and who is not guilty, of the serious accusations they described.

Judges were asked to complete a questionnaire after viewing each stimulus tape of a confederate. The primary measures were perceptions of guilt, as recorded on a 9-point scale and a dichotomous report of guilt or innocence. Other measures, as well as manipulation checks, were also included in the questionnaire (see Appendix C for the complete list). After judges viewed and rated all 12 confederates, they were thanked for their time, given course credit, and debriefed.

Results

Judges were the units of analysis in a series of four repeated-measures 2 (confederate's gender) × 6 (confederate's defense against the accusation) ANOVAs.

In the first ANOVA, the question "How likely is it that the accused person is guilty of [the serious offense]?" served as the dependent measure. Answers were on a 9-point scale, in which "5" was the midpoint, and in which higher numbers denoted greater levels of perceived guilt. The mean across all conditions was 5.04, indicating that there was not a truth bias in this study (unlike in most studies of deception detection).

As predicted, the type of defense confederates used to explain the accusation significantly affected their perceived guilt, $F (5, 33) = 11.25$, $p < .001$. A planned contrast was computed to test the prediction that the defense of denying the accusation and admitting to a relevant lesser offense would result in lower perceptions of guilt than the other five defenses. The contrast weights were +5 for the "deny accusation and admit to a relevant lesser offense" defense and −1 for each of the other defenses. This contrast was significant, $F (1, 185) = 8.32$, $p = .004$, indicating that the key condition resulted in lower perceptions of guilt than the mean of all of the other conditions. To determine whether that condition differed significantly from each of the other conditions, considered individually, protected t-tests were computed. Results indicated that the defense of denying the accusation and admitting to a relevant lesser offense differed significantly from three of the other five conditions: denying the accusation, denying the accusation and offering an explanation, and denying the accusation and making a counter-accusation. However, confederates who admitted to a relevant lesser offense did not elicit significantly different perceptions of guilt than confederates who denied the accusation and admitted to an irrelevant offense, or who offered no defense against the accusation.

There was an unpredicted interaction between confederate gender and the type of defense confederates used, $F(5, 33) = 8.78$, $p < .001$. Results showed that the perceptions of guilt elicited by the male confederates were more in line with the hypothesis than were the perceptions elicited by the female confederates. Specifically, the men who denied the accusation and admitted to a relevant lesser offense elicited significantly lesser perceptions of guilt than those who simply denied the accusation, who denied the accusation and offered an explanation, who denied the accusation and made a counter-accusation, or who denied the accusation and admitted to an irrelevant offense. However, men who denied the accusation and admitted to a relevant lesser offense did not elicit significantly different perceptions of guilt than men who offered no defense against the accusation, $F(1, 185) = .37$, $p = .54$.

Female confederates, on the other hand, were perceived as significantly less guilty when they denied the accusation and admitted to an irrelevant offense than when they used any other kind of defense. Women who denied the accusation and admitted to a relevant lesser offense were only perceived as significantly less guilty than women who offered no defense against the accusation, or who denied the accusation and offered an explanation.

The male and female confederates differed most strikingly in the condition that was supposed to be a simple control group: the condition in which confederates described the accusation supposedly made against them but said nothing more. In that condition, the men were seen as especially innocent ($M = 3.77$) and the women as especially guilty ($M = 5.79$). As I will explain in more detail below, it is not possible to discern from this study why the men and women were perceived so differently in the condition in which they offered no defense at all. However, that difference, regardless of its origins, leads to another pair of questions that can be addressed with these data. First, men start out seeming relatively innocent; what strategies are effective in maintaining that perception of innocence? The only strategy that does not result in men being perceived as more guilty is admitting to a lesser offense. All other strategies result in increased perceptions of guilt. Second, women start out seeming relatively guilty; what strategies are effective in changing that perception to one of innocence? Only admitting to an offense of some kind (either a relevant lesser offense or an irrelevant offense) significantly decreases judges' perceptions of women's guilt from the control condition.

Another mixed-design 2 (confederate's gender) × 6 (confederate's defense against the accusation) × 2 (judge's attribution) ANOVA was conducted, in which the question "Is the accused person guilty of [the serious offense]?" served as the dependent measure. This dependent measure was dichotomous; judges responded with either a "yes" (coded as 1) or "no" (coded as 0).

The dichotomous measure was merely different in format from the 9-point rating scale measure of guilt, and the results, as expected, were substantially similar. The type of defense confederates used to explain the accusation significantly affected their perceived guilt, F (5, 33) = 8.32, p < .001. A planned contrast (in which the "deny accusation and admit to a relevant lesser offense" defense was assigned a weight of +5 and all other defenses were assigned a weight of –1) was significant, F (1, 185) = 4.09, p = .04. Pairwise comparisons indicated that the key defense of denying the accusation and admitting to a relevant lesser offense resulted in significantly lesser perceptions of guilt than denying the accusation and offering an explanation. In addition, the key defense resulted in nearly significantly lesser perceptions of guilt than simply denying the accusation, F (1, 185) = 3.18, p = .08, or denying the accusation and making a counter-accusation, F (1, 185) = 3.26, p = .07. However, confederates who admitted to a relevant lesser offense did not elicit significantly different perceptions of guilt than confederates who denied the accusation and admitted to an irrelevant offense, or than confederates who offered no defense against the accusation.

Also consistent with the results of the continuous dependent measure of guilt, the results of the dichotomous measure of perceived guilt showed an unpredicted interaction between confederate gender and the type of defense confederates used, F (5, 33) = 5.77, p = .001. The pattern of results was also similar. Male confederates were perceived as most innocent when they described the accusation and gave no defense at all, whereas female confederates were perceived as most guilty, though not significantly so, when they described the accusation and gave no defense. Note that none of the strategies used by men were effective in maintaining the baseline perception of innocence except for the strategy of admitting to a relevant lesser offense. Also, none of the strategies used by women were effective in reducing the baseline perception of guilt except for the strategies of admitting to either a relevant lesser offense or an irrelevant offense.

In summary, the results of Study 2 were somewhat consistent with predictions, but more so for the perceptions of the male confederates than of the female confederates. On both the continuous and dichotomous measures of guilt, the men who denied the accusation but admitted to a relevant lesser offense fared significantly better than the men who offered every other defense except no defense at all. Women, in contrast, fared best when they admitted to an irrelevant offense. Perhaps more importantly, the men and women were perceived very differently in the control condition in which confederates described the accusation but said nothing further. Men were seen as especially innocent when they offered no defense, and they maintained their innocence more effectively in the condition in which they admitted to a relevant lesser offense than in any other condition. The women, on the other hand, were seen as especially guilty when they offered no defense, and they were able to undo those negative perceptions most effectively in the condition in which they admitted to an irrelevant offense. Admitting to a relevant lesser offense was the only other defense that helped women appear significantly less guilty than they did in the control condition.

Study 3

Participants

A total of 87 undergraduates (52 females and 35 males) at the University of Virginia took part in the third study. Participants received credit toward the experiment participation requirement for an introductory psychology course.

Twenty-four of the participants (12 men and 12 women) were designated as "senders." In a questionnaire from a related study, all senders had mentioned recalling a time when they had been accused of a serious offense of which they were guilty, and a time when they had been accused of a serious offense of which they were innocent. Senders were run individually.

The other 63 participants (40 females and 23 males) were designated as "judges." Judges were run in groups of 4 to 12.

Design

Judges were the units of analysis in a 2 (sender was guilty vs. not guilty) × 6 (sender's defense against the accusation) within-participants design. The dependent measures consisted of the questionnaire with direct and indirect measures of judges' perceptions of guilt (see Appendix C).

Procedure

Senders were run through the procedure individually. After filling out a consent form, senders were asked to confirm that they could think of either a time they were accused of a serious offense of which they were guilty, or a time they were accused of a serious offense of which they were innocent. Senders were asked to recount the events immediately preceding and during the accusation. When necessary, the experimenter gave senders a few minutes to recall an appropriate event. After senders recalled an event, they were instructed to do one of the following:

1. Describe the accusation, but do not present any additional information.

2 Describe the accusation and deny that it was true.
3. Describe the accusation, deny that it was true, and offer a brief explanation for the accuser's suspicions.
4. Describe the accusation, deny that it was true, and make a counter-accusation against the accuser.
5. Describe the accusation, deny that it was true, and admit to a relevant lesser offense than the one of which they were accused.
6. Describe the accusation, deny that it was true, and admit to an irrelevant lesser offense (of which they were not accused).

When they were ready, senders were asked to recount their accusation event for approximately 20 to 40 seconds. Senders were videotaped recounting the event. Upon completion of the videotaping, senders were thanked for their time, given course credit, and debriefed.

Six videotapes were created, each with 12 senders, presented in six counterbalanced orders. In the second phase of the study, a different set of participants ("judges") viewed these videotapes in groups of 4 to 12. After filling out consent forms, judges viewed a videotape of 12 senders, and followed the same procedure as in Study 2. After judges viewed and rated the 12 senders, they were thanked for their time, given course credit, and debriefed.

The stimulus videotapes included a total of 24 senders (four senders from each of the six defense conditions. One male and one female sender from each defense condition described an event in which they were falsely accused, and the other male and female sender described an event in which they were justly accused; see Appendix E). However, in each experimental session there was only enough time for judges to watch a videotape of 12 of the senders. There were six different orders of 12 senders. These six orders can be matched together as three pairs of "orthogonal" orders; in each pair of orders, every sender is shown once and only once. In order to facilitate analysis of the data, each judge was matched with another judge who viewed and rated the corresponding "pair" order of senders. Thus, matched pairs of judges were created; while each judge viewed only 12 of the senders, each matched pair of judges watched all 24 senders between the two of them. Three of the 63 judges did not have a "match" among the other judges; thus, data from these three judges were eliminated from the analyses. The remaining 60 judges (23 males and 37 females) were matched with each other, to create a final 30 matched pairs of judges.

Results

The matched pairs of judges were the units of analysis in a series of four 2 (sender's guilt/innocence) × 6 (sender's defense against the accusation) within-participants ANOVAs. Senders' gender was not included as a factor in these ANOVAs because there was only one female and one male sender in each condition.

Responses to the question, "How likely is it that the accused person is guilty of [the serious offense]," recorded on a 9-point scale, were the dependent measures in the first analysis. The mean across all conditions was 5.37, indicating that, as in Study 2, judges did not exhibit a truth bias.

As predicted, the type of defense senders used to explain the accusation significantly affected their perceived guilt, $F (5, 25) = 20.25, p <$ .001. These main effect results were similar to those in Study 2. The planned contrast (in which the "deny accusation and admit to a relevant lesser offense" defense was assigned a weight of +5 and all other defenses were assigned a weight of −1) was significant, $F (1, 145) = 15.43, p < .001$. Individual comparisons showed that denying the accusation and admitting to a relevant lesser offense resulted in significantly lesser perceptions of guilt than simply denying the accusation, or denying the accusation and offering an explanation.

Senders who admitted to a relevant lesser offense were seen as less guilty, but not significantly so, than senders who offered no defense against the accusation, senders who denied the accusation and made a counter-accusation, and senders who denied the accusation and admitted to an irrelevant offense.

Because the senders in Study 3 really were guilty or innocent of the serious accusations they described, it was possible to determine whether the judges could reliably discriminate the guilty senders from the innocent ones. The main effect of actual guilt showed that they could do so, $F (1, 29) = 6.82, p = .01$. Judges rated the senders who were actually guilty ($M = 5.56$) as more guilty than the senders who were actually innocent ($M = 5.17$).

A 2 (sender's guilt/innocence) × 6 (sender's defense against the accusation) within-participants ANOVA for the dichotomous measure of guilt also produced the predicted main effect of type of defense, $F (5, 25) = 13.52, p < .001$. The planned contrast was also significant, $F (1, 145) = 12.62, p < .001$. Individual comparisons indicated that denying the accusation and admitting to a relevant lesser offense resulted in significantly fewer perceptions of guilt than simply denying the accusation, or than denying the accusation and offering an explanation. Senders who denied the accusation and admitted to a relevant lesser offense elicited fewer, but not significantly fewer, judgments of guilt than did senders who offered no defense against the accusation, senders who denied the accusation and made a counter-accusation, or senders who denied the accusation and admitted to an irrelevant offense.

The analysis of the dichotomous measure of guilt also showed that judges were able to discriminate senders who were actually guilty from senders who were actually innocent of the serious accusations they described, $F(1, 29) = 12.38$, $p = .002$. Guilty senders were judged as guilty 58.3% of the time, whereas innocent senders were judged as guilty 46.8% of the time.

The interaction between actual guilt and type of defense was also significant, $F(5, 25) = 13.52$, $p < .001$. The difference in perceived guilt between guilty senders and innocent senders depended on the type of defense senders used. When judging senders who denied the accusation and made a counter-accusation, judges were most accurate (i.e., more likely to rate the innocent senders than the guilty senders as innocent), though not significantly more accurate than when senders offered no defense.

In summary, the results of Study 3 were similar in important ways to the results for the male confederates in Study 2. Although it was not possible to test sender gender effects in Study 3, the results that emerged across senders indicated that the strategy of admitting to a relevant lesser offense was significantly more effective than simply denying the accusation, or denying the accusation and offering an explanation. Also consistent with the results for the male confederates of Study 2, senders who admitted to a relevant lesser offense were not perceived as any less guilty or more honest than senders who offered no defense at all.

Discussion

Effectiveness of the Six Defenses Against an Accusation

How can people who are accused of serious wrongdoing most effectively defend themselves? I predicted that one particular strategy, denying the accusation but admitting to a relevant lesser offense, would be especially convincing. Initially, in Study 1, I compared that strategy only to the strategy of simply denying the accusation. In Studies 2 and 3, I added a control condition in which the accused simply described the accusation without saying anything further. I also added a condition in which the accused person offered an explanation for why the accuser may have misconstrued the situation, and a condition in which the accused person made a counter-accusation. Finally, to test the notion that perhaps confessing to a lesser offense is effective because it give the appearance of having an honest character, I added a final condition in which the accused person admitted to an irrelevant offense.

Admitting to a Lesser Offense vs. Simply Denying the Accusation

Results consistently demonstrated that, among strangers, confessing to a lesser offense elicited greater perceptions of innocence than simply denying an accusation. In Study 1, hypothetical strangers accused of cheating on a test were seen as nonsignificantly less likely to be guilty, and significantly more honest, when they admitted to the lesser offense of failing to prevent a friend from cheating than when they denied any wrongdoing. In Studies 2 and 3, people who denied a serious accusation but admitted to a lesser offense were seen as significantly less likely to be guilty than those who simply denied the serious accusation. On the dichotomous measure of guilt, Study 2 confederates who admitted to the lesser offense were also perceived as nonsignificantly less likely to be guilty than confederates who simply denied the accusation. In Study 3, this difference was significant.

The consistency of these results across different methodologies provides ample evidence that, when people describe an accusation made against them, they are better off admitting to some wrongdoing than to simply denying an accusation. Results from Studies 1 and 2 indicate that this effect was not due to differences in the type of accusations people discussed, because the same accusations were discussed in all conditions. Results from Study 3 demonstrate that this pattern was true for real-life accusations in which people had a genuine emotional investment.

Admitting to a Lesser Offense vs. Other Defenses

Results were somewhat consistent with the prediction that denying the accusation and admitting to a lesser offense would be more effective than the various other strategies used to defend against an accusation. Despite the differences in methodology, results from Studies 2 and 3 were remarkably consistent with each other. In both Studies 2 and 3, no defenses were significantly more useful than admitting to a lesser offense; this pattern was consistent across the continuous and dichotomous measures of perceived guilt as well as the measure of perceived honesty. However, in Study 2, confederates who admitted to a lesser offense did not elicit significantly lesser perceptions of guilt, or greater perceptions of honesty, than confederates who admitted to an irrelevant offense or who offered no defense. Differences were even less marked in the dichotomous measure of guilt, for which admitting to a lesser offense elicited significantly fewer perceptions of guilt than only one other defense: simple denial of the accusation. Results for Study 3 were similar: Admitting to a lesser offense resulted in the least perceptions of guilt and greatest perceptions of honesty; however, this defense did not differ significantly from admitting to an irrelevant offense, making a counter-accusation, or offering no defense.

In both studies 2 and 3, simply denying an accusation, as well as denying an accusation and offering an explanation, elicited the highest levels of perceived guilt and the lowest levels of perceived honesty. The purpose of the present study was not to determine why these strategies are so ineffective, so here I will just offer a few speculations. Simply denying an accusation may leave people wondering why the accusation was made in the first place. When then-President Clinton simply told Americans, "I did not have sexual relations with that woman—Ms. Lewinsky," many people felt unsatisfied with the answer; they wondered why the issue had been brought to national attention. However, results of this study indicate that simply coming up with an explanation for the accusation, without insulting or attacking the accuser, is also an ineffective strategy. For an explanation to work by the coolly logical way of accounting for a misperception on which the accusation was based, the explanation would have to be convincing. The "there's a perfectly reasonable explanation!" reply may come all too readily to the lips of those who are caught with their hands in the cookie jar. Such a defense may be found lacking in emotion; it may not offer the judges a way to explain away any discomfort they are feeling, and it may do nothing to establish the integrity and honest character of the accused.

The findings for only one of the defenses differed between Study 2 and Study 3, and even this difference was a small one. Denying the accusation and making a counter-accusation was shown to be a reasonably effective strategy for the senders in Study 3; in fact, it was not significantly less effective than admitting to a relevant lesser offense. In Study 2, it was significantly less effective than admitting to a relevant lesser offense, though still more effective than attempting to explain the accusation away.

From a rational perspective, it is surprising that making a counter-accusation works as well as it does, because it fails to account for why the accusation was made. The greater effectiveness of this strategy in Study 3 than in Study 2 may provide a clue to this puzzle. The Study 3 senders, unlike the Study 2 senders, really had been accused of the defense they were describing, and half of them had been unjustly accused. As they recounted their genuine life experiences, they likely re-experienced their anger and resentment toward their accuser (see Coats & Feldman, 1996; Sternglanz & DePaulo, 2004). Senders' personal investment in their stories may have been evident to the judges. Perhaps the aggrieved senders also elicited empathy from the judges; the judges, as a result, may have been somewhat more lenient in their judgments of guilt. If this is the case, then (as I will discuss in more detail below) judges should be especially likely to find the truly innocent senders compelling.

The most effective defenses, other than admitting to a relevant lesser offense, were admitting to an irrelevant offense, and offering no defense at all. However, an interaction of type of defense with confederates' gender in Study 2 suggests that there may be another important twist to the interpretation of these results.

Sex Differences in the Control Condition

On the continuous measure of guilt, the dichotomous measure of guilt, and the perceptions of honesty, the men who denied the accusation but admitted to a relevant lesser offense fared significantly better than the men who offered every other defense except no defense at all. Women, in contrast, fared even better when they admitted to an irrelevant offense than when they admitted to a relevant lesser offense.

Perhaps more importantly, the men and women in Study 2 were perceived very differently in the control condition in which confederates described the accusation but said nothing further. Men were seen as least guilty when they offered no defense, and they maintained their innocence more effectively in the condition in which they admitted to a relevant lesser offense than in any other condition. The women, on the other hand, were seen as especially guilty when they offered no defense, and they were able to undo those negative perceptions most effectively in the condition in which they admitted to an irrelevant offense. Admitting to a relevant lesser offense was the only other defense that helped women appear significantly less guilty than they did in the control condition.

These sex differences leave us with several puzzling questions. First, why did male confederates who merely described the accusation appear so innocent, while female confederates who did the same thing appeared so guilty? There are several possible answers. First, the stories told by male confederates were based on other men's responses to a questionnaire about serious accusations; likewise, the stories told by female confederates were based on women's responses to the same questionnaire. One possibility is that the accusations described by women were seen as the kind of transgressions anyone is more likely to have committed than were the kind of accusations described by men. This difference could be in the kinds of transgressions men and women actually committed, or in the kinds of transgressions they reported. Upon first examination, there appeared to be very few differences between the transgressions discussed by men and the transgressions discussed by women. Men's and women's transgressions were about similar topics, such as breaking rules set by authorities (generally either parents or school), and relationship infidelities (see Appendix D). However, possibly the same kinds of transgressions were interpreted differently when they were attributed to men than when they were attributed to women. For instance, it may have been more socially acceptable for men than for women to talk about being unfaithful to their romantic partner (see Sprecher, McKinney, & Orbuch, 1991); perhaps judges thought that a woman who brought up such a serious norm violation was most likely guilty. A goal for future research is to determine whether the exact same accusation elicits greater perceptions of guilt when attributed to women than to men.

Even if men and women were describing transgressions that were similar in content and in social acceptability, they could convey different impressions if they felt differently about their transgressions. For example, if women felt more embarrassed or more defensive than men while describing an instance when they were accused of sexual infidelity, their feelings might be evident in their word choice, their tone of voice, their overall demeanor, or some combination of these. The contributions of different kinds of cues to conveyed impressions can be disentangled by standard nonverbal communication methodologies. For example, men's and women's descriptions of being accused of infidelity could be video-taped, transcribed, and then shown to raters who would judge only the transcripts, only the audio portions of the videotapes (i.e., sound turned off), only the visual portion of the videotapes (i.e., picture turned off), or the complete videotapes.

Finally, there may have been differences in the way men and women were expected to give an explanation. Perhaps it was considered more socially acceptable for men than women to be less forthcoming and talk-ative in their explanation of the accusation. Researchers have shown that traditional behavioral norms inhibit self-disclosure in men and encour-age it in women (Dolgin, Meyer, & Schwartz, 1991; Shaffer, Pegalis, & Cornell, 1992); thus, a very brief, incomplete explanation of a per-sonal event offered by a man may elicit less suspiciousness than the same explanation offered by a woman.

The present research was not designed to determine which of the aforementioned explanations can best account for the large differences in how men and women were perceived when they described an accusa-tion. In any case, it is likely that in many real-life situations, people do not volunteer stories in which they were accused by others, but rather are unwillingly put on the spot to respond (or fail to respond) to an accusation made by someone else. Are there differences in the way men and women are perceived when accused in this manner? Future research should address this question.

Sex Differences in Admitting to an Irrelevant Offense

One possible mechanism by which confessing to a lesser offense was pre-dicted to work was by giving senders the appearance of having an honest character. O'Sullivan (2003) proposed that we judge the truthfulness of people's statements not so much by the cues they give off as by our judg-ments of their honesty more globally. People who admit to something when they do not have to do so may be seen as inherently honest people. This was the rationale used for including the condition in which send-ers and confederates admitted to an irrelevant offense. This condition, unlike the other defense conditions, was not included because it was presumed to be a likely way for people to defend themselves against an accusation. Rather, it added a test of the hypothesis that admitting to a lesser offense works because it is a taken as a sign of honest character.

This hypothesized mechanism was supported only for female confederates in Study 2, who were even better off using this defense than they were admitting to a relevant lesser offense. Perhaps because of the aforementioned gender differences in disclosure norms, men found it difficult to pull off admitting to a wholly irrelevant offense in a way that seemed natural, whereas women were able to talk about an irrelevant offense in a way that seemed more comfortable. Women are more expressive and have more legible expressions than men generally (Hall, 1984); perhaps such skills are especially advantageous when discussing something a little bit odd, such as an irrelevant offense.

Differences in Accuracy

Because the senders in Study 3 really were either innocent or guilty of the serious accusations they described, it was possible to determine whether judges could reliably discriminate the innocent senders from the guilty ones. As predicted, judges rated the guilty senders as more guilty than the innocent senders on both the continuous and dichotomous measures of guilt. However, judges' ratings of honesty did not differ between senders who were actually innocent and senders who were actually guilty. This last finding may have been due to judges' differing levels of accuracy depending on the defense senders used.

Accuracy at Differentiating Innocent from Guilty Senders for the Six Defenses

Regardless of whether senders were innocent or guilty of the serious accusations they described, no defense was significantly more successful than confessing to a lesser offense. Confessing to a lesser offense was especially useful for the guilty senders; only 43.1% of guilty senders who used this defense were seen as guilty on the dichotomous measure, which was fewer (though not always significantly fewer) than any other defense. Likewise, 65.5% of innocent senders who confessed to a lesser offense were seen as innocent, which was not significantly fewer than for any defense, and significantly more than for the defense of simply denying the explanation or offering an explanation for it.

Confessing to a lesser offense was also a wise defense for both innocent and guilty senders in their attempts to come across as honest. Both innocent and guilty senders were seen as more honest (though not always significantly so) when they confessed to a lesser offense than when they used any other defense.

As stated earlier, most senders were seen as more guilty when they were actually guilty than when they were actually innocent. However, for most defenses these differences were small. Judges perceived guilty senders as significantly more guilty than innocent senders only when senders offered no defense or when they made a counter-accusation. Innocent senders who made a counter-accusation were seen as honest a striking 77.6% of the time. It is possible that judges were able to recognize the genuine anger and righteous indignation experienced by the senders who used this defense.

Conclusions and Directions for Future Research

Partial support was found for the hypothesis that admitting to a relevant lesser offense was helpful in maintaining the appearance of innocence. It was the only defense, other than offering no defense, by which men were able to maintain their innocence. It also helped women appear significantly less guilty than they did by offering no defense.

Women were also able to appear innocent by admitting to an irrelevant offense. This provides some support for the notion that admitting to an offense makes one seem more innocent by lending the sender the appearance of having an honest character. It is not clear why this should only be the case for women, but perhaps only women have the verbal and nonverbal communication skills necessary to talk about something irrelevant without appearing awkward.

It is important to investigate further the reasons why simply describing an accusation, without offering a defense, made men appear so innocent, and women so guilty. I suspect this finding was caused by gender norms which implicitly suggest that being untalkative is more acceptable for men than women. Differences in the way the men and women told their stories, either verbally or nonverbally, could also be important.

Earlier I suggested that people may respond differently to an accusation when they first hear the charge, often standing face-to-face with the person who is making it, than when they later tell the story of having been accused. This process may be different for perceivers as well. Defenses that seem compelling in the heat of the moment may seem less so during a subsequent retelling. And of course, the person leveling the accusation may well see things differently than an uninvolved observer.

The present research was an examination of the efficacy of various defenses, rather than an exploration of the frequency with which these defenses really are used. This question is also important. In one example from 2003, basketball star Kobe Bryant, who was accused of sexual assault, used the strategy of admitting to a lesser offense. In an emotional press conference, Bryant vehemently denied the rape but confessed to adultery. How typical is Bryant's response? It is not known how often the defenses explored in this study are used, nor whether there may be other defenses people use regularly. Understanding the defenses people use when accused of a serious offense may help elucidate the processes involved in the communication and detection of lies and truths more generally.

Acknowledgment

Portions of this chapter are based on the author's doctoral dissertation in the Department of Psychology at the University of Virginia. The author wishes to thank Jerry Clore, Dan Wegner, Karen Schmidt, Ann Lane, Bobbie Spellman, and especially Bella DePaulo for their comments on earlier drafts of this chapter.

References

Anderson, D. E., DePaulo, B. M., & Ansfield, M. E. (2002). The development of deception detection skill: A longitudinal study of same sex friends. *Personality and Social Psychology Review, 28*, 536–545.

Coats, E. J., & Feldman, R. S. (1996). Gender differences in nonverbal correlates of social status. *Personality and Social Psychology Bulletin, 22*, 1014–1022.

DePaulo, B. M. (1992). Nonverbal behavior and self-presentation. Psychological *Bulletin, 111*, 203–243.

DePaulo, B. M. (1994). Spotting lies: Can humans learn to do better? *Current Directions in Psychological Science, 3*, 83–86.

DePaulo, B. M., Ansfield, M. E., Kirkendol, S. E., & Boden, J. M. (2004). Serious lies. *Basic and Applied Social Psychology, 26*, 147–167.

DePaulo, B. M., Charlton, K., Cooper, H., Lindsay, J. J., & Muhlenbruck, L. (1997). Accuracy and confidence in the detection of deception. *Personality and Social Psychology Review, 1*, 346–357.

DePaulo, B. M., Kashy, D. A., Kirkendol, S. E., Wyer, M. M., & Epstein, J. A. (1996). Lying in everyday life. *Journal of Personality and Social Psychology, 70*, 979–995.

DePaulo, B. M., Lanier, K., & Davis, T. (1983). Detecting the deceit of the motivated liar. *Journal of Personality and Social Psychology, 45*, 1096–1103.

DePaulo, B. M., LeMay, C. S., & Epstein, J. A. (1991). Effects of importance of success and expectations for success on effectiveness at deceiving. *Personality and Social Psychology Bulletin, 17*, 14–24.

DePaulo, B. M., & Morris, W. L. (2004). Discerning lies from truths: Behavioral cues to deception and the indirect pathway of intuition. In P. A. Granhag & L. Stromwall (Eds.), *Deception detection in forensic contexts* (pp. 15–40). New York: Cambridge University Press.

DePaulo, B. M., & Pfeifer, R. L. (1986). On the job experience and skill at detecting deception. *Journal of Applied Social Psychology, 16*, 249–267.

Dolgin, K. G., Meyer, L., & Schwartz, J. (1991). Effects of gender, target's gender, topic, and self-esteem on disclosure to best and middling friends. *Sex Roles, 25,* 311–329.

Ekman, P., & Friesen, W. V. (1964). Nonverbal leakage and clues to deception. *Psychiatry, 32,* 88–106.

Folkes, V. S., & Sears, D. O. (1977). Does everybody like a liker? *Journal of Experimental Social Psychology, 13,* 505–519.

Gilbert, D. T. (1991). How mental systems believe. *American Psychologist, 46,* 107–109.

Gilbert, D. T., Krull, D. S., & Malone, P. S. (1990). Unbelieving the unbelievable: Some problems in the rejection of false information. *Journal of Personality and Social Psychology, 59,* 601–613.

Goffman, E. (1959). *The presentation of self in everyday life.* Garden City, NY: Doubleday/Anchor Books.

Hall, J. A. (1984). *Nonverbal sex differences: Communication accuracy and expressive style.* Baltimore: Johns Hopkins University Press.

Heinlein, R. A. (1953). *If this goes on–.* In *Revolt in 2100* (pp. 11–129). New York: The New American Library.

McCornack, S. A., & Levine, T. R. (1990). When lovers become leery: The relationship between suspicion and accuracy in detecting deception. *Communication Monographs, 57,* 219–230.

O'Sullivan, M. (2003). The fundamental attribution error in detecting deception: The boy-who-cried-wolf effect. *Personality and Social Psychology Bulletin, 29,* 1316–1327.

Park, H. S., Levine, T. R., McCornack, S. A., Morrison, K., & Ferrerra, M. (2001). *How people really detect lies.* Presentation at the National Communication Association, Atlanta, GA.

Rosenthal, R., & Rosnow, R. L. (1991). *Essentials of behavioral research (2nd ed.).* New York: McGraw-Hill.

Shaffer, D. R., Pegalis, L. J., & Cornell, D. P. (1992). Gender and self-disclosure revisited: Personal and contextual variations in self-disclosure to same-sex acquaintances. *Journal of Social Psychology, 132,* 307–315.

Snedecor, G. W., & Cochran, W. G. (1967). *Statistical methods (6th ed.).* Ames: Iowa State University Press.

Sprecher, S., McKinney, K., & Orbuch, T. L. (1991). The effect of current sexual behavior on friendship, dating, and marriage desirability. *The Journal of Sex Research, 28,* 387–408.

Sternglanz, R. W., & DePaulo, B. M. (2004). Reading nonverbal cues to emotions: The advantages and liabilities of relationship closeness. *Journal of Nonverbal Behavior, 28,* 245–266.

Toris, C., & DePaulo, B. M. (1985). Effects of actual deception and suspiciousness of deception on interpersonal perceptions. *Journal of Personality and Social Psychology, 47,* 1063–1073.

Vrij, A. (1994). The impact of information and setting on detection of deception by police detectives. *Journal of Nonverbal Behavior, 18,* 117–136.

Wegner, D. M. (1994). Ironic processes of mental control. *Psychological Review, 101,* 34–52.

Wegner, D. M., Wenzlaff, R., Kerker, R. M., & Beattie, A. E. (1981). Incrimination through innuendo: Can media questions become public answers? *Journal of Personality and Social Psychology, 40*, 822–832.

Winer, B. J. (1971). *Statistical principles in experimental design (2nd ed.)*. New York: McGraw-Hill.

Appendix A

"Deny Accusation Completely" Vignette (Study 1)

Imagine that _____, a fellow student at the University of Virginia, has been accused of committing an honor violation. He/she has been accused of exchanging answers with a fellow student during the exam. A teaching assistant for the class allegedly witnessed the cheating and informed the professor.

_____ has denied these accusations completely, stating that he/she was looking at his/her own exam the whole time, and that at no time did he/she either give or receive assistance on the exam.

In your own words, please describe this hypothetical scenario taking place. Use the space below on this page. Use the back of this page if necessary.

Appendix B

"Admit to Lesser Offense" Vignette (Study 1)

Imagine that _____, a fellow student at the University of Virginia, has been accused of committing an honor violation. He/she has been accused of exchanging answers with a fellow student during the exam. A teaching assistant for the class allegedly witnessed the cheating and informed the professor.

_____ has admitted that he/she was sure he/she saw a friend looking at his/her answer sheet during the exam, and that because this person was a friend he/she didn't report this friend's suspected cheating. However, he/she also states that at no time did he/she receive any assistance on the exam.

In your own words, please describe this hypothetical scenario taking place. Use the space below on this page. Use the back of this page if necessary.

Appendix C

Questionnaire of Dependent Measures (Studies 2 and 3)

The following questionnaire asks some questions concerning your views about the person who has been accused of a serious offense. There are no right or wrong answers, and your answers will be kept confidential. Therefore, please respond as openly as possible.

The response choices for the following questions are ordered on a 1 to 9 scale. To respond, please circle the number that best fits your beliefs.

1. How likely is it that the accused person is guilty of [THE SERIOUS OFFENSE]?

1	2	3	4	5	6	7	8	9
Not At All			Likely					Very Likely

   (Questions 2 through 12 are not included here; participants were asked to rate the "accused person" on several other dimensions, including suspiciousness, confidence, and likability.)

13. Is the accused person guilty of [THE SERIOUS OFFENSE]? (Circle one answer)
    Yes   No

14. Have you ever met the accused person before?
    Yes   No

15. In your own words, briefly summarize the accused person's response to the accusation. Do you think it was a good response? (Write your answer below.)

Appendix D

Confederates' Serious Offenses (Study 2)

Phrases substituted for "[THE SERIOUS OFFENSE]" in Questions 1 and 13 on the Questionnaire of Dependent Measures (see Appendix C) in Study 2.

The first six offenses were described by male confederates; the last six were described by female confederates.

1. purposely cheating with a fellow student on the exam
2. sleeping with the other girl whom he was friends with

 3. driving home while drunk
 4. breaking his father's record player
 5. knocking the kid off his bike
 6. throwing a big party in the house while his parents were away
 7. sneaking out to go to a party after her parents went to sleep
 8. cheating on her boyfriend with the other guy
 9. purposely letting her friend cheat off of her during the test
10. writing the nasty anonymous note to the girl
11. purposely going out in order to hang around with the older guy whom she was forbidden to date
12. telling her best friend that her boyfriend could be in danger of getting herpes, and that therefore she should get tested

Appendix E

Real Senders' Serious Offenses (Study 3)

Phrases substituted for "[THE SERIOUS OFFENSE]" in Questions 1 and 13 on the Questionnaire of Dependent Measures (see Appendix C) in Study 3.

The first 12 offenses were described by female senders; the second twelve were described by male senders.

 1. dating a guy who was much older than the age she had told her mother
 2. chewing gum while in the museum
 3. going to a co-ed sleep-over (rather than just a dance team sleep-over)
 4. giving the other girl her I.D.
 5. telling her suite-mate's boyfriend (directly) that the suite-mate had been cheating on the boyfriend
 6. smoking marijuana
 7. cheating on her boyfriend with the other guy
 8. crashing the car due to carelessness (rather than in order to avoid a truck)
 9. being interested in her roommate's boyfriend
10. plagiarizing the paper
11. trying to take her sister's lotion back to school with her
12. throwing away her mother's lasagna
13. jumping (rather than falling) off the swingset
14. having a party while his parents were away
15. going out with friends instead of to the hospital
16. stealing printing paper from the computer lab

17. drinking a lot (rather than just once in a while)
18. leaving his class early
19. cheating on his Latin test by writing on the board
20. cheating on his chemistry homework
21. cheating on his math test
22. cheating on his girlfriend
23. driving around and causing havoc (instead of watching a movie at his friend's house)
24. striking his friend on the back of the head

Index

Page numbers in italic refer to figures or tables.